PRAISE FOR THE BUSINESS BULLSHIT BOOK

"If you're sick of deep dives and webinars, exhausted by a world of re-baselining and Death by PowerPoint, or enraged by endless guff about goal-focused learnings and opening the kimono, Kevin Duncan's refreshingly no-nonsense guide will put a smile back on your face."

Henry Hitchings, author of *The Language Wars*

"Latest research in neuroscience shows that words really matter, and have a chemical reaction in the brain, causing us to switch off, reject and turn away, or accept and take action. This is a guide to put you on alert to the phrases that might just be turning people away from you!"

Kevin Murray, author of *The Language of Leaders*

"Despite Mr. Duncan's sterling efforts one can only wonder at the blamestorm that arose from the omission of 'blamestorming'. (Vb. The practice of attributing blame in advance of a known outcome)."

Rob Norman, Chairman Group M North America

THE BUSINESS BULLSHIT BOOK

THE WORLD'S MOST COMPREHENSIVE DICTIONARY

Published by
LID Publishing Ltd
One Adam Street
London
WC2N 6LE
United Kingdom

31 West 34th Street, Suite 8004,
New York, NY 10001, US

info@lidpublishing.com
www.lidpublishing.com

A member of:

BPR
Business Publishers Roundtable

www.businesspublishersroundtable.com

Printed in Spain

ISBN: 978-1-910649-85-5

Cover and page design: Caroline Li

THE BUSINESS BULLSHIT BOOK

THE WORLD'S MOST COMPREHENSIVE DICTIONARY

KEVIN DUNCAN

LONDON   NEW YORK   BOGOTA
MADRID   BARCELONA   BUENOS AIRES
MEXICO CITY   MONTERREY   SAN FRANCISCO
SHANGHAI

To Rosanna, Shaunagh and Sarah.

CONTENTS

Foreword..10

Introduction...12

Aa..14

Bb..26

Cc..47

Dd..65

Ee..78

Ff..87

Gg..100

Hh..108

Ii..118

Jj..125

Kk..127

Ll..130

Mm 138

Nn 150

Oo 157

Pp 166

Qq 185

Rr 187

Ss 199

Tt 213

Uu 226

Vv 230

Ww 234

Xx 244

Yy 245

Zz 246

FOREWORD

"This dictionary easily ranks as one of the greatest single achievements of scholarship, and probably the greatest ever performed by one individual who laboured under anything like the disadvantages in a comparable length of time."
Walter Jackson Bate

No, not this one in your hand, but rather the one compiled by the dyspeptic poet, essayist, and all-round Enlightenment man, Dr Samuel Johnson.

That one was written primarily to settle the use and spelling of English at a time when more and more of the population needed to know the agreed definitions of meaning, usage and spelling. And it was at least partly funded by printers who had real need of knowing the correct way to spell, for example, the word 'dictionary' and understanding what it meant.

Johnson went about his task by using 'custom' as the equivalent of legal precedent to set the standard on all these dimensions.

"The rules of stile, like those of law, arise from precedents often repeated, collect the testimonies of both sides, and endeavour to discover and promulgate the decrees of custom, who has so long possessed whether by right or by usurpation, the sovereignty of words," he explained.

This dictionary has a very different purpose: it collects our terribly loose custom in a catechism of cliché and an encomium of euphemism, not merely to describe our dire contortions of the language and logic, but to condemn them and shame us from using them.

Too often we simply glue words and ideas together and – pleased by the familiar ring of them - attach them to some more loosely related ones.

George Orwell pointed out in *Politics and the English Language* that too much of our prose is like this:

"Prose consists less and less of words chosen for the sake of their meaning, and more and more of phrases tacked together like the sections of a pre-fabricated hen-house."

All of which might make you think this book sounds like a terrible old bore. But, like all of Kevin Duncan's writing, it's actually incredible fun. I keep dipping into the copy I've got as a kind of anti-thesaurus (no, you can't use that phrase).

It's sharp, tight, and all too true.

So here's my proposal.

Buy one of these for a businessperson in your life and challenge them not to use any of the words and phrases in Duncan's Dictionary.

In fact, why don't you buy several? The more the... (*Ed: Is that allowed?*)

Do it and we might start to speak more clearly in business, and in doing so, think more clearly.

Which would be an excellent thing all round.

Mark Earls
Author of *Herd*, *I'll Have What She's Having*, and *Copy, Copy, Copy*

INTRODUCTION

At first glance, the topic of bullshit is very much filed under comedy.

It's hilarious, isn't it?

Or is it?

When it replaces clear communication it can be no laughing matter.

Those of us who talk straight are entitled to ask:

"What the hell are these people talking about?"

You hold in your hand three decades of nonsense that I have collected.

It's a never-ending task, and we will probably never eradicate it.

But once you have had a laugh with it, at least you can use this book to name and shame the worst offenders in your company.

Your boss, perhaps?

Keep sending me your most egregious examples.

Kevin Duncan, Westminster 2016

ABC, easy as: 1. A complete doddle; something you could do in kindergarten. 2. A task only suitable for total idiots, which probably says more about the person being asked to do the job than they would care to admit; pisseasy; pride before a fall, as in: *"This is easy as ABC, Derek,"* shortly before realizing that it is in truth quite complicated. *(see Art form, got it down to an; Cooking on gas; Falling off a log)*

ABC session: 1. Meeting in which all staff are graded in their absence. 2. Management immediately use findings of said session to instigate a ruthless cull; superb opportunity to display flagrant nepotism and favouritism. *(see Axe, face the; Destaff; Headcount: LIFO; Phone list, go down the; Powwow)*

A-Z: 1. Fully comprehensive; covering absolutely everything. 2. We can't decide which bit to concentrate on, so we're asking you to do everything before we decide; not comprehensive at all, but claiming to be so for marketing purposes; starting at A, but petering out horribly after E and F. *(see Chapter and verse; Full Monty, the; Zee, we've covered everything from A to)*

Above and beyond: 1. More than was originally asked for. 2. Totally unnecessary over-delivery fuelled by rampant ambition and sucking up to the boss – guaranteed to annoy all colleagues; plaintive mantra of Terylene-wearing sales directors from Land's End to John o' Groats, as in: *"Come on guys, we need to go above and beyond in this sales period!"* *(see Quarter, one, two, three, four; Team, take one for the)*

Above board: 1. Correct, proper, or legal. 2. This is a bit dodgy but we need to create the semblance of being whiter than white otherwise we'll be fired; barely legal; just about okay; marginal. *(see Cook the books; Fiscal juggling)*

Abruption: 1. Abruptly interrupting someone. 2. Macho, rather aggressive advertising term for stopping someone in their tracks, probably with undesirable consequences for the consumer in question. *(see Disruption)*

Absolutely: 1. Totally or completely. 2. Maybe, actually probably not; I've just added an authoritative-sounding adverb to reassure you, but I'm none the wiser frankly; not in the slightest; it's never going to happen. *(see At the end of the day; Basically, Frankly; Literally)*

Accelerator, take one's foot off the: 1. Lose energy and enthusiasm for a project or initiative. 2. Decide you can't be arsed because the whole thing's pointless; one of many automotive analogies that makes wishy-washy male executives feel particularly virile; suggestion of speed and power, but in reality slowing down; much-loved rallying cry for oppressed managers, as in: *"Guys, we mustn't take our foot off the accelerator on this one."*

Access to information: 1. Ability to see what a department or company is up to. 2. You can't have access; 'Restricted Access', otherwise known as none at all; a cover up; a sham; don't ever let this get out or else we're all doomed. *(see Need to know basis)*

Accountable, accountability: 1. We are truthful and reliable, and our numbers really do add up if you check them. 2. We will never be held accountable, because we have set up impenetrable and arcane structures so you can't get us; we have absolutely no accountability; we don't trade in this country at all – it's all based overseas, but we're not telling you where. *(see Buck stops here, the)*

Achieve learning outcomes: 1. Get something done based on sensible information. 2. Set woefully low standards and repeatedly fail to live up to them, despite plenty of warning signs. *(see Fall short)*

Achilles heel: 1. Back of the ankle (anatomical). 2. Fatal flaw suddenly exposed through fundamental incompetence, especially of those who lied on their CV. *(see CV)*

Acid test: 1. A rigorous test of authenticity, from the testing of gold with nitric acid. 2. Nasty moment when it becomes apparent that it's simply not going to work; time to retire hastily to the pub to lick wounds and have a re-think; conclusive proof that it's a shambles; irrefutable evidence of incompetence. *(see Blue touch paper, light the; Proof of concept)*

Acquihire: 1. An elision of acquire and hire; someone who became an employee without going through the usual process. 2. Dreadful term that can refer to a good or bad state of affairs – good if the employee cleverly managed to bypass all the usual nonsense that goes with getting a job, or bad if a boss has inherited a complete dimwit, and nobody knows how he or she got there. *(see Bodyleasing)*

Across the board, right: 1. Everywhere. 2. Sweeping implementation that will give everyone an unexpected surprise; complete closure of company; meltdown; Armageddon; comprehensively wrong everywhere; not everywhere actually, just at head office in Aldershot. *(see Across the piste; Across the whole piece; Niche, carve out a, market ____; Pan-global, -European; Swingeing cuts)*

Across the piste: 1. Everywhere. 2. Disastrous confusion between piece and piste, inadvertently leading to saying the opposite of what was intended; a piste is a restricted strip of land, and so by definition narrow, whereas the idea here was to suggest a wide expanse. *(see Across the board, right; Across the whole piece; Off-piste)*

Across the whole piece: 1. Everywhere. 2. Baffling conflict between one piece (presumably singular) and pieces (presumably several); vague suggestion of a lot of stuff; comprehensive, but uncertain in what way; grandiose; omnipresent; often accompanied with a world domination sweep of the arm, as in: *"I want Project Duckboard implemented across the whole piece, Barry."* *(see Across the board, right; Across the piste)*

Act, getting our ___ together: 1. Being competent. 2. We are not competent and we're about to be found out. *(see Ducks in a row, get our)*

Act out: 1. Demonstrate; do a run through. 2. Use kindergarten techniques to explain to a halfwit what the f**k you are talking about; simulate for those too thick to get it; try a dry run to see if it's going to work. *(see Test-drive)*

Action (vb), actioned, actioning: 1. Taking action. 2. Taking no action at all; ignoring completely; delegating by email in order to avoid; idling; going to the pub; taking the day off; skiving; buying an extra jacket and hanging it over your chair so that people think you are in the office; blocking; obstructing; making niggardly changes to a draft so that it has to be done again. *(see Goal-oriented; -driven; Outcomes, negative, positive; Outputs)*

Action list: 1. A list of things to do. 2. A bird's nest of jumbled notes shoved into a drawer. *(see Snake's honeymoon)*

Activation: 1. Making something happen. 2. Pretending to make something happen, but not really doing much.

Activity, lack of, planned: 1. Planning or doing stuff. 2. Not planning or doing stuff; cleverly creating the appearance of activity when nothing much is really happening; calling a meeting to avoid having to do any proper work.

Acumen, commercial: 1. Smart business intelligence. 2. Judgment utterly warped by the filthy lucre; blind obsession with cash; money at all costs; an eye for a dollar; quality much prized in finance directors, who then spend all their time generating impenetrable spreadsheets that no one can fathom.

Adhocracy: 1. Management that reacts to urgent problems rather than planning to avoid them. 2. Company in which everything is done on the hoof as a matter of course; most companies. *(see Pants, fly by the seat of our; SNAFU)*

Administrivia: 1. Trivial administration. 2. Civil servant job description. *(see Bread and butter; Bureaucracy; Jobsworth; Panjandrum; Process; Target manager; Timesheets)*

Advisorial: 1. Relating to advice. 2. Fabricated Americanism alluding to taking advice; a euphemism for a direct order; word to the wise; side remark that is weightier than the main thrust of the meeting. *(see FAQs; Hints and tips; Practical advice; Shell-like, a word in your)*

AFLO: 1. Another f**king learning opportunity. 2.Dismayed acronym often heard by those consistently asked to fix issues for which they have not been trained; usually prevalent in companies who make no effort to enlighten their staff. *(see Learning opportunity; SNAFU)*

Again: 1. Once more; for the second time; for the umpteenth time. 2. Mindless preface to repeating oneself, as in: *"Again, as I say, the market is depressed, Nigel"*; regular refuge of all idiots who either have nothing to say or only the one thing which they then feel duty-bound to repeat over and over again. *(see As I say; OCD)*

Agenda, hidden: 1. Meeting plan, concealed. 2. Devious intention to hijack or derail intended topic of meeting; scheme to ignore topic altogether, or table a completely new one; murder plot, Ides of March style; plan for *coup d'etat*, usually of managing director or chief executive. *(see Agenda, own the, set the)*

Agenda, own the, set the: 1. A list of items to be discussed. 2. A list of items you had no idea existed; swathes of material for which you have done no preparation at all; topics deliberately kept secret from you to retard your career progress. *(see Agenda, hidden)*

Agree violently: 1. Have a heated discussion while having the same view. 2. A frequent state of affairs in business, where two people or companies generate huge amounts of hot air when in truth there is no need because in fact they agree with each other; failure to see wood for trees; generation of much static with little tangible result; standard practice in all-day meetings. *(see Wood, can't see the ___ for the trees)*

Aha moment: 1. Moment of realization or sudden understanding. 2. Fanciful notion that someone will see your amazing product or presentation and shout out loud: *"Aha! Finally I get it! Thank you so much for enlightening me!" (see Bob's your uncle; Enlighten me; FMF; Light bulb experience)*

Aims: 1. Intentions or purpose. 2. Hopelessly unachievable targets that will never be met; comprehensive fiction invented at the beginning of every financial year. *(see BHAG; Fiscal juggling; Objectives; Target, hit the___, miss the point, miss the ___left, right and centre, moving)*

Air cover: 1. Protection from above to allow 'the troops' to get on with their work. 2. Total absence of management, whose main role seems to be to go on holiday precisely when any important issue needs to be addressed. *(see Empower; Enablement; Forces of darkness, deploy the; Piggyback; Shit hits the fan, when the)*

Air sandwich: 1. The layer of management between senior and junior people in a company. 2. Vacuous jobsworths who spend most of their time criticizing management and the people at the bottom who do all the work – in equal measure.

Alarm bells, set the _____ ringing: 1. Trigger warning system because there is a fire. 2. Cause total panic among colleagues by doing something distinctly unnerving, such as wearing trainers with suits, reaching inside a room from the corridor when a meeting is in session and turning the light switch repeatedly on and off for five minutes, or insisting on being called Colin when your real name is Samantha. *(see AWOL, go; Ballistic, go; Box of frogs, mad as a; Bundle, one stick short of a; Gene pool, swimming in the shallow end of the; Mid-life crisis; Moon, barking at the, over the, through the; Picnic, one sandwich short of a; Plot, lose the; Pram, to throw one's toys out of the; Radar, off; Rails, gone off the)*

Albatross around our necks: 1. A burden. 2. Poorly-informed bastardization of Coleridge's *The Rime of the Ancient Mariner* metaphor, without any particular knowledge of the origin or context.

Align, aligned: 1. In line with. 2. Categorically not in line with; unaligned; nowhere near agreeing; not interested; in desperate need of a complete rebrief. *(see FIFO (2); Hymn sheet, singing from the same; Realignment)*

All over bar the shouting: 1. Finished, unless something truly unexpected happens at the very last minute. 2. This was dead in the water years ago; it always was a non-starter; misguided from the outset; doomed. *(see Fat lady, it's not over till the ___ sings; Horse, flogging a dead)*

All-singing, all-dancing: 1. The full works, with no expense spared, particularly with regard to presentation. 2. Much fanfare with precious little content. *(see Bells and whistles; Hype; Pull out all the stops; Push the boat out)*

All staff memo: 1. Announcement to the whole company. 2. Momentous announcement for three possible reasons: 1) Most of you are fired. 2) We've gone bust. 3) Just to let you know that you may spot in the papers tomorrow that the board have awarded themselves a massive pay rise when none of you have got one – this is because we have hit the targets we set for ourselves and you haven't.

Alpha male: 1. Highest rank in a community of social animals, some of them human; also applicable to females. 2. Usually an annoying individual who simply cannot bear to be subservient; typically characterized by an unstinting belief that they are always right; frequent possessor of 'daddy issues', in which an overbearing father regularly beat them to a pulp for failing to emulate their success; increasingly manifested in the female of the species in a work context. *(see Apex predator; Ballbreaker; Control freak; Gynocracy; Nutcracker; Rottweiler)*

Alphanista: 1. Elite band of successful women in powerful positions who appear to have it all. 2. Curiously pseudo-glamorous way of describing people who lead businesses, in this case females; hints of the mafia, or some revolutionary group, when in fact the protagonists are merely perfectly ordinary executives in heels and shoulder pads being little more intrepid than convening meetings and holding court all day. *(see Alpha male; Apex predator; Ballbreaker; Consigliere; Gynocracy; Nutcracker; Rottweiler)*

Always in beta: 1. Forever in test mode. 2. Rather hip phrase adopted by digital natives to suggest that they are constantly improving their work; failure to note that this means they never arrive in alpha, so nothing is permanent and there is always an excuse as to why something doesn't work because it is still work in progress; additional insinuation that anyone in alpha is some kind of stick-in-the-mud dinosaur. *(see Digital native; MVP; WIP)*

Always on: 1. Paying attention at every moment of the day. 2. Intensely annoying to colleagues and family due to total inability to relax or generate any form of work-life balance. *(see Amber as red, treat every; Constantly striving; Expectations, exceeding; Mission statement; Sun, the _____ never sets at; Passion, passionate; 24/7/365; Work-life balance)*

Am I right, or am I right?: 1. I'm right. 2. I'm right and I'm in charge, so do what you're bloody well told or you'll be fired. *(see Dejob; Follow, do you)*

Ambassador, brand, team: 1. A person who represents the cause in an appropriate way. 2. C-list celebrity signed up at great expense who will probably disgrace the company when found face down in a pole dancer's lap after a night of drunken debauchery.

Amber as red, treat every: 1. Be on permanent alert, even if nothing is urgent or critical. 2. Panic every working moment; generate paranoia among all colleagues; fret unnecessarily; mainline on coffee and hard drugs to stumble through; lose wife and family due to permanent obsession with trivial work matters. *(see Always on; 24/7/365)*

Ambition, ambitious: 1. Intent on making progress. 2. Prepared to kill women, children and colleagues in order to secure promotion; ruthlessly selfish. *(see Driven)*

Ambulance chasing: 1. Following emergency services in the hope of picking up business (insurance industry). 2. Frantic and merciless pursuit of any business at any cost. *(see Bottom feeding; Scraping the barrel)*

Analysis, paralysis by, in the final: 1. Incapable of taking action due to being overwhelmed by too much data. 2. Too dim to understand basic numbers. *(see Brain dump; Crunch the numbers; Data dump)*

Anonymize: 1. Make anonymous. 2. Don't tell a soul I did this or I'll get the boot. *(see Team, take one for the)*

Another day another dollar: 1. I earned some money yesterday and I intend to do the same thing again today. 2. I am obsessed with making money and will do anything to get it, including parroting trite aphorisms like *"another day another dollar"*.

APAC: 1. Shorthand for Asia Pacific region. 2. Job title offering the broad excuse to fly round the Far East hurling abuse at the locals and surreptitiously shagging diminutive hookers and/or ladyboys. *(see EMEA)*

Apex predator: 1. Animal at the top of the food chain, characterized by its ability to eat everything else. 2. Grumpy, hectoring boss with appalling bullying habits; despotic twat who believes he is Hitler; world domination freak hell-bent on control and power. *(see Alpha male)*

Apples with apples, not comparing: 1. These two data sets cannot be compared. 2. I am totally baffled; my brain is too small to compare two slightly different things without melting down; I am dim and blinkered; unless it's blindingly obvious I simply won't get it; please don't show me any facts because I'll just apply the same bias I always have anyway. *(see Merger; Mix, the right, the wrong)*

Apple cart, don't upset the: 1. Don't make a fuss. 2. The chairman is always right, even when he is wrong. *(see Natural order of things, don't upset the)*

Appraisal, one degree: 1. An authoritative one-dimensional view of a subordinate. 2. Utterly prejudiced view that flies in the face of all prevailing opinion; one-eyed bias. *(see Appraisal, 360 degree; Riot act, read the)*

Appraisal, 360 degree: 1. Appraisal in which everyone with whom you work is consulted, regardless of status. 2. Annoying, touchy-feely modern HR development in which the tea lady has a say about whether you get a pay rise or not; fertile opportunity for colleagues to shaft you completely, while hiding behind the veil of anonymity; erratic and inconsistent scoring system which seems to have no pattern from one review to another; confused even further by having a different appraiser every time; pointless, ill-informed chat with so-called line manager who doesn't give a shit. *(see Appraisal, one degree; Line manager; Performance review; Shafted down the river, yourself)*

Architect (vb): 1. To design or organize something. 2. Nasty transmogrification of a noun (denoting a venerable profession) into a verb suggesting that something has been prepared with diligence and no little skill; almost invariably overclaim, as in: *"Once we have the blueprint, we can really architect this comprehensively, Rupert."* *(see Crafting, it needs a bit of)*

Architecture, brand___, business___: 1. The component parts of a brand or business. 2. Classic wank word to suggest that the brand or business has solid foundations. *(see Foundations, lay the, firm, shaky; Overarching; Positioning)*

Armageddon plan: 1. Crisis management plan. 2. Daily occurrence; permanent panic mode; firefighting; tail chasing; chaos. *(see Doomsday scenario; Efficiency drive; Scenario, best-case, nightmare, worst-case; Scorched earth policy; SNAFU)*

Arse about face, you've got that: 1. The wrong way round. 2. Hopelessly inappropriate; so bad that it is effectively the opposite of what is needed to do the job; completely off brief; useless (item or person).

Arse covering: 1. Protecting one's position or job. 2. All-pervasive frame of mind in which the perpetrator can never admit that it was their fault; generating a massive email trail proving that everyone else is responsible, but not me; enormous dossier of evidence that verifies beyond a shred of doubt that the client is in the wrong, because I am perfect; sole activity of control freaks who don't care what they work on, so long as they are always right. *(see BCC; Belt and braces; Call report; CC; Control freak; FYI)*

Arse in alligators, up to my: 1. In danger of being eaten by an aggressive crocodilian; very busy; in a spot of bother. 2. About to be fired, or carried away by a team of medics in white coats; not coping at all; stacking lie upon lie to get out of a metaphorical hole that is only getting bigger by the minute; seconds away from defenestrating a colleague, or oneself; seriously considering self-immolation. *(see Defenestrate, defenestration; Full-on; Postal, go)*

Arse, up your own: 1. Self-obsessed and usually spouting nonsense. 2. Utterly unbearable; insufferable; effectively impossible to work with, as in: *"He was so far up his arse they could have shared a hat."* *(see Loose cannon)*

Art form, got it down to an: 1. Mastered a successful formula that can be repeated again and again. 2. Taken a series of crass shortcuts to knock something up in as quick a time as possible so we can all go to the pub; skimmed it; mapped out a simplistic framework that will just about do; plagiarized someone else's method and passed it off as our own; stole intellectual copyright lock, stock and barrel, while claiming barefaced that it was all your work. *(see ABC, easy as; Cooking on gas; Falling off a log)*

ASAP: 1. As soon as possible. 2. Now; yesterday; actually any time you like, I'm just trying to make it sound as though everything is vitally urgent when it isn't really, which makes me feel important and gives me wood. *(see ETA; PDQ)*

As I say: 1. Just to let you know that I am repeating myself. 2. Just to let you know that I am repeating myself. *(see Again; OCD)*

Ask, big: 1. A substantial request, usually involving a lot of work or onerous responsibility. 2. Impossible task dressed up as a flattering and significant thing to do; a project that genuinely cannot be completed in time or for the budget; a pup; an instruction that will almost certainly lead to termination of employment. *(see Hospital pass; Opportunity; Poisoned chalice; Team, take one for the)*

Asking a duck to bark: 1. Requesting something impossible. 2. Deliberately requesting something impossible in order to humiliate a subordinate, preferably in public; blindly refusing to accept that something cannot be done. *(see Bark into the wind, up the wrong tree; Impossible, nothing is)*

Aspirational: 1. Something to aspire to. 2. Vain and insubstantial; deeply unfulfilling within seconds of purchase; fleeting dopamine high followed by profound and sustained depression; addictive and yet unsatisfying; jealous yearning for someone else's job or possessions; shallow characteristic displayed by thousands of talent show contestants; in total denial about skills and wanting something beyond one's capability. *(see Capability gap; Deeply shallow)*

Asset: 1. Anything valuable or useful. 2. Anything we can flog, frankly, and quite a lot of things that we can't; toadying descriptor of workforce often deployed by HR directors, as in: *"Our greatest assets walk out of the office every night – our staff!"*; any cash we can get for nothing, usually filed under 'goodwill' in the accounts so that shareholders can squeeze more money out of ignorant investors.

Assimilation: 1. Process of absorbing. 2. Process of ejecting, such as during mergers and takeovers when half the staff are sacked; of individuals, total failure to absorb any relevant information due to daydreaming, hangovers, or plain boredom. *(see Merger; Mix, the right, the wrong; Integrate, integral, integration)*

ASTRO: 1. Always stating the really obvious. 2. Intensely annoying characteristic of those who have little to contribute but are desperate to make it look as though they do. *(see Jobsworth; Obvious, a firm grasp of the)*

Astroturfing: 1. When a movement is portrayed as a grassroots initiative but is actually run on behalf of corporate interests. 2. Curious, semi-sporting, analogy that takes a playing surface noun and turns it into a verb, all for the sake of a pun about grass; almost certainly invented by people who have never played football in their lives, but think it might be trendy to do so.

At a stroke: 1. In one go, sometimes of a pen. 2. In a horrible split second, as in: *"Did you hear about Darren? He was dejobbed at a stroke."* *(see Dejob; One fell swoop, in)*

A team, this calls for the: 1. We urgently need our senior team on this. 2. The management has severely neglected this project and now it's a monumental cockup so they are going to position themselves as the only people who can get us out of a hole; B, C, or D Team – we don't actually have an A Team. *(see Cavalry over the hill; Dream team; Eleventh hour, at the)*

At, where I'm: 1. This is my point of view. 2. Nowhere – my brain is so small I just can't work it out; I've made cock-all progress on this since I last saw you because I am too (a) busy, (b) lazy, (c) retarded to have a view. *(see Coming from, where I'm)*

At the end of the day: 1. When a day is finishing, somewhere between 11pm and 12pm. 2. Totally pointless beginning or ending to a sentence that adds nothing to its meaning whatsoever. *(see Absolutely; Basically; End of play; Frankly; Literally; Net net; Put to bed)*

At this moment in time: Now. *(see At this point in time; End of play)*

At this point in time: Now. *(see At this moment in time; End of play)*

Attention-getting: 1. Someone who gets attention, usually Sally on reception with the large Charlies. *(see Attention-seeking)*

Attention-seeking: 1. Someone who seeks attention, usually Sally on reception with the large Charlies. *(see Attention-getting)*

Augmented Business Visualization: 1. Information you may or may not understand. 2. As defined by the originators: *"ABV is a new paradigm in visualization which provides rich and actionable visual decision making environments on all delivery platforms by connecting portions of documents to business data found in enterprise applications. With ABV, information and business data is synthesized from multiple sources into a single visual environment, delivering rich information context to users."* Quite.

Aunt Sally: 1. Something set up as a target for disagreement. 2. Egregiously sub-standard proposal or piece of work that has no hope of doing the job, but is lobbed into the presentation anyway to make it look as though more work has been done than truly has; item included on the agenda for the sole purpose of rejecting it and humiliating your main rival for promotion. *(see Agenda, hidden; Know it when I see it, I don't know what I want but I'll _____; Sacred Cow; Straw Man)*

Authenticity: 1. Relating to anything that is authentic. 2. Totally false, such as: *"This product was lovingly forged in the crucible of time"*; quality constantly demanded of staff in over-earnest companies. *(see Back story; Passion, passionate; Provenance; Rebrand)*

Autocorrect: 1. Feature that corrects spelling on computers and mobile devices. 2. Frequently annoying function that makes you say something you don't want to; source of occasional massive *faux pas* such as: *"I can't* *come out tonight, I'm cleaning my Mum's vagina,"* shortly followed by, *"China, I meant china!!" (regular examples of this phenomenon at www. damnyouautocorrect.com)*

Autonomy: 1. Ability to do something on your own, and without interference; complete executive authority. 2. No freedom in which to move whatsoever; constantly being monitored. *(see Control freak; Micromanaging)*

Autopilot: 1. Machine that can control a plane. 2. Zombie-like state prevalent first thing in the morning after the office party or a bank holiday; near total absence of brain activity, often witnessed on the second day of an 'off-site' awayday after overshooting in the hotel bar the previous night. *(see Awayday; Office party; Off-site)*

Awayday: 1. A day away, usually from the office. 2. Large-scale excuse for the board or an entire department to wear ill-advised 'mufti' clothes, play golf badly, and eat unfeasible quantities of boiled sweets and biscuits; embarrassing escapade to an eye-wateringly expensive country retreat, accompanied by a programme of excruciating team bonding exercises, facilitated by a ruddy-cheeked woman called Amanda. *(see Autopilot; Bad idea, there's no such thing as a; Bonding, team; Brainstorm; Executive retreat; Flip chart; Off-site; Workshop)*

AWOL, go: 1. Absent without leave (military). 2. Nowhere to be seen, as in: *"Where the f**k is Dave?"*; throw a sickie; not turn up; do a runner; leg it; quit the scene at once, sometimes permanently. *(see Ballistic, go; Pear-shaped, it's all gone; Plot, lose the; Postal, go; Pram, to throw one's toys out of the; Radar, off; Rails, gone off the; Tits up, it's all gone)*

Axe, face the: 1. Be a candidate for dismissal. 2. Be summarily dismissed, despite a sham of a 'consultation period'. *(see ABC session; Can, carry the; Consultation period; Decruit; Dejob; Downsize; Phone list, go down the)*

Back burner, we'll have to put that on the: 1. Make that low priority from now on. 2. We announced this project in a blaze of glory but it has now become apparent that it's doomed, so ignore it – but if anyone asks, don't tell them we cocked it up. *(see Front burner, let's bring that onto the)*

Back end architecture: 1. The design bit at the end of the project or product. 2. Desperate scrambling around at the last minute to rectify all the bugs in the project or product that were never anticipated due to lack of foresight or blatant incompetence. *(see Front end)*

Background noise: 1. Irrelevant static that should be ignored. 2. Vital signals that would have warned us that the whole project would be a disaster if only we hadn't been so intent on doing it anyway because the boss insisted on it, despite all sensible advice to the contrary. *(see Static; White noise)*

Backlash: 1. Nasty reaction to an action. 2. Vicious witch-hunt to find someone else to blame. *(see Blame culture; Witch-hunt)*

Backroom: 1. The room at the back where no one ever goes. 2. The place where all the truly valuable work is done, despite the claims of the self-appointed glory boys from the sales department. *(see Frontline; Jazz hands)*

Back stabbing: 1. Apportioning blame to someone when they are not present to defend themselves, or even deny that they were responsible. 2. Merciless accusation of a colleague in order to save your own skin. *(see Blitz; Front stabbing; Rowing in the same boat, direction)*

Back story: 1. History of something; events which took place before, usually necessary to explain action in a film. 2. Often deceitful attempt to suggest provenance for a product where there is none; fanciful guff trumped up by marketing department along the lines of *"forged in the crucible of time"*, *"lovingly handpicked by Masai virgins"*, or *"individually blessed by the Pope". (see Authenticity; Provenance)*

Back-to-back: 1. A segue between one thing and another, with no gap in between them. 2. A relentless mad scramble caused by chronic lack of organization and institutional incompetence. *(see Cocks on the block; Stacked, completely; Under siege; Wall-to-wall)*

Back to basics: 1. A return to first principles, also often referred to as the drawing board, or square one. 2. We massively over-elaborated this due to a mixture of hubris, overconfidence and sheer arrogance – simple would have been far better. *(see Drawing board, back to the)*

Backs to the wall: 1. A desperate rearguard action. 2. We could well be fired for this, mainly due to amateurish misjudgment and overconfidence. *(see Cocks on the block)*

Backwards, bend over: 1. Do everything possible to help. 2. Drop all the important stuff and leave everyone else in the lurch just to brown-nose the boss. *(see Brown-nosing)*

Bacon, bring home the: 1. Get the job done. 2. Take all the credit for a successful sale or presentation when in fact other people did all the work.

Bad apple: 1. Rotten piece of fruit. 2. Poisonous member of staff with a dreadful attitude. *(see Draining the swamp)*

Bad idea, there's no such thing as a: 1. Say what you like – all thoughts are welcome, no matter how poor they sound. 2. We are incapable of distinguishing between a good and bad idea; most ideas are rubbish and these are no exception; we don't care how much crap we generate in this session so long as it looks as though we are working when in fact we are just eating biscuits. *(see Awayday; Brainstorm; Conceptual thinking; Idea, big; Lateral thinking; Off-site)*

Baked in: 1. An intrinsic part of the whole, as in a thoroughly cooked pie or loaf of bread. 2. Tragically inane metaphor drawn from the culinary world, much loved of 'digital natives' (qv) as in: *"We must ensure that social media is fully baked into the brand's DNA." (see Digital native; DNA)*

Balanced scorecard: 1. A wider set of measurements of business performance than simply finances, invented by Harvard Business School professor

Robert Kaplan in 1992. 2. Semi-useless ragbag of vague characteristics only loosely relevant to the business, most commonly used as a smokescreen to disguise inept performance; godsend for poor managers, giving the impression of a pseudo-science and thereby adding legitimacy to shocking failures in competence. *(see Snake oil salesman; Vin ordinaire)*

Ball, take one's eye off the: 1. Fail to concentrate sufficiently. 2. Fail to concentrate sufficiently, for a split second or several years, resulting in dismissal; daydream; cockup. *(see Decruit; Drop a ricket)*

Ballbreaker: 1. Tough female executive. 2. Tough female executive who revels in the ritual humiliation of male colleagues just for the sport of it; woman with 'issues'; resentful divorcee; aggressive lesbian on a mission; miserable harridan without an inch of compassion. *(see Control freak; Gynocracy; Nutcracker; Rottweiler)*

Ballistic, go: 1. Adopt an approach relating to the flight of projectiles; become enraged or frenziedly violent. 2. Hurl objects around the office, sometimes including members of staff; go AWOL; have a paddy; embark on childish tantrum; have a fit; become incandescent with rage. *(see AWOL, go; Defenestrate, defenestration; Midlife crisis; Moon, barking at the, over the, through the; Nuclear, go; Plot, lose the; Postal, go; Pram, to throw one's toys out of the; Radar, off; Rails, gone off the)*

Ball juggling: 1. Handling several issues or projects at the same time. 2. Failing to cope on all fronts; attempting to create the impression of all-round competence but failing miserably; standing up in the middle of an open plan office and shouting: *"I've got fifteen balls up in the air on this project and two of them are mine!"*; surreptitiously fiddling with one's testicles in a tiresome board meeting. *(see Balls in the air, on the block, to the wall; Plate spinning; Python, wrestling with a)*

Balloon has gone up, the: 1. The action has started. 2. Quick, leave the building immediately and don't ever go back – we've been rumbled; sudden and fatal discovery of financial mismanagement. *(see Fiscal juggling)*

Ballpark figure: 1. An estimated number. 2. Comprehensive fiction; nowhere near the true amount; out to the tune of millions; flagrant lie; random guesswork. *(see Cover all the bases; Zone, in the)*

Balls in the air, on the block, to the wall: 1. Genitals not entirely where they should normally be. 2. Reputation in near-tatters; chances of ever working again diminishing by the second; sweating profusely on the outcome of a tribunal after a misdemeanour with Jemma from the typing pool.

(see Ball juggling; Cocks on the block; Plate spinning; Python, wrestling with a; Under siege)

Banana, stabbing a seal with a: 1. Using a tropical crescent-shaped fruit to terminate the life of an aquatic mammal of the *phocidae* or *otariidae* families. 2. Hopelessly equipped for the job; using entirely the wrong tool to get something done; repeatedly using the same technique again and again hoping in vain for a different result; too dim to change tactics. *(see Bark into the wind, up the wrong tree; Grasping at fog; Nailing a jelly to the wall, trying to)*

Banana skin, political: 1. Issue with the power to trip someone up. 2. Terminal booby trap that leads to dismissal, either via the window or after a slow, painful death. *(see Consultation period; Defenestrate, defenestration)*

Bandwagon, jumping on the negative ___,positive ___: 1. A wagon carrying a band in a parade. 2. Blindly following what everyone else is doing for no particular reason, for better or worse; joining in a craze without thought; triumphantly shouting "I am an individual!" while joining a million other people doing the same thing; failing to have an original thought, ever. *(see Outcomes, positive, negative)*

Bandwagoneering: 1. There is no correct definition for this word, because it doesn't exist. 2. Exploiting a trend in order to make stack loads of cash out of it; agreeing with lots of other hip people in the vain hope that you will look hip too. *(see Midlife crisis)*

Bandwidth, he doesn't have the: 1. Not intelligent. 2. He's thick as a brick; dead from the neck up; relentlessly useless at work; no help at all, in fact, a downright hindrance; 100% incompetent. *(see Intelligent, if you were any less ___, I'd have to water you once a day; Mental furniture; Obvious, firm grasp of the; Psychic RAM; Shilling, not the full; WOMBAT)*

Bang the drum: 1. Hit a percussion instrument. 2. Make a disproportionate racket about something in a futile attempt to rally support or gain interest. *(see Tub thumping)*

Bar chart: 1. Histogram showing data or sales performance. 2. Work of fiction designed to mislead potential customers or shareholders; cunning deployment of distorted axes to create the impression of success; baffling array of similarly-coloured towers depicting nothing intelligible whatsoever; one of 127 similar charts in a tedious research debrief with no discernable conclusion. *(see Histogram)*

Bark into the wind, up the wrong tree: 1. Attempting something that is never going to work. 2. Too unintelligent to rumble that the current approach will consistently fail. *(see Asking a duck to bark; Banana, stabbing a seal with a; Dialogue, continuous consumer, meaningful; Herring, chasing a different)*

Barnstorm: 1. To tour rural districts putting on shows (chiefly USA). 2. Take a meeting by storm, for better or worse; be brilliant and win; be utterly useless and fail miserably in public; throw a wobbly and lose it completely in front of the entire board; experience a burst of Tourette's in front of a senior visiting customer.

Barriers: 1. Things in the way. 2. Thoroughly legitimate reasons why prospective customers refuse to buy your sub-standard products, as in so-called 'barriers to purchase'; obstructive colleagues who block your every proposal.

Baseline: 1. An agreed point from which other points can be measured or compared. 2. Ever-shifting criteria only called upon to trumpet imaginary success; infuriating chimera that never quite arrives nor truly exists. *(see Ballpark figure; Fiscal juggling; Hopper, pour into the; Horizon, above the, change the, below the, small ripple on the; Re-baselining; Touch base)*

Basically: 1. In a fundamental or elementary manner. 2. This word has marginal meaning and rarely adds anything no matter where it is used. *(see Absolutely, At the end of the day; Frankly; Literally)*

Basket case: 1. Merciless US slang term for a person with all limbs amputated. 2. Total buffoon; complete no-hoper; an idiot in search of a village. *(see Box of frogs, mad as a; Mid-life crisis; Picnic, one sandwich short of a; Postal, go)*

Bath, take a: 1. Conduct ablutions in a body-sized water-bearing vessel. 2. Lose the lot; nose dive spectacularly; crash violently in full view of all colleagues; experience absolute humiliation in all-company meeting. *(see Catch a cold; Gung ho)*

Battleground: 1. Place where a battle is fought. 2. Pathetic deployment of the military metaphor to something truly bland, such as toilet cleaner market; heroic but pointless attempt to make dreary subject matter seem more appealing, as in: *"We're going to take the curtain ring market by storm guys!" (see Flagpole, run it up the____ and see who salutes; Jungle out there, it's a)*

Bazooka after a fly, we're not going to send a: 1. We won't devote disproportionately large resources to this. 2. It's a piss-pot little project so we'll let it wither on the vine; outrageous budget request, as in: *"Brian, the board has decided that the £1 million sign-off for the jasmine and sesame seed line extension will sadly not be forthcoming." (see Drop a ricket; Feet, to dive in with both; Nut, sledgehammer to crack a; Platform, eat one's own)*

BCC: 1. Blind carbon copy. 2. My intention is to humiliate you convincingly in public by letting everyone see your crass rantings in full; tangible equivalent of a vindictive outburst along the lines of: *"Don't f**k with me you little shit, I have the proof!" (see Arse covering; Blame culture; CC; Email; FYI; Voice mail)*

Beaconicity, predictors of: 1. Factors that will indicate what will stand out. 2. Truly shocking piece of government rubbish, inventing 'beaconicity', the capacity to shine or stand out; originating from the correct word for a signal fire or light on a hill, and horribly migrated to any areas acquiring 'beacon status', and thus qualifying for special funding; the addition of the suffix –icity and a predictive element make this a car crash of gargantuan proportions.

Be-all-and-end-all: 1. Ultimate; final; crucial. 2. Nothing of the sort; quintessentially unimportant, but dressed up to sound as though it is; irrelevant; incidental; of no real interest; inconsequential.

Beanbags: 1. Large soft cushions. 2. Large soft cushions much loved by reclining semi-stoned hippies; similar brightly-coloured 'furniture' totally unsuited to the office environment; popular, in-vogue items to scatter around so-called 'soft areas'; near-flattened blob of material still bearing the unmistakable imprint of the rear end of Sylvia from HR, who has a 'big personality'. *(see Blue sky thinking; Brainstorm; Breakout groups; Soft area)*

Bean counter: 1. Accountant or finance director. 2. Intensely irritating man in a bad suit who is never seen without a spreadsheet; incapable of any basic social skills; champion of the hilarious Donald Duck tie; also inclined to wear hooped red socks with unpolished brown shoes; likely resident of Ruislip or Rickmansworth; humourless numbers person with borderline halitosis and a disconcerting leer – to be avoided at all costs at the Christmas party.

Beans, spill the: 1. Drop a number of leguminous plants of the genus *phaseolus* on the floor. 2. Let slip something highly inappropriate in a crucial meeting; get pissed and reveal vital trade secrets to a competitor; blurt out confidential information at a trade conference or interview. *(see Chinese whispers; Drop a ricket; Loop, out of the, keep in the)*

Beavers, defending it like: 1. Tenaciously backing a cause. 2. Completely inaccurate analogy attempting to specify anthropomorphic qualities which the beaver does not in fact possess; starting a sentence without knowing how to finish it and randomly grabbing at a member of the animal kingdom to finish the job. *(see Seals, left them clapping like; Wildebeest in a row, has the lion got his)*

Bear with me: 1. Give me a moment. 2. I desperately need to stall for time; I have no executive authority to deal with this problem, despite claiming I did.

Bee's knees, it's the: 1. It's brilliant. 2. It's the same as the leg joints of a hymenopterous insect of the superfamily *apoidea*, which is really saying something; curious piece of vernacular with no discernible purpose. *(see Dog's bollocks; Mustard, cut the, that's ___ that is)*

Begs the question: 1. Why? 2. Why oh why?

Behavioural economics: 1. Pseudoscience suggesting that pure economic theory is a poor indicator of human behaviour. 2. Spectacular smoke and mirrors job much loved by advertising agencies; random series of anecdotes about the vagaries of human decision-making; not a discipline at all, having resisted a clear definition in the entire academic canon that describes it. *(see FAQs; Grasping at fog; Hints and tips; Smoke and mirrors job)*

Behaviours: 1. Ways of behaving. 2. Ugly plural meaning not a lot, other than ways of behaving.

Bells and whistles: 1. Lots of fancy stuff. 2. Pointless superfluous fanfare surrounding something actually quite ordinary; scores of additional features on a piece of technology that nobody uses but which make the designer look clever and get him promoted. *(see All-singing, all-dancing; Hype; Pull out all the stops; Push the boat out)*

Belt and braces: 1. Trousers held up by two equally good methods. 2. Needless duplication of task or method. *(see Arse covering)*

Bench, has this got: 1. Does this team have strength in depth, as verified by the quality of the players on the substitute's bench? 2. Truly dire phrase pilfered, once again, from the verbal swamp that is American sport; is this idea any good, or is it pure bollocks? *(see Legs, it's got; Real estate, how much ___ does this have; Success, what does ___ look like?)*

Benchmarking, category, industry: 1. Making a mark as a reference point for surveying. 2. Incessant paranoid comparison between the performance of your business and that of a competitor; incapacity to have one iota of original thought; relentless plundering of copycat ideas from a more inventive rival. *(KPIs; Markers, put some ___ down; Metrics; Milestones)*

Bench time: 1. Amount of time spent sitting on a bench, for reasons unclear. 2. Nauseating American expression for how many meetings are held with prospective customers, believing (often erroneously) that the more you talk to someone, the more likely they are to buy; despairing cry of sales directors throughout the USA, as in: *"Jeez Brad, your team are failing to generate enough quality bench time!" (see Bench, has this got)*

Beneficiate: 1. To treat a raw material to improve properties. 2. Inappropriately used to denote chairing a meeting with kindness, or giving it one's blessing, as in: *"Beloved monarch (insert name here), would you be so kind as to beneficiate this convention for us?" (see Headline benediction)*

Best of need offering: 1. An elision of best of breed and need – best of breed that meets a need. 2. Circular twaddle vainly trying to suggest that something is as good as it can possibly be.

Best is the enemy of better: 1. Poorly articulated transposition of "better is the enemy of best", intending to suggest that settling for simply okay won't do, while conveying precisely the opposite. 2. Tired mantra usually delivered by people desperately trying to be more creative than they truly are; frequently misstated through trying to be just a little too glib. *(see GEIGE; Great, good is the enemy of)*

Best practice: 1. How something should be done, i.e. properly. 2. Standard that companies and individuals consistently fail to reach; shoddy fudging; skimming; quality never achieved, but regularly hyped up; something that is practiced but never enacted; abstract concept often discussed without any reference to how it can actually be done.

BHAG: 1. Big hairy audacious goal, invented by Jim Collins in 2001 in his book *Good To Great*. 2. Tediously macho 'vision' mapped out by unintelligent business leader, usually just after reading said book or failing to complete an MBA; vacuous collection of bland and predominantly meaningless adjectives supposedly intended to 'direct' the staff; random verbal guff entirely interchangeable with that on the boardroom wall of a main rival. *(see Aims; Aspirational; Greatest Imaginable Challenge; Impossible, nothing is: MBA; Objectives; Unthinkable, think the)*

Bias for action: 1. Tendency to get things done rather than just talk about them, first proposed by business writers Peters and Waterman in their 1982 book *In Search of Excellence*. 2. Loud but hollow mantra frequently peddled by vacuous macho managers, as in: *"We need a bias for action on this one guys!"*, when in truth they have no intention of lifting a finger to help, ever.

Big boys, playing with the: 1. Competing against the biggest and best there is. 2. Scrabbling around with the same old has-beens; frantically playing catch-up; vainly trying to move out of the second or third division.

Big data: 1. A lot of information. 2. Small moniker for a lot of twaddle; suggestion that anyone using the phrase is also big, although they may have little grip on the subject; catch-all trumped up to blur the fact that most companies have so much information they haven't a clue what to do with it all.

Big fish: 1. Large marine animal; significant player or prize. 2. Tired aquatic scale reference, usually involving being a big fish in a small pond, or a small fish in a big pond; rarely mentioned as a big fish in a big pond for some unknown reason.

Big cheese: 1. Large chunk of dairy produce, such as Gorgonzola. 2. The boss; the person at the top; supposedly famous visiting dignitary. *(see Fromage, grand; Head honcho; Head office, I'm from ___ and I'm here to help; Player, big)*

Big enchilada: 1. Large tortilla fried in hot fat, filled with meat and covered in chilli sauce. 2. The boss, or if not, then a big presence in the office. *(see Big cheese)*

Big match temperament: 1. Disposition suitable for important occasions. 2. Disposition utterly unsuitable for important occasions; prone to childish outbursts. *(see Pram, to throw one's toys out of the)*

Big picture: 1. A large painting. 2. Apparent ability to see beyond the trivia, when the trivia is actually more interesting; strategic wibble that excuses someone from having to do any work, on the grounds that they are 'strategizing'. *(see Blue-sky thinking; Brainstorm; Helicopter view; Holistic; Strategy, strategize)*

BIMBO: 1. Buy in management buy out. 2 Financial gymnastics that incorporate characteristics of both a management buy in and buy out – the existing management and outside managers buy out a company in a form of fiscal hokey cokey, thereby ensuring that at any given moment they may be unsure as to whether they are in or out.

BlackBerry prayer: 1. Leaning forward, as if praying, to check emails surreptitiously in meetings. 2. Incapable of paying attention to those present due to absolute addiction to one's own mobile device; total ennui with regard to present company; belief that one's own affairs are intrinsically more interesting than anyone else's; odd belief that activities elsewhere must somehow be more interesting than what is happening in front of you, despite repeated evidence to the contrary. *(see Death by PowerPoint; Meetings; Moi presentation)*

Black arts: 1. Black magic used for evil purposes. 2. Obscure chicanery used by shady executives to achieve their nefarious ends. *(see Cook the books; Fiscal juggling)*

Black hole, disappeared into a: 1. Astronomical phenomenon so dense that its escape velocity exceeds the speed of light. 2. Catastrophic loss of income or flaw in system; near-total loss of customer base overnight; instant sacking, never to be seen again; immediate imprisonment for fraud. *(see Blood bath, on the walls; Game is up, the; Leaky bucket)*

Black swan: 1. Large and dark aquatic bird; random event that cannot be predicted, as explained by Nassim Nicholas Taleb in his 2007 book of the same name (all swans were assumed to be white until overseas travel revealed the existence of black ones). 2. Disastrous development that no one saw coming, and that destroys everything; total crash; meltdown; catastrophe; career-threatening cockup. *(see Bounce out of the norm; Crystal ball; Event; Futureproof; Game plan; Head office, I'm from ___ and I'm here to help; Navel gazing; Risk management)*

Blame culture: 1. Work place in which people have to prove that they are genuinely doing something constructive, or face the consequences. 2. Vicious atmosphere in which finger pointing and character assassination are the norm – it's dog eat dog, and anything goes so long as it's definitely not your fault. *(see BCC; Backlash; Back stabbing; Fear; Front stabbing; Hospital pass; In the same boat; Witch-hunt)*

Blank canvas: 1. A clean sheet; starting from scratch. 2. Highly dangerous non-brief allowing a completely free rein, often leading to disastrous consequences; permission to run riot and go completely off-piste, much loved of creative and design folk; irresponsible grey area allowing people to do exactly what they want, which usually means going to the pub.

Bleeding edge: 1. Blood dripping from the corner of a sharp object such as a knife. 2. Hideous bastard son of the phrase 'leading edge', impossibly suggesting something even more advanced than the most advanced thing. *(see Cutting edge; Leading edge; Next-generation; Pioneering)*

Blitz: 1. Violent and sustained attack. 2. Violent and sustained attack on a colleague after years of persecution. *(see Back stabbing; Front stabbing)*

Blood bath, on the walls: 1. Massive fight, leaving significant evidence. 2. Total carnage in the office; wholesale sacking of an entire department; full-scale walkout of majority of the board to form a rival breakaway; dramatic eviction of finance director in hand cuffs following appalling exposé of malfeasance. *(see Armageddon plan; Black hole, disappeared into a; Fiscal juggling)*

Blow it: 1. Fail to take an opportunity. 2. Crash and burn at the vital moment, such as breaking wind loudly at interview; allow inner monologue to surface during a crucial client meeting, as in: *"Oh for f**k's sake Brian, just get on with it!"*

Blue-chip: 1. A company whose stock is considered reliable for dividend income and capital value, named after the gambling chip with the highest value. 2. Lazy catch-all descriptor to suggest anything of high quality, particularly by companies claiming that all their customers are 'blue-chip', or by job candidates portraying a supposedly 'blue-chip' CV; not high quality at all – in fact, distinctly average; just as likely to go bust tomorrow as an iffy start up. *(see CV)*

Blue in the face, talk until you're: 1. Talk for a long time. 2. Say nothing of consequence for a whole day. *(see Awayday; Brainstorm)*

Blueprint: 1. Photographic print of technical drawings, using white lines on a blue background; a cyanotype; an original plan or prototype. 2. Crap diagram with a few blobs on it purporting to hold the key to world domination; frequently not even blue, and almost certainly not worthy of print. *(see Brand onion; pillars, pyramid)*

Blue sky, to: 1. To think theoretically without any regard to future application of the result. 2. Shocking verb-cum-noun-cum-adjective much loved of Americans, roughly denoting to think broadly and vaguely; useless hot air session in which many attendees talk drivel for a sustained period, congratulate themselves on a 'highly constructive session,' and then sod off to the golf course to wear dreadful trousers. *(see Blue-sky thinking)*

Blue-sky thinking: 1. Purely theoretical thinking. 2. Waffle; static; hot air; piffle; inconsequential rubbish; stuff that will never happen in a million years. *(see Beanbags; Big picture; Blue sky, to; Blue yonder; Brainstorm; Static; White noise)*

Blue touch paper, light the: 1. Set something running, then stand back and watch the consequences. 2. Cause complete chaos; do something thoughtless without due regard for the consequences; set in train a cataclysmic chain reaction; fail to spot the link between several related things. *(see Acid test; Dropping grenades in fishponds; Proof of concept)*

Blue yonder: 1. A long way over there in the distance. 2. Metaphorical place where all the pointless blue-sky thinking ideas go, never to return or be enacted. *(see Blue-sky thinking; Head of the valley syndrome; Horizon, above the, change the, below the, small ripple on the)*

BOAC: 1. Bit of a c**t. 2. Totally profane reference to someone who just about gets away with it, and yet everyone knows they are fundamentally untrustworthy, as in: *"Geoff's great at the numbers but in all honesty he's a BOAC, isn't he?"*

Bob's your uncle: 1. Robert is your father's brother. 2. Hey presto!; there you have it; trite throwaway phrase much loved by self-appointed office wags who are never as funny as they think they are; daft nonsensical aphorism frequently trumpeted by the annoying maintenance man when completing a perfectly simple task such as fixing a shelf. *(see Aha moment)*

Bodies are buried, where the ___: 1. Dark secrets, of individual or company. 2. One of the primary reasons why long-serving (but often incompetent) members of staff never get fired – because they know the CEO shagged the receptionist, or worse. *(see Skeletons in the cupboard; Smoking Gun)*

Bodyleasing: 1. Lending personnel to a client company, either cheaply or for free. 2. Somewhat impersonal term likening people to cars or similar. *(see Acquihire: Human resources)*

BOGOFF: 1. Buy one get one for free. 2. This tat is so low quality we're giving it away.

BOHICA: 1. Bend over here it comes again. 2. Look out, you're about to get shafted for the umpteenth time; scatological rallying call for procurement executives about to screw their suppliers for the fourth year in a row. *(see Compliance; Cost effective; Drop our trousers; Sprat to catch a mackerel)*

Boil the ocean, you can't: 1. It's impossible to make the sea turn from liquid to vapour. 2. This task simply can't be done; somewhat over dramatic analogy, as in: *"We're not trying to boil the ocean here, Steve."* *(see Rocket science, it's not)*

Bollocks, talking: 1. Testicles that can speak. 2. Sustained burst of total rubbish blurted out in answer to an unexpected interview question; patchwork of platitude and cliché designed to confuse; mission statement contents; any acceptance speech; 100% of proclamations made by politicians or sportsmen. *(see Bullshit; Obfuscation)*

Bombs, box of: 1. Container of explosives. 2. Lethal, career-threatening material lurking ominously in in-box, whether physical or electronic; accident waiting to happen; project that will detonate the moment it is touched; important meeting with trouble written all over it; annual review at which a severe dressing down will undoubtedly be administered. *(see Ask, big; Catching a falling knife; Curve ball; Dyke, finger in the; Hospital pass; Minefield, complete, tiptoeing through a; Poisoned chalice)*

Bombshell: 1. Unexpected news; attractive blonde woman. 2. Combination of the two, as in discovering that the attractive blonde woman is up the duff, and the child is yours; marching orders. *(see Bullet, get the; Marching orders, get your)*

Bonding, team: 1. Joining together, not always using adhesive. 2. Dreaded verb referring to the abhorrent process of 'getting to know your colleagues better', probably originated by well-meaning and touchy-feely HR people intending to improve morale; butt of thousands of awayday jokes referring to disastrous 'team bonding' exercises, typically building a pontoon over a river with limited materials, or having the courage to fall backwards into the team's arms from a great height. *(see Awayday; Partners; Share and air; Show and tell; Strategic alliance; Touchy-feely)*

Bones, put flesh on the: 1. Provide detail to explain the broad concept. 2. Add extraneous layers of blether when the gist is already evident; massively pad out with dross; confuse the issue with irrelevant material; obfuscate; waffle; drone on purely to hear one's own voice; showboat; bore for England, or any nation that will listen.

Boomerang effect: 1. A person or thing that comes back. 2. Awful unintended repercussion; unexpected reaction to something you originally thought was of no great consequence; trainee you badly mistreated returning to company some years later as chief executive, with inevitable effect; tit for tat retaliation to office prank leading to dismissal.

Boss: 1. Person in charge. 2. Incompetent prat.

Bottleneck: 1. The top of a bottle where the flow of liquid is most squeezed. 2. Chaotic log jam of projects and workload that can cripple a company in a matter of days; complete deadlock when no one will work with you because of your appalling office habits; paralysis caused by one power-crazed maniac insisting on signing off every bit of paper in the company. *(see Control freak)*

Bottom feeding: 1. Eating material on the floor of a river, sea or fish tank. 2. Hoovering up any crap that has settled on the bottom; dealing solely in the dross; working with or for the cheapest and worst possible exponents in the market; actively pursuing low-rent customers, and to hell with the consequences. *(see Ambulance chasing; Scraping the barrel)*

Bottom line: 1. The figure at the bottom when all the others have been added and subtracted. 2. Maze of chicanery and falsehoods, bearing no resemblance to the true state of the business; work of supreme fiction. *(see Fiscal juggling; Topline)*

Bottomed out: 1. No longer falling, having reached the floor. 2. Sales figures that have nowhere else to go, having collapsed catastrophically and hit their lowest possible point. *(see Entering a new plateau; Flatline; Negative growth)*

Bounce ideas off: 1. Discuss a concept with a colleague. 2. Random word dump after jumping a colleague unexpectedly in the corridor just outside the toilets; sustained monologue trying to impose one's own view; blunt refusal to accept any idea deviating from one's own preconceived bias; bawl out subordinate for no particular reason other than being in a bad mood. *(see Brain dump; Brainstorm; Word dump)*

Bounce out of the norm: 1. Deviate from what is normal. 2. Veer horribly off-piste; discover utterly unexpected sales figure (almost always negative); random occurrence that really should have been anticipated. *(see Black swan)*

Box, think outside the, try and put a ___ round that one: 1. Nine-dot matrix game usually called the Gottschaldt figurine, which challenges the solver to join all nine dots with four lines without removing the pen from the paper – it can only be solved by taking the lines outside the perceived square, hence the phrase. 2. Hackneyed piece of nonsense used as a euphemism for having a perfectly average thought; plaintive plea for originality that is almost never answered; all-round conspiracy designed to convince one and all that everyone is rather intelligent. *(see Blue-sky thinking)*

Box of frogs, mad as a: 1. Mad. 2. Utterly ga-ga; loopy; not well, by any stretch of the imagination; incomprehensible; likely exponent of bullshit.

(see Basket case; Gene pool, swimming in the shallow end of the ___; Mid-life crisis; Moon, barking at the, over the, through the; Postal, go; Picnic, one sandwich short of a)

Braggadocious behaviour: 1. Vainglorious, empty boasting, after a character in Spenser's *The Faerie Queene*. 2. Vainglorious, empty boasting, all day every day at work; tedious windbag very keen on him- or herself; convinced of one's own self-importance; principle characteristics of chairman. *(see Chairman; Large, giving it)*

Brain dump: 1. Outpouring of thoughts. 2. Outpouring of thoughts on a colleague without any warning; random musings of a muddled fool; ill-prepared ragbag of half-baked clichés; so-called briefing. *(see Analysis, paralysis by, in the final; Bounce ideas off; Breeze, shooting the; Data dump; Waffle; Word dump)*

Brainstorm: 1. Ideas session. 2. Curious gathering of hapless individuals who have never had a decent idea in their lives, in the vain hope that suddenly they will; badly cast group who neither know nor like each other; international coming together of global network staff who claim they are 'one big family' when in fact they have never met before; tedious powwow in which Geoff from production puts a downer on everything with the immortal phrase: *"That'll never work will it?" (see Aha moment; Awayday; Bad idea, there's no such thing as a; Beanbags; Big picture; Blue-sky thinking; Flip chart; Lateral thinking; Light bulb experience; NPD; Off-site; Outcomes, negative, positive; Outputs; Think-tank; Workshop)*

Brain surgery, it's not: 1. It's not like cutting someone's head open and performing an intricate operation. 2. Actually it is – politics and backstabbing make this an impossible task. *(see Open-heart surgery, it's not; Rocket science, it's not)*

Brand ambassador: 1. Celebrity paid to endorse a brand. 2.Often little-known or irrelevant individual with no discernible relevance to the brand, often seen extolling its virtues on television, only to bring down said brand after some horrible exposé in the tabloids ruins the reputation of all involved.

Brand onion, pillars, pyramid, values: 1. Diagram designed to clarify what a brand stands for. 2. Horribly contrived bastard son of a management consultancy chart, densely populated with meaningless catch-all adjectives such as 'passion', 'innovative' and 'leading edge'; unintelligible child's drawing resembling a car crash of imagery and words, vaguely reminiscent of Stonehenge, the Egyptian pyramids, or an unspecified vegetable.

(see Brand strategist; Foundations, lay the; Guardian, brand ; Guidelines, brand; corporate; Innovation, innovative, innovatively; Passion, passionate; Positioning; Promise, brand, broken:)

Brand strategist: 1. Person in charge of the direction a product or service is taking. 2. Purveyor of endless diagrams; generator of impenetrable jargon; conjurer. *(see Architecture, brand ___, business ___; Brand onion, pillars, pyramid, values, Marketing; Marketing guru; Needs and wants; Overarching; Positioning; Rebrand; Smoke and mirrors job; Time-poor, time-rich; User experience)*

Bread and butter: 1. Standard, workaday stuff; ordinary 2. Drudgery; slave labour; tedious, relentless administration. *(see Administrivia; Target manager)*

Break the ice: 1. Smash up frozen water. 2. Frantically attempt to butter up a frosty customer; smile weakly and ask a question about the family, where they live, or the weather; try to establish basic eye contact despite the other person having disconcerting designer glasses that create an impenetrable, inscrutable impression.

Break the mould: 1. Take a mould and break it, for reasons unknown; try to do something different. 2. Hackneyed catch-all phrase meaning: *"For God's sake, we've seen all this stuff before, Derek. Can't you do something original for once?"*; oft-used expression in creative industries, as in: *"Come on guys, we need to break the mould here!"*, although why anyone would want to break a mould when they have spent so long designing it remains unclear. *(see Game-changing; Groundbreaking)*

Breakout groups: 1. Small sub-sets of a larger group, not necessarily broken. 2. Supposedly trendy term for awayday attendees when asked to sod off from the main room and have a decent idea for once; all the smokers at said event standing on the balcony puffing furiously under the guise of thinking; similar gathering at coffee refill station, where Brenda and Stephanie from accounts can be found scoffing custard creams and moaning about the management. *(see Awayday; Bean bags; Come on people; Off-site; Soft area)*

Breath of fresh air: 1. A person or idea that brings something entirely new to the matter in hand. 2. Thoroughly dangerous new recruit, often senior, who wants to change everything on their first day; terminal bore who keeps repeating: *"That's not how we did it at my old place"*; genuinely inspiring new person with loads of good ideas who only lasts a few months before being fired. *(see Bull in a china shop; Broom, new; Compatible, not)*

Breathes through his arse: 1. Physical impossibility, alluding to an ability to talk consistently without appearing to breathe. 2. This bastard never comes up for air; talks non-stop; only interested in the sound of one's own voice. *(see Bark into the wind; Dialogue; Fire hydrant, trying to drink from a; Human wind tunnel)*

Breeze, shooting the: 1. Firing shots into thin air. 2. Wibbling for no apparent reason; boring a colleague senseless; boring an entire audience senseless. *(see Blue-sky thinking; Brain dump; Word dump)*

Bridge too far, it may be a: 1. This may be more than we can handle. 2. This is definitely more than we can handle so we may as well admit defeat now. *(see Capabilities)*

Bring to the table: 1. Carry item to (usually) four-legged structure, presumably for some purpose. 2. Rather condescending reference to whether someone has anything to contribute, as in: *"What exactly is Veronica going to bring to the table?"*; shades of Jam and Jerusalem, along the lines of bringing cake or other foodstuff to a village gathering of some kind; furthermore, hints of ritual sacrifice or some other arcane religious activity, in which the supplicant individual has to bring something to a central point of major significance; more prosaically, just arriving at the boardroom table for yet another dreary meeting.

Broad brush: 1. Wide painting utensil for covering a wide area. 2. Total fudge; failure to come to point; obfuscation; vagueness; sweeping attempt to avoid coming to the point. *(see Gloss over; Keep it dark; Strategy)*

Broad canvas: 1. A big surface area on which to paint. 2. Massive subject area about which a person knows very little, or naff all; diffuse area of overclaim, as in: *"Of course, Nigel, these proposals can be applied across a very broad canvas,"* without actually specifying what, when or where; favourite hazy domain of politicians and chief executives where no one can be held accountable.

Broad church: 1. Religious building with a wide aisle; diverse gang of people, or broad-minded attitude. 2. Suggestion that work force is drawn from a wide spectrum, as in: *"Of course we have a very broad church here, Martin."* *(see Diversity; Multicultural)*

Broom, new: 1. Freshly-purchased household cleaning instrument. 2. New boss, who knows nothing, and never will. *(see Breath of fresh air; Bull in a china shop)*

Brownie points: 1. Notional mark to one's credit based on the mistaken idea that the Brownies earn points for good deeds. 2. Seldom-quantified suggestion that a number of good achievements at work all add up to something helpful, such as promotion or a pay rise; odious sucking up to the boss in a pathetic attempt to curry favour. *(see Brown-nosing)*

Brown-nosing: 1. Scatological reference to placing one's nose where the sun doesn't shine. 2. Obsequious behaviour towards anyone in a more senior position; toadying approach; automatic agreement with whatever the boss says; blind acceptance of what management decrees. *(see Backwards, bend over; Brownie points; Ego; First past the post; Hedge our bets; Team, take one for the; Where the sun don't shine, stick it)*

Buck, pass the: 1. In poker, a marker that reminds a player they are the next dealer. 2. Outrageous abdication of responsibility; total failure to live up to job description; automatic raising of hands as if to say: *"Nothing to do with me!"*, almost always preceded by complaint that said individual is not being given enough respect or responsibility. *(see Empower; Hospital pass; Micromanaging; Pass the baton; PDQ; Riot act, read the; Wash our hands of it)*

Buck stops here, the: 1. I/we am/are fully responsible for everything, and am/are prepared to take the consequences. 2. I/we truly love everything that power brings – the money, the status, the women on tap – but try to hold us to task for anything untoward and we'll deny everything. *(see Accountable; Delegate, delegation)*

Bucketize: 1. Segment costs or revenues into separate buckets for analysis. 2. Another in the long and hideous line of adding the –ize suffix to any perfectly good word. *(see Diarize; Incentivize; –ize; Maximize; Optimize; Prioritize; Productize; Professionalize; Utilize)*

Bucks, bang for your: 1. Number of satisfying explosions, or possibly orgasms, for an amount paid. 2. Value for money; nothing whatsoever to do with value for money – more a case of desperately trying to receive more for less; vain cry of under-resourced manager, as in: *"I need more bangs for my buck, Fiona!" (see Dial up)*

Bugs, iron out the: 1. To remove beetles from an article of clothing with a hot pressing implement. 2. To eliminate critical flaws in a product or service; start from scratch; return to the drawing board. *(see Crafting, it needs a bit of; Drawing board, back to the; Optimal; Sub-optimal)*

Build an opportunity: 1. Generate a chance to do something entirely from scratch. 2. Fly solo; be left in the lurch; make something out of nothing;

make the best of a bad job. *(see Opportunity; Putting lipstick on a pig; Turd, polishing a)*

Building bridges: 1. Constructing ways over water or valley. 2. Try to make amends after a total breakdown in relations; bring flowers to colleague after throwing up on them at the office party; offer olive branch to new boss who beat you to the promotion; buy chocolate biscuits for receptionist following highly inappropriate physical approach the day before. *(see Burning bridges)*

Building the plane as we fly it: 1. Literally, aeronautical construction on the wing, if it were possible. 2. Overly-macho notion that we are so clever we can rectify any unforeseen problem as it arises, without preparing first; hubris; misplaced confidence, usually followed by a loud crash; phrase much loved of self-styled internet entrepreneurs. *(see Digital native; Fly by the seat of one's pants; Flying unstable; SOP)*

Builds: 1. Other ideas adding to what has been said already. 2. Awful bastardization of a verb into a noun, as in: *"If we can have your builds on this, please Ron?"*; also applied to ever-increasing number of points on an already-overloaded chart. *(see Point, to your)*

Built to last: 1. Classic management book written by Jim Collins and Jerry Porras in 1994, explaining how companies can generate long-term success. 2.Peculiar exhortation of short-term managers who have no intention of staying in the job for more than 18 months; sham expression designed to fool colleagues into believing that you give a damn, as in: *"We need this built to last, guys!"* *(see Good to great)*

Bull in a china shop: 1. Someone causing a lot of trouble in a delicate environment. 2. Loose cannon; horribly off-brief colleague; all chairmen who haven't read their briefing notes and who think they can wing it; every politician that ever existed. *(see Breath of fresh air; Broom, new; Catalyst; Dropping grenades in fish ponds; Flight path; Gung ho; Loose cannon)*

Bullet, bite the: 1. Face up to; be stoical. 2. Run for the hills; leave the building; resign; shift the blame onto someone else. *(see Blame culture; Bombshell; Hospital pass)*

Bullet, get the: 1. Experience execution. 2. Be fired. *(see Decruit; Defenestration; Marching orders, get your)*

Bullet, magic, silver: 1. Single cure, answer or solution. 2. Deflective verbal ruse of squirming bosses and politicians, as in: *"There is no silver bullet here, guys!"*; weak excuse; unwanted component if playing Russian roulette.

Bullet points: 1. A series of points on a chart. 2. PowerPoint's undying lethal gift to the world of business; list of objectives on a brief, whose true number is infinite; number of things required by customer yesterday; competition to see how many items can be placed on a chart before they are illegible, or the audience shoots the presenter. *(see Bullet, silver; Death by PowerPoint)*

Bullshit: 1. The excreta of a large male bovine. 2. Technically endless supply of waffle and nonsense uttered in business meetings; cunning wordsmithery that is neither on the side of the false nor the truth; verbal expedience; the entire contents of this book. *(see Bollocks, talking; Doughnut rather than the hole, it would be wise to concentrate on the; Obfuscation; Off the top of my head; Static; Talking out loud; Waffle; White noise; Word dump)*

Bun fight: 1. Violent disagreement in a bakery (causes various). 2. Dust up; brawl; mild difference of opinion leading to outright fisticuffs; suit-ripping incident at sales conference; abuse (or vegetables) thrown at awards ceremony; principle activity at office party. *(see Consensus)*

Bundle, one stick short of a: 1. A lightweight collection of fire wood. 2. Not the full shilling, not quite the ticket; slow; dim. *(see Box of frogs, mad as a; Gene pool, swimming in the shallow end of the; Mid-life crisis; Picnic, one sandwich short of a; Shilling, not the full)*

Bureaucracy: 1. System of administration. 2.Pointless rules and processes that take all the fun out of business; pen-pushing twaddle; form filling. *(see Administrivia; Jobsworth; Panjandrum; Process; Target manager)*

Burn the candle at both ends, the midnight oil: 1. Stay awake too long; get very little sleep. 2. Be worked like a dog by one's boss; have a job with perfectly ordinary working hours but then spend inordinate amounts of time in bars and nightclubs; sleep under one's desk.

Burning bridges: 1. Set light to bridge and thus prevent the chance of going back. 2. Tell the boss in no uncertain terms to f**k off; deliver similar message to important customer; shag secretary; shag boss's wife; shag both; ruin one's life in an ill-advised instant. *(see Building bridges)*

Burning platform: 1. Rostrum or dais in flames; impossible position that will inevitably end in disaster. 2. A firm favourite of sales people who have boxed themselves into an awkward corner; death wish; shades of self-immolation; suggestion of so-called platform as physical manifestation of ethereal concept such as customer base. *(see Foot, shoot oneself in the; Hoist by one's own petard; Kamikaze; Object, defeating the;*

Own goal, spectacular; Platform, online, sales, user; Platform, eat one's own; Platform, exceed the)

Bus, who's driving the: 1. Is this double-decker operated by a robot? 2. Who the f**k's in charge here?!; euphemism for weak, or totally absent, senior direction; strategy-free zone; complete lack of leadership. *(see Rowing in the same boat, direction; Train, who's driving the)*

Buy-in: 1. State of purchasing something and consuming it at home. 2. Agreement or approval from a colleague, as in: *"We'll need Geoff's buy-in on this one."*; poisoned blessing which doesn't mean approval at all, simply permission to go ahead and humiliate yourself. *(see Green light; Greenlit; Issues , I have ___with that; Problem, I don't have a ___with that; Redlit; Run it past; Unhappy, I'm not ___with)*

Buzz: 1. Annoying sound made by insect. 2. Annoying sound made by public relations executives called Emma when waxing lyrical about the coverage they will achieve for a client; static; hot air; gossip; wibble; abject failure of said campaign to generate any publicity at all; sound of chief executive's intercom when calling the PR agency into his office to be fired for failing to 'generate buzz'. *(see Hype)*

By the board: 1. Next to a piece of board, just there. 2. Absolutely nowhere at all; certainly not there; redundant; dead; passed over.

B2B: 1. Business to business. 2. Squeamish mnemonic denoting subject matter between two businesses; childish shorthand; wince-making collision of verbal and numerical components. *(see B2C; One-to-one)*

B2C: 1. Business to consumer. 2. Something straight out of kindergarten class; random abuttal of letters and a number; lazy shorthand to suggest that the writer is 'in the know' when it comes to industry lingo. *(see B2B)*

CADET: 1. Can't Add, Doesn't Even Try. 2. Egregiously poor mathematician.

Calibrate: 1. Determine the accuracy of a measurement. 2. Fabricate a totally false scale in order to make sales or profits look impressive, when in fact they are disastrous. *(see Cook the books; Fiscal juggling)*

Call report: 1. Record of conversation between a company representative and a client or customer. 2. Pack of lies noted down as an afterthought to protect oneself from gross incompetence and failure to complete a simple instruction; additional pack of lies that uses the spurious authority of type to note things that were never agreed at all; pure fiction. *(see Arse covering; Contact report)*

Call to action: 1. Request to do something. 2. Desperate plea for a colleague or customer to acknowledge that your hopeless job or product is even worth a second of their time.

Campaign: 1. Sustained programme of events to achieve an objective. 2. Overly-macho expression plundered from the military to lend undeserved credence to a random selection of lacklustre ideas.

Can, carry the, left holding the: 1. Take the blame, right now or at some later time. 2. Get it comprehensively in the slats when it was absolutely nothing to do with you. *(see Above and beyond; Team, take one for the)*

Can, we need to ___ it: 1. We need to stop doing something. 2. This is utter crap – cease work on it immediately.

Can do attitude: 1. A constructive, positive approach. 2. Pointless blind optimism flying in the face of all sensible known information, deployed to impress a boss or colleague of the opposite sex. *(see Doable; Easy tiger; Failure is not an option; Impossible, nothing is)*

Cane it: 1. Beat something too hard or go too fast. 2. Completely overshoot despite all previous experience, usually in reference to alcohol or drugs.

Capabilities: 1. Range of skills. 2. Enormous selection of lies perpetrated on one's CV. *(see Bridge too far, it may be a; CV; Competencies, core)*

Capability gap: 1. Difference between what can and can't be done. 2. Sudden revelation that a colleague is incapable of doing the job in hand, despite their claims at interview. *(see Aspirational; CV; Potential)*

Carbuncle, unwanted: 1. A nasty boil. 2. Undesirable colleague who really should have a bath.

Card, red: 1. Severe or final warning; outright dismissal. 2. Removal from job, or meeting room; humiliating public dress down; red card offence that strangely results in no disciplinary procedure or dismissal, but is merely described as such by relieved macho colleagues; awestruck reflections of other members of team in the pub after a disgraceful scene at work, as in: *"Gary should have had a red card for that."*

Carrot, big, ___and stick: 1. Incentive to do something; blend of reward and sanction. 2. Blend of slave-driving and pitifully small 'bonus' much loved by macho organizations trying to suggest they have a passable approach to staff welfare; small carrot; no carrot at all; a derisory £25 shopping voucher apparently as reward for twelve months of hard labour; bowl of gruel. *(see Incentive, staff; Incentivize)*

Cascade (vb): 1. Of water, to fall down, as in a waterfall. 2. To tell the other people in a company something, usually subordinates; to pass on information; to inform (a quality often beyond most large companies); to keep in the dark; to fail comprehensively to mention anything helpful at all; to patronize with kindergarten observations or bland, uninformative platitudes; to say nothing at all. *(see Mum, keep)*

Cash flow: 1. Flow of cash through the company accounts. 2. Complete absence of flow of cash through the company accounts. *(see Cook the books; Fiscal juggling)*

Casting: 1. Choice of personnel for a task, or to work on a particular account or customer. 2. Huge error of judgment in choosing the wrong person for the job; erroneous selection of bearded, skateboarding digital native for serious piece of corporate business; futile attempt to match the right people to the right business, as in: *"We really need to get the casting right on this one guys!"* (see *Digital native; Dress to impress; Fish up a tree, he looks like a; Food chain, a long way down the, higher up the; Mix, the right, the wrong*)

Catalyst: 1. Person or substance that causes change. 2. Reckless newcomer, usually a sales director or managing director, who changes everything and wrecks it in the process; annoying, self-appointed 'minister for fun' who pisses everyone off so badly that they all leave. (see *Bull in a china shop; Broom, new; Loose cannon; Minister for fun*)

Catastrophize: 1. Turn something into a catastrophe, presumably when it is nothing of the sort. 2. A verbal catastrophe in its own right, yet another example of turning a noun into a verb by adding the –ize suffix; in all probability says more about the parlous state of the person uttering it than the situation itself. (see *Diarize; Incentivize; Internalize; -ize; Maximize; Mondayize; Optimize; Prioritize; Productizel; Professionalize; Utilize*)

Catch a cold: 1. Contract viral infection of the upper respiratory tract; lose on an investment. 2. Lose everything after a gung-ho bet; blow everything on the nags; under estimate the amount of preparation required for a crucial meeting. (see *Bath, take a; Gung ho*)

Catch-22: 1. Paradoxical set of rules that always lead nowhere, or to disaster, coined in the book of the same name by Joseph Heller in 1961. 2. Deadlock state of affairs; personal dilemma involving only nasty options such as dismissal, embarrassment, demotion, humiliation in front of the whole company, or wife. (see *Square the circle*)

Catching a falling knife: 1. Foolishly attempting to grab a sharp kitchen implement when it slips off the work surface. 2. Idiotic attempt to intervene that will only lead to pain or severe injury; stupidly claiming to be able to save the day in order to impress, only to discover the true horror of the problem. (see *Bombs, box of; Hospital pass; Poisoned chalice*)

Category of one: 1. Area of business with no other competition. 2. Mathematically inane suggestion that the company or brand is invincible; abject failure to spot that an as yet unknown rival will steal all your customers by Christmas; tub-thumping claim to uniqueness, almost always false.

Cavalry over the hill: 1. It's time to put proper resources on this for once. 2. It's all hands to the pump and those senior people who have horribly neglected the task will be the first to claim hero status for apparently bailing everyone else out when in fact they should have paid proper attention to it in the first place. *(see A Team, this calls for; Eleventh hour, at the; Lead from the front)*

CC: 1. Carbon copy. 2. Sustained campaign to smear a colleague for incompetence; relentless email trail proving that you are in the right and it's everyone else's fault; career-spanning arse-covering exercise, much loved of administrators the world over. *(see Arse covering; BCC: Email; FYI; Voice mail)*

Centre of excellence: 1. Place where stuff is done well. 2. All-too-rare outpost of an organization where they really do know what they are doing; somewhere, but not in your organization; in the head office of your main rival, but not in yours.

-centred, -centric: 1. Having a centre; anchored in the middle. 2. Nasty, roughly interchangeable, suffix pairing; frequently added mindlessly to any word the author can get their hands on; examples include customer-centric, goal-centred, and media-centric, when in fact the correct usage is to be found in words such as concentric, eccentric, and heliocentric. *(see – driven; -focused, people-, goal-; -oriented)*

Chairman: 1. Person, annoyingly usually male, who looks after, or sits in, a chair. 2. Mysterious shadowy figure at the top of many companies; so-called *éminence grise*; unnecessary overhead; inveterate meddler in other people's work; person whose role is almost entirely unknown; walking embodiment of the phrase 'out of touch'; consistently unaware of what the company is actually doing; elderly irritant who should in all probability be put out to grass; prone to making long, rambling speeches about nothing in particular; windbag. *(see Braggadocious behaviour; Gloss over; Heavy hitter; Player, big)*

Chairman's wife: 1. Woman married to your boss. 2. Extremely attractive woman married to your boss, with whom eye contact must be avoided at all costs; extremely unattractive woman married to your boss, with whom eye contact must be engaged at all costs; knackered old harridan who has the chairman under her thumb and as such runs the company in a surrogate fashion; woman with irrational objections to simple things, such as the colour blue, as in: *"The 3,000 outlet refit has been shelved at the last minute because the chairman's wife doesn't like blue."* *(see Charisma bypass; Movers and shakers; Prejudice)*

Challenger brand: 1. Any brand that isn't number one but would like to be. 2. Clapped out selection of has-beens and also-rans in any market; semi-macho lingo designed to improve morale in mediocre companies, as in: *"Good news, guys, we're not bottom of the market – we're challengers!"* (see Market-leading; Mediocracy; Thought leadership; World class)

Challenges: 1. Things to do, some of them quite tricky. 2. Things to do, all of them very tricky; impossible selection of tasks set out thoughtlessly by boss; so-called 'opportunities' that are actually booby-trapped. *(see Ask, big; Opportunity; Poisoned chalice; SWOT analysis)*

Champion (vb): 1. To be an ambassador for; to support; to promote something. 2. To take the credit when everyone else has done all the work; to agree to back a proposal and then vote against it in a crucial meeting, to the amazement of all colleagues; to vacillate and prevaricate; to lie outright in order to avoid a conflict with one's team members.

Change drivers: 1. To give control of the steering wheel to someone else. 2. Factors that might affect whether things change or not; factors that probably won't affect anything at all; bleating set of mission or 'value' statements that all staff will ignore as a matter of urgency; hypothetical blether that probably has no bearing on anything; axiomatic twaddle hastily woven together in order to secure a publishing contract. *(see Drivers, key; Values; Vision, visioning)*

Chapter and verse: 1. Exact authority for something. 2. Tautological battle cry usually decreed by desperate managers wanting to know why something has failed miserably, as in: *"I want chapter and verse on this one, guys!"*; catch-all receptacle for anything supposedly comprehensive, but in truth shallow and hastily cobbled together. *(see A-Z; Full Monty, the; No-quibble guarantee; Zee, we've covered everything from A to)*

Charisma bypass: 1. Total absence of character. 2. Sales director; finance director; Geoff in production; Alan in IT; any of various insufferably dull people one has to endure at work. *(see Chairman's wife)*

Chasing eyeballs: 1. Pursuing vital visual organs, for reasons unknown. 2. Unspeakably bad phrase for encouraging people to watch something on a screen, usually the television or their computer.

Chatty dolphin: 1. Marine cetacean mammal that talks a lot. 2. Dreadful expression dreamt up by online technorati to describe volume of website comment, as in: *"This site has more clicks than a chatty dolphin, Sean."* *(see Techno-babble; Technorati)*

Cherry pick: 1. Pluck red round fruit of the rosaceous genus *Prunus*. 2. Take all the interesting work for yourself; demonstrate disgraceful favouritism by only selecting your drinking buddies for a project, or the well-stacked Julia from procurement for slightly different reasons; ask Julia for a 'one-to-one' after work to discuss some 'issues'. *(see One-to-one)*

Chinese walls: 1. Structures that hold up ceilings in China. 2. Metaphorical barriers between teams or departments, purported to retain client confidentiality; free-for-all of information exchange for maximum benefit; hotbed of gossip; industrial espionage; flagrant cross-fertilization of market knowledge to increase bonus levels.

Chinese whispers: 1. Chain of message passing that results in a distortion of the original message. 2. Thoroughly illegal passing on of information, all of it 100% accurate and highly damaging; ill-advised momentary lapse of discretion at office party usually leading to dismissal. *(see Beans, spill the; Loop, out of the, keep in the)*

Choiceful: 1. Full of choice. 2. Offering no choice at all, as in: *"Guys, can we make this offering more choiceful?"* *(see Insightful; Meaningful)*

Chop, for the: 1. About to be fired. 2. About to be physically removed from the building. *(see Decruit; Defenestrate, defenestration)*

Christmas party: 1. Festive celebration. 2. Carnage; unwanted collision between management and staff; only moment when Phil from IT is brave enough to tell the managing director what he always thought of him; bacchanalian orgy in which an appalling volume of bodily fluids is exchanged; vomitfest best avoided, every year. *(see Office party)*

Chuggers: 1. Elision of 'charity' and 'muggers'; charity representatives in the street who press unsuspecting pedestrians to sign up to the cause. 2. Feral gangs of students with clipboards and relentlessly cheerful smiles; gap year mercenaries intent on securing a sale to bolster their Peruvian cycling trip fund. *(see Cold calling; Experiential marketing; Hot lead)*

Churn and burn: 1. Process fast and move on; attend to, then ignore or discard. 2. Cynical exploitation of customer base; obsession with winning new customers, only to ignore existing ones; similar attitude to staff, utilizing a hire and fire policy. *(see In for the long haul; Leaky bucket)*

Circular file: 1. Wastepaper basket. 2. Last resting place of sanctimonious all-staff memos; unsavoury mélange of old banana skins, nail clippings and desk detritus; health hazard; fire hazard; surreptitious dumping ground for illicit porn; occasional vomit bucket. *(see Christmas party; FIFO; LIFO)*

Clapham omnibus, man on the: 1. Male of the species, found aboard a London bus in the SW4 postcode. 2. Derogatory descriptor for an 'average' customer, whatever that may be; Joe Bloggs; John Doe; John Smith; supposed pig-ignorant mug who will buy our sub-standard product regardless of all evidence to the contrary. *(see Consumer focused; Focus group)*

Clarity: 1. Clearness, of expression or water. 2. Total absence of clarity; opacity; obscurity; scrabbling around trying to find out the truth. *(see Focus; Obfuscation)*

Clear-cut: 1. Evident. 2. Vague as hell; trumped-up; biased; loaded to suit one's needs.

Clicks and mortar: 1. Related to online assets and retail estate. 2. Awful bastard son of 'bricks and mortar', in which the genuine components of a building have been twisted to suit online needs; the total value of our online assets is nothing, as is the value of our shops; inability to distinguish between the value of either. *(see Concretize; Foundations, lay the; Offline, let's take this)*

Close but no cigar: 1. Not bad, but you don't win a prize. 2. Utter second-rate rubbish; woefully inadequate; failing even to reach a very low standard; shoddy; crap.

Closer look, stand back and take a: 1. Curiously contradictory phrase suggesting that a broader view may allow greater understanding of the detail. 2. Supreme example of management bollocks, in which distant managers envy the detail shown by micro managers, and vice versa. *(see Big picture; Deep dive; Helicopter view; Loose-tight properties; Micromanaging; Marathon not a sprint, it's a; No stone unturned; Overview; Witch-hunt; Wood, can't see the ___ for the trees)*

Closure: 1. To declare the end of an issue; 2. Peculiar matrimonial Americanism originally referring to a person who is finally able to stop bleating about their ex and boring everyone rigid, including their therapist; business equivalent in which a member of staff simply will not stop referring to a long-gone disastrous project or obsolete working practice that went out with the ark. *(see Jobsworth)*

Clout: 1. To cuff stiffly, usually on the head; degree to which an executive can pack a metaphorical punch. 2. Dick-swinging bravado; testosterone-fuelled show of strength evident in any all-male boardroom; peacock-strutting display of power, often with no back-up whatsoever. *(see Cojones; Dick swinging)*

Coalface: 1. The exposed seam of coal in a mine. 2. Patronizing management term for the environment in which the people who do all the work have to operate; bear pit; shit hole; dump; pressurized customer interface; the sharp end; appalling frontline job that no one should have to endure; sales region in Wales. *(see Frontline; Ground, on the)*

Coals, hauled over the: 1. Given a severe dressing down. 2. Humiliated in public in front of everyone who needs to know.

Coals, send ___ to Newcastle: 1. Something supplied where it is already plentiful. 2. Pointless duplication; misguided decision; adding resource where none is needed; attempt to fix something that isn't broken.

Coals, walk on hot: 1. Tread dangerously. 2. Embark on a perilous sequence of blunders, such as losing a major customer, insulting the chairman, and sleeping with the receptionist, often all in the same day. *(see Hand rails, hold the; Last chance saloon, drinking at the; Postal, go; Riding the razor blade; Saddle, cycling with no)*

Cocks on the block: 1. In an extremely uncomfortable position. 2. With genitals metaphorically on the chopping block, knife poised. *(see Backs to the wall; Back-to-back; Cojones; Hand rails, hold the; Last chance saloon, drinking at the; Over a barrel; Postal, go; Riding the razor blade; Saddle, cycling with no)*

Cockup: 1. Something done badly. 2. Poor show; disaster; lousy job. *(see Pig's ear)*

Coffee, wake up and smell the: 1. Face up to reality. 2. Emerge from haze of self-delusion; stop pretending to have skills you don't possess; cease and desist from Nero-like delusions of power; resign and let someone properly qualified handle it. *(see Nero syndrome)*

Cohesive: 1. Sticking together. 2. All over the place; not joined together at all; random and unrelated, as in 'a cohesive package of measures'.

Cojones: 1. Spanish word for testicles. 2. Sheer front; balls; guts; chutzpah; audacity. *(see Clout; Cocks on the block; Dick-swinging)*

Cold calling: 1. Soliciting people you have never met for business. 2. Relentlessly hard sell business approach; systematically telephoning hapless potential customers; doorstepping; chugging (charity mugging), usually in busy streets. *(see Chuggers; Doorstepped; Doorstopped; Hot lead)*

Collaboration: 1. Working together. 2. Totally shafting a colleague or sister company by pretending to work together while undermining their efforts and/or taking all the credit for anything good, and denying responsibility for anything bad. *(see Turf wars)*

Collaborvation: 1. A combination of collaboration and innovation. 2. Hideous union of two of the most trendy ideas in recent times, aka getting together and having some decent ideas. *(see Innovation, innovative, innovatively)*

Collars and cuffs, I bet the___don't match: 1. All is not what it seems. 2. Sleazy, sexist remark referring to a woman's hair colour being unlikely to match that of her pubic region; linguistic genre much used by greasy Terylene-clad salesmen who have never had a decent shag in their life; regular refuge of ugly, lecherous men often working the security night shift. *(see Kimono, open the; Matching luggage; Playtex strategy)*

Collateral: 1. Security pledged for a loan repayment; situated or running side by side, literally co-lateral. 2. Perfectly good word hi-jacked by Americans to denote a suite of stuff or materials (no genuine dictionary contains this definition); arsenal, and probably deployed by an arse; faux suggestion of a vast phalanx of resources when there are none; mock toolkit that is in fact empty. *(see Cross-collateralization; Tools, management, unique)*

Collect your P45: 1. Visit the finance department and pick up your last evidence of employment. 2. Take marching orders; move on; leave in disgrace; precursor to setting fire to the boss's desk and marching triumphantly to the pub.

Come a cropper: 1. Hurt oneself, or fail badly at something. 2. Cock it up completely; crash and burn; sustain severe injury (often self-inflicted) and report to hospital forthwith. *(see AWOL, go; Ballistic, go; Crash and burn; Fly in the face of; Full-tilt boogie; Postal, go; Radar, off; Rails, gone off the)*

Come on guys: 1. Pay attention you bastards. 2. Plaintive cry of anyone trying to bring a meeting to order; exhortation used indiscriminately, regardless of whether one is addressing male or female attendees; in fact, often used by women when talking to other women. *(see Come on people)*

Come on people: 1. Please back me up. 2. Plaintive request in the face of widespread derision, as in: *"Come on people, all join hands in the team bonding game!"*; happy-clappy exhortation much loved of hippy HR managers. *(see Bean bags; Breakout groups; Come on guys; Off-site; Soft area)*

Come up to scratch: 1. Reach the required level. 2. Exasperated exhortation to reach the required level, for once in your life; desperate plea from boss to ineffective and feckless subordinate; set low standards for oneself and consistently fail to meet them; underachieve.

Comfort zone, out of one's: 1. Beyond the level or nature of work in which one feels comfortable and competent. 2. A tiny fraction of what a person is asked to do; unpleasant sinking feeling that you haven't a clue what you are doing; blatantly ill-equipped; in a canoe without a paddle. *(see Micromanaging)*

Coming from, where I'm: 1. Direction of travel based on where I was before. 2. Directionally-challenged remark confusing opinion with physical position; this is my view and I wish to prevail over yours; I'm your boss so shut up and get on with it. *(see At, where I'm; SUMO)*

Coming or going, he doesn't know if he's: 1. He is confused, or dithering. 2. He's a blithering idiot; incompetent; indecisive; conflicted; self-styled 'entrepreneur' who makes a lot of U-turns and then claims they were intentional 'pivots'. *(see Evolving to meet customer demand; Pivot; Tweak; U-Turn)*

Commercial wife-beating: 1. Constantly beating up a supplier who offers no resistance. 2. Disgraceful one-sided business relationship in which a dominant partner screws the other party on every dimension – price, service levels, professional intimidation, and personal abuse. *(see BOHICA; Partners; 60:50 relationship, this is the perfect)*

Commit, committed, commitment: 1. Pledge or align oneself to a particular cause. 2. Run a mile from any such agreement; use macho vocabulary to imply 'commitment' while intending nothing of the sort; hang colleague out to dry by suggesting backing and then pulling it in a crucial meeting; quality perpetually demanded by macho sales directors but rarely delivered; principle that flies straight out of the window in the face of a job offer with a bigger salary.

Commoditized: 1. Turned into a commodity. 2. Horrible addition to the seemingly endless production line of Americanisms in which a perfectly good noun has once again been turned into a verb; paranoid (or possibly quite true) feeling that one's product is bog standard, despite brash marketing claims to be 'premium'. *(see Concretize; Democratize; Diarize; -ize; Monetize; Premium; Socialize)*

Communication, lack of, plan, skills: 1. Convey something to someone else. 2. Total breakdown in understanding; complete failure to have a meeting of minds; static; hot air; piffle; conveying the opposite of what was intended. *(see Non-verbal; Static; White noise)*

Community: 1. Group of people. 2. Hackneyed and over-used word to describe people linked together on the internet; random collection of hangers-on determined to receive free samples of any product, in return for hitting the like button.

Compatible, not: 1. Unable to exist together harmoniously. 2. Totally incompatible; at loggerheads; likely to come to blows; daggers drawn; full of hate for each other; extremely likely to take a swing after a few drinks. *(see Breath of fresh air; Office party)*

Competencies, core: 1. Things a company or person can do properly. 2. Utterly bizarre extension of the word competence, in itself perfectly capable of conveying precisely the same meaning; stuff that any fool or organization worth its salt should be doing; basics; lowest common denominator activities to even warrant being in business in the first place; bog standard stuff. *(see Bridge too far; Capabilities; Core; CV; Knitting, stick to the)*

Competitive advantage, edge: 1. Something compelling that makes us better than our competitors. 2. Sinking feeling based on the dawning realization that we are clearly no better than our competitors; on further examination, alarming discovery that we are actually much worse than our competitors; trumped up piece of corporate puffery to claim competitive advantage where there patently is none. *(see Leverage)*

Competitive heat: 1. Ability to compete. 2. Pathetic phrase to suggest that one's efforts somehow generate thermal energy that will 'turn the heat on' one's competitors; abject failure to understand the basics of physics; misguided effort to envisage a market as a place in which temperature has any bearing whatsoever; utter twaddle.

Competitive review: 1. Analysis of what your competitors are doing. 2. Paranoid sweep of what all the others are doing; flagrant theft of ideas from all competitors in the absence of having any decent ones of one's own; pointless collection of tedious data that will never lead to action. *(see Data dump)*

Competitiveness: 1. Desire to compete; winning drive. 2. Determination to win at all costs, regardless of the effect on others; ruthless streak; thoughtless quality; macho tendency to stomp all over colleagues, women, children, puppies, and anything else than gets in one's way. *(see Ambition; Drive)*

Compliance: 1. Act of complying; acquiescence. 2. Shadowy department that insists that everyone 'follows the rules'; total capitulation; giving in; getting shafted comprehensively; dropping one's trousers; losing out completely on price to the extent that one will make a whopping loss. *(see BOHICA; Drop our trousers; Jobsworth; Panjandrum)*

Conceptual thinking: 1. Thinking concerned with concepts. 2. Ludicrously abstract; so-called 'ideas' that are impossible to implement; hot air; waffle; the entire output of an awayday; intellectually lazy bollocks with no practical application whatsoever. *(see Awayday; Bad idea, there's no such thing as a; Lateral thinking; Off-site)*

Concretize: 1. To turn into concrete; make solid. 2. Thoroughly annoying noun-turned-verb suggesting the solidification of an idea; pseudo construction industry term suggesting strength, usually where the idea is intrinsically flimsy; vain attempt to make a weak thought into a better one; yet another attempt to make a non-physical entity appear physical. *(see Clicks and mortar; Commoditized; Democratize; Diarize; Foundations, lay the; Granular, let's get; Monetize; Premium; Socialize)*

Conductor's baton, wave the: 1. To direct effectively; issue instructions. 2. Tenuous attempt to imbue the world of business with some of the subtleties of the world of music; futile suggestion that mundane business operations can somehow be compared with lyricism or melody; vainglorious claim by deluded boss to be 'conducting an orchestra' when in reality he or she is in charge of a ragbag of greasy executives in a warehouse in Redcar. *(see Orchestra Model; Pull out all the stops)*

Conference call: 1. Phone conversation with more than two people. 2. Total waste of time in which several people in a badly decorated room address their remarks to a box in the middle of the table, loudly; superb opportunity to hit the mute button and spend an hour looking at porn; excuse to do nothing in bursts of fifteen minutes, interspersed with an occasional comment, such as: *"I completely concur with David on this – we've had exactly the same experience here in the UK."*; technique designed to assert authority over executives in a different time zone without the faff of having to get on a plane and visit them in person. *(see Head office, I'm from ___ and I'm here to help)*

Connect with our audience: 1. Have a customer pay attention or react in some way to one's marketing. 2. Catch-all wibble to suggest some sort of emotional connection with customers; concept that becomes more and more improbable the less interesting a sector is, as in: *"Come on guys, we really need to connect with our audience over these panty pads!"* *(see Consumer focused; Customer experience)*

Connectivity: 1. State of connecting. 2. Ubiquitous term describing things that join together, particularly in technology companies; obsession with joining everything together. *(see Joined-up thinking; Seamless; Segue)*

Consensus: 1. Widespread agreement. 2. Widespread disagreement; anarchy; what the boss says. *(see Bun fight)*

Consigliere: 1. Adviser or counsellor to the boss. 2. Rather unnerving lifting of mafia term to refer to what should be quite innocent advisory board duties; hints of the mob and nefarious dealings. *(see Alphanista; Consultant; Non-exec)*

Constantly striving: 1. Trying all the time. 2. Being very trying all the time; dreary overclaim suggesting that the company thinks about its customers incessantly. *(see Always on; Continual improvement; Expectations, exceeding; Passion, passionate; Sun, the ___ never sets at; 24/7/365; Work-life balance)*

Consultant: 1. A specialist who gives expert advice. 2. Charlatan who charges a fortune for simply chatting; silver-haired *éminence grise* who cruises their former industry dispensing pearls of apparent wisdom; person with no executive responsibility or accountability at all; shadowy septuagenarian who really should have hung up his boots years ago; annoying occasional presence at advisory board meetings who refuses to write anything down lest it destroy the conversation flow, and then fails to remember to do any of the items discussed. *(see Consigliere; Non-exec)*

Consultation period: 1. Time span in which discussions can be had. 2. Time in which no discussions are had at all; silent spell when all those due to be axed are kept in the dark and ignored; frustrating month for management in which all the people they have decided to fire are annoyingly still in the building. *(see Axe, face the; Banana skin, political; Can, carry the; Decruit; Downsize)*

Consumer focused: 1. Concentrating on what customers want. 2. Ignoring what people want while claiming rapt attention; incapable of having an original idea before asking a group of housewives in Bromley. *(see –centred, -centric; Clapham omnibus, man on the; Connect with our audience; Constantly striving; Customer experience; Focus group)*

Contact report: 1. Record of meeting between two parties. 2. Fantastic work of fabrication that bears no relation at all to what was discussed; heavily-biased representation of the issues at hand; close cousin of Tolstoy's *War and Peace* outlining in minute detail a near-verbatim account of immensely tedious meeting. *(see Arse covering; Call report)*

Context, the power of: 1. Significant influence of circumstances on subject matter. 2. Brilliant deception in which style overcomes substance; spectacular charade disguising utter lack of content; any presentation by an advertising agency.

Contiguous niches: 1. Series of small pockets that join together. 2. Forlorn effort to suggest that a few patches of hopeful activity can somehow be viewed as a universal success; deliberate use of an obscure adjective in order to imply competence. *(see Coterminous; Long tail, the; Niche, carve out a, market ___)*

Continuous improvement: 1. Getting better all the time. 2. Consistent underachievement; relentless programme of HR initiatives designed to buck up an ineffectual workforce; work in progress. *(see Always on; Constantly striving; CPD; Expectations, exceeding, 24/7/365; Sun, the ___ never sets at)*

Control freak: 1. Executive who cannot delegate. 2. Executive who cannot delegate due to (a) a fear that everyone else will discover how mundane their work is, or (b) an unstinting belief that they are the only person capable of doing something. *(see Arse covering; Autonomy; Ballbreaker; Bottleneck; Comfort zone; Micromanaging; Nutcracker; Rottweiler)*

Conversation, have a ___with: 1. Talk to. 2. A perfectly reasonable statement, now hijacked by pompous brands who want to "have a conversation" with their customers; as for the customers, they would just prefer the brands to produce quality products and stop broadcasting mindless drivel that costs a fortune.

Conversation marketing: 1. Paying attention to what customers want. 2. Not really a conversation at all – more like brands pestering people all the time on social meeja in language that suggests they are personal friends.

Cooking on gas: 1. Performing really well. 2. Giving the impression of outstanding forward motion, but only because the job is piss-easy to do. *(see ABC, easy as; Art form, got it down to an; Falling off a log)*

Cook the books: 1. Move money around to make things look better. 2. Lie comprehensively about projected income to justify bonuses for the directors or impress ignorant shareholders. *(see Above board; Black arts; Calibrate; Fiscal juggling; Crunch the numbers; Massage the numbers; Numbers, the)*

COP: 1. Close of play; before everyone has gone home. 2. By 5 o'clock; by 6 o'clock; by whatever time I decide to leave, since I gave you the order;

unspecified moment before the cleaners come into the office; somewhat bizarrely vague phrase given that if said item is indeed needed today, then mentioning a clear deadline would surely be advisable; throwaway flourish suggestive of authority, as in: *"Get that to me by close of play will you, Alice?"* (see End of play)

Core: 1. The innermost part of something; the bit in the middle. 2. Lazy catch-all for anything routinely done; dull, workaday; perfectly serviceable as a noun but sorely abused as an adjective, as in: *"Guys, let's stick to our core beliefs here."*(see Competencies; Non-core; Knitting, stick to the; Principle, core)

Corporate governance: 1. Correct and proper running of a company. 2. Flabby and pompous phrase that somehow tries to raise the status of running a company to that of running a nation.

Cost-effective: 1. Good value. 2. We screw our suppliers so hard that we make a massive profit and they can barely eat. *(see BOHICA)*

Coterminous: 1. Having a common boundary. 2. Colliding nastily. *(see Contiguous niches; Niche, carve out a, market ___)*

Cover all the bases: 1. Be prepared for any eventuality. 2. Another in the seemingly never-ending supply of American sport phrases; fail to make a decision. *(see Ballpark figure; Zone, in the)*

CPD: 1. Continuous professional development. 2. Erratic, occasional bursts of staff motivation; naked favouritism shown to a favoured few. *(see Continuous improvement; Fast track)*

Crack it: 1. Break the code. 2. Rather over dramatic way of saying that you have worked out how to do something, or completed even the simplest of tasks.

Crafting, it needs a bit of: 1. Further work is required on this. 2. This is sub-standard rubbish and needs to be done again. *(see Bugs, iron out the; Drawing board, back to the; Optimal; Sub-optimal; Tools, management, unique; Woodwork, spanners in the, spanners jumping out of the)*

Crash and burn: 1. Sustain impact, then burst in flames. 2. Fail spectacularly; fly high, then fall to earth; pride before a fall, followed by fall; public display of incompetence, preceded by hubristic claims of technical expertise. *(see Come a cropper; High risk; Maxed out; Needle, moving the; Needle, pushing the; Nightmare, utter; Plate spinning; Pushing the envelope; Wheels coming off; Wind, sailing close to the)*

Credentialing: 1. Presenting credentials. 2. Awful way to encapsulate describing what you do, much loved by over enthusiastic American companies, as in: *"Hey Brad, we have developed a breakthrough external-relations and credentialing programme."*

Credo: 1. Belief or principle. 2. Self-aggrandizing word, much loved by advertising agencies, to explain what they stand for; how we do it round here.

Crisis: 1. Crucial development or unhelpful period. 2. Permanent state of affairs in many companies; meltdown; systemic inability to cope.

Criteria, key: 1. Some important points. 2. One criterion after another in a seemingly never-ending list; not 'key' at all; cobbled together ragbag of disparate thoughts masquerading as a brief. *(see Key learnings; Word dump)*

Critical path: 1. Timing plan. 2. Perfectly ordinary sequence of events that should occur in order to make something happen effectively; not critical at all, in fact, quite humdrum and workaday; almost nothing to do with a path in the normal sense of the word.

Crossback impact (vb): 1. Affect something somewhere else. 2. Messy and quite unsatisfactory combination of two notions – that an idea can travel across and backward at the same time, and that there might be some kind of collision as a result; dreary wibble that effectively means nothing at all, as in: *"We're convinced that Project Sticking Plaster will crossback impact on Q3 sales, Roger."* *(see Impactful)*

Cross-collateralization: 1. Blending of various materials. 2. Woeful verbal car crash combining incorrect use of the word collateral, the classic American suffix –ize extended into an -ation, and a cross- prefix thrown in for good measure. *(see Collateral, -ize)*

Crunch the numbers: 1. Do some calculations. 2. Make a big deal out of doing some calculations; use a calculator; flounder around, having barely any capability at maths; design a ridiculously large spreadsheet to disguise the fact that the numbers are either unhelpful or unintelligible. *(see Analysis, paralysis by, in the final; Brain dump; Cook the books; Data dump; Fiscal juggling; Massage the numbers; Numbers, the)*

Crystal ball (vb): 1. Predict the future. 2. Risible attempt to work out what will happen next, with absolutely no chance of getting it right; plaintive call to action all-too-familiar to economists and weathermen everywhere, as in: *"We need to crystal ball this guys!"* *(see Black swan; Futureproof; Navel gazing; Strategy, strategize)*

CSR: 1. Corporate social responsibility – a policy explaining how a company conducts its business in an ethical and appropriate manner. 2. Fawning set of half-truths and broken promises that comes nowhere near explaining the full operational horror of what the company does; all-encompassing manifesto explaining whiter-than-white approach to everything from employee benefits to working conditions; joyous geographical trip around the globe showing delirious, exotic workers in conditions of sheer bliss; improbably equal set of photographs representing every race, colour and creed, all smiling by the company logo. *(see Exit interview; Transparency)*

C-suite: 1. The floor in an office block on which the titles of all the occupants begin with the letter C, as in chief executive. 2. Last resting place of all those whose jobs involve the C word; home of pompous twats lounging around and firing out orders from a self-constructed ivory tower; home to deep shag pile carpets, expensive art, randomly-dispersed fruit bowls and a vainglorious folly of an aquarium.

Culture, company: 1. The atmosphere in a company. 2. Curious, ethereal attempt to describe what companies are like; strange belief that what people are like may have a bearing on whether they can do the job. *(see Grasping at fog; Values; Vision, visioning)*

Culture, blame: 1. Company mood in which it is always someone else's fault. 2. Vicious, selfish and ungrateful collection of spiteful individuals who don't give a shit about anyone else; strange gathering of people who come together despite not liking other people; users out for themselves; collective atmosphere generated by the world's worst people, with the possible exception of Morris dancers.

Curve ball: 1. A ball that swerves in mid air. 2. Another baseball reference courtesy of the USA, referring to something that's quite tricky to deal with; nasty booby trap. *(see Ask, big; Bombs, box of; Catching a falling knife; Hospital pass; Poisoned chalice)*

Cushion management: 1. New team of company directors who do exactly the same as their predecessors, simply following on from the impression left before. 2. Nothing really changes in companies – despite triumphant announcements and mighty fanfares, it's the same old stuff every year; world-weary maintenance of the status quo.

Custodian: 1. Somebody looking after the welfare of something or someone. 2. Somebody totally ignoring the welfare of something or someone; just passing through; deriving maximum personal benefit and then sodding off; itinerant job hopper: self-appointed 'brand guardian' who ruins it completely before being ceremonially fired. *(see Guardian, brand)*

Customer experience, -centric, -facing, -focused, journey, satisfaction, value: 1. Talking to customers, looking after them and making them happy. 2. Hotchpotch of drivel designed to convince customers that anyone gives a damn about them; not facing the customer at all, in fact probably looking the other way; self-deluding fabrication of so-called 'customer journey' to suggest proper service; consistently low ratings for satisfaction and value. *(see Connect with our audience; Expectations, exceeding, failing to achieve, living up to, managing, meeting; Journey, customer; Seamless)*

Cut our losses: 1. Quit while behind. 2. Compound our losses; go bust; fail; file for bankruptcy.

Cut through, cut-through: 1. Sever something. 2. Odious verb-cum-noun prevalent in the communications industry; strange allusion to media messages somehow being physically tangible, as in: *"We need to cut through the clutter here, guys"*; even worse: *"We need to generate cut-through"*, thus turning an active verb into a spurious noun.

Cutting edge: 1. The sharp edge of something like a knife. 2. Macho, semi-military descriptor to suggest that something is particularly advanced or ingenious, when it probably isn't; noun morphed into an adjective, as in: *"This is truly cutting-edge technology, Malcolm,"* when referring to something perfectly straightforward such as a bicycle or paper clip. *(see Bleeding edge; Leading edge; Next-generation; Pioneering)*

CV: 1. Curriculum Vitae (Latin). 2. A total pack of lies and fabrication bearing no relation to the true (in)competence of the candidate. *(see Achilles heel; Blue-chip; Capabilities; Capability gap; Drop a ricket; FNG)*

DABDA: 1. Denial, anger, bargaining, depression, acceptance. 2. Sequence identified by Swiss-American psychiatrist Elisabeth Kubler-Ross for those confronting terminal illness; not dissimilar to the sequence of panic experienced by fraught businessmen when realizing for the first time that everything has gone horribly wrong.

Daily basis, on a: 1. Daily. 2. Completely redundant addition of three extra words to a perfectly good one with the sole purpose of wasting all our time; favoured fallback of all panjandrums and jobsworths, as in: *"Of course Bernard, I shall be checking the entire department's timesheets on a daily basis." (see Administrivia; Bureaucracy; Jobsworth; Panjandrum; Timesheets; Vis-a-vis)*

Damage, collateral: 1. Unintentional damage caused to civilians and property by military action. 2. Disastrous chain reaction following an appalling blunder – easily capable of bringing an entire brand or company down if the person is stupid or clever enough, as in Leeson or Ratner.

Data dump: 1. Download of large amount of information. 2. Large scale vomiting of factoids or statistics without due heed for the intended audience, or indeed any useful outcome – much loved by researchers with only average intelligence. *(see Analysis, paralysis by, in the final; Brain dump; Competitive review; Crunch the numbers)*

Datafy: 1. To convert into data. 2. Loathsome verb spawned from the modern obsession with 'big data', as in: *"Of course now that we have datafied it, we can really exploit the customer base, Brendan."*

Dead cat bounce: 1. Temporary recovery in prices after a substantial fall, but not a true recovery. 2. Futile attempt to suggest there is still potential in a project or product when the wheels fell off ages ago; desperately clinging on to any tiny glimpse of good news while simultaneously flying in the face of all rational information. *(see Entering a new plateau; Flatline; Negative growth, profit; SNAFU)*

Dead wood: 1. Arboreal matter that is no longer growing. 2. Any long-term colleague you genuinely dislike and would like to see fired, or an entire department meeting the same criteria.

Death by PowerPoint: 1. Extremely long and boring presentation. 2. Interminable drivel given credence by near-universal software package; default setting for all bad presenters who, on being asked to write a presentation, rush to their work station and immediately open a PowerPoint file called 'Presentation to X', without any thought about the line of argument; deck of impenetrable charts offered up by fawning management consultancy to justify exorbitant fee; receptacle for juvenile clip art; vehicle for thunderously boring research debrief; all-day briefing nightmare; cure for insomnia; showboater's paradise; colossal time wasting mechanism. *(see BlackBerry prayer; Bullet points; Full Monty, the; Kitchen sink; Meetings; Moi presentation)*

Decision maker, decision-making process: 1. An individual or system whose purpose is to decide what to do. 2. A dithering individual or neutered committee whose sole purpose is in fact to avoid decisive action. *(see Deconflicted)*

Deconflicted: 1. Free of conflict. 2. Emerging from a dark period of indecision and self-loathing. *(see Decision maker)*

Decruit: 1. Relieve of employment. 2. Fire; sack; physically eject from the building without warning; defenestrate spontaneously (advertising industry only). *(see Axe, face the; Defenestrate, defenestration; Delayering; Dejob; Downsize; Human resources; Phone list, go down the)*

Dedication: 1. Complete and wholehearted devotion. 2. Pathetic adherence to the corporate creed, and the working of inhumane hours, in the vain hope of a pay rise or viable pension.

Deep dive: 1. Close and detailed look. 2. Frantic plunge into the issues to see what exactly has gone so horribly wrong, usually following a holiday or sustained period of reckless neglect of a project. *(see Closer look, stand back and take a; Drains up, have the; Drill down; No stone unturned; Root-and-branch review; Witch-hunt)*

Deeply shallow: 1. Of nearly no substance. 2. Inspired oxymoron defining someone's complete lack of backbone or integrity, as in: *"One thing one can say about Barry is that he is deeply shallow."* *(see Aspirational)*

Defenestrate, defenestration: 1. The act of throwing someone out of a window. 2. Dismissal from a company by the same technique, sometimes followed by a range of office furniture and a pot plant; swift eviction method much loved by advertising agencies. *(see Alligators, up to my arse in; Ballistic, go; Bullet, get the; Chop, for the; Exit strategy; FIFO (2); Marching orders, get your; Mid-life crisis; Moon, barking at the, over the, through the; Postal, go; Radar, off; Rails, gone off the; Show the door)*

Degrow: 1. Shrink; decline. 2. Disgraceful attempt to suggest that something is going up rather than down – usually sales or profits; another in the large lexicon of words attaching the de- prefix to an otherwise positive word in the vain hope that no one will notice the bad news. *(see Decruit; Dejob; Delayering; Destaff)*

Dejob: 1. Remove from current job. 2. Construct a farrago of lies to suggest why one's current role is no longer valid, thereby justifying firing, redundancy, or a move to the Faroe Islands, or Staines-on-Thames. *(see At a stroke; Axe, face the; Decruit; One fell swoop, in; Phone list, go down the)*

Delayering: 1. Taking away layers. 2. Firing everyone except the management. *(see Decruit; Dejob; Destaff)*

Delegate, delegation: 1. Pass on a job to a subordinate. 2. Get rid of entire workload to subordinates; do nothing; idle. *(see Buck stops here, the; Deploy energies, resources)*

Delighting customers: 1. Making customers happy. 2. Annoying customers over a sustained period through persistent pestering. *(see Customer journey; Desired consumer response; Expectations, exceeding; Loyalty beyond reason, customer, staff, team)*

Deliver: 1. Cause to arrive. 2. Often, completely fail to arrive, as in fail to deliver.

Deliverables: 1. Things that should be delivered. 2. Condemning rap sheet of items that palpably failed to happen; wish list; wishful thinking; not a cat in hell's chance of occurring; much-abused default position for lazy managers wishing to appear practical, as in: *"What are the deliverables on this guys?"*

Delivery of outputs: 1. Things that should be delivered. 2. Even longer-winded and more pointless phrase for stuff that hasn't been done. *(see Inputs; Outputs)*

Demise (vb) : 1. Make redundant. 2. Execute; kill; ill-conceived euphemism for throwing a human being (or many) out of the company, deployed by a major bank when dismissing thousands; morbid conversion of a noun into a verb, as in: *"As of today we are announcing that 5,000 jobs are to be demised,"* or *"We are henceforth demising these roles,"* as though the undertaker has been called to the office – which may not be far off the mark for many of those involved. *(see Decruit; Dejob; Delayer; Downsize)*

Democratize, democratizing the idea: 1. Make the people's property. 2. 'Down with the kids' verb invented by self-styled 'hip populists' in social media, having established that all companies and capitalists are bad, 'democratizing the idea' returns power to the people, apparently. *(see Commoditize; Digital native; -ize; Monetize; Productize)*

Demographic: 1. Relating to demography. 2. Hybrid noun referring to a demographic segment, as in: *"Hey guys, let's not forget which demographic we are targeting here."* *(see Target)*

Deploy energies, resources: 1. Decide how to spend time or effort. 2. Put feet up and get everyone else to do the work. *(see Delegate, delegation)*

De-risk: 1. Reduce or remove likelihood of failure. 2. Wince-inducing application of the de- prefix to a perfectly normal word to spawn a six-letter monster; weasel expression to disguise the fact that a proposal is intrinsically dangerous; downgrade from suicidal to merely foolhardy. *(see Decruit; Dejob; Destaff)*

Derive synergies: 1. Create benefit(s) from working well together. 2. Squeeze extra profit out of already strained workforce by combining two departments and sacking half the people. *(see Synergy)*

Desired consumer response: 1. How a customer will ideally respond. 2. Vacuous wish list of reactions that will never come to pass. *(see Customer journey; Delight customers; Expectations, exceeding)*

Destigmatize: 1. Remove stigma from. 2. Try to resuscitate project or colleague when all hope of survival is long gone; attempt to improve image but actually make it worse. *(see Turd, polishing a)*

Destaff: 1. Reduce number of employees. 2. Fire as many people as possible, as fast as possible. *(see ABC session; Defenestrate, defenestration; Dejob; Decruit; Delayering; Marching orders, get your; Phone list, go down the)*

Details, God is in the: 1. Phrase coined by Mies van der Rohe to suggest that the importance of detail cannot be overstated. 2. Mindless, glib parroting of same phrase by smug managers when horribly out of their depth; desperate attempt to plaster over the cracks of vacuous waffle outburst with a semblance of practicality; massive hospital pass masquerading as a compliment. *(see Buck, the ___ stops here; Hospital pass)*

Development: 1. Unfinished work; new event. 2. Work that will never be finished because it is, and always will be, 'in development'; nasty turn of events that will ruin everything. *(see Black swan; WIP)*

Devil and the deep blue sea, between the: 1. On the horns of an uncomfortable dilemma. 2. Clichéd excuse of all lazy sales executives; suggestion of conflict where none exists; weary bleating of executive who has never seen (a) the devil, or (b) the deep blue sea, having never left Solihull.

Devil's avocado: 1. Fruit owned, or indeed possessed by, Lucifer. 2. Variation on devil's advocate; deliberate taking of the opposite view; attempt to diffuse uncomfortable conflict in meeting, as in: *"I'm just trying to play devil's avocado for a minute here, guys."*

Dial up: 1. Telephone a number. 2. Irritating modern expression for increasing the strength of something; much used in the world of media, as in: *"We need to dial up this TV plan, guys."*; randomly used regardless of resources, budget or any reference to investment likelihood. *(see Bucks, bang for your)*

Dialogue (vb): 1. To talk with. 2. Redundant noun-cum-verb, as in: *"I'm going to dialogue with Nigel on this one tomorrow." (see Triangulate)*

Dialogue, continuous consumer, meaningful: 1. Conversation with customer or colleague, intended to have some meaning. 2. Intersecting monologues; no conversation at all; shouting into the void. *(see Bark into the wind, up the wrong tree; Human wind tunnel)*

Diarize: 1. To put in a diary. 2. Lamentable 'action oriented' verb created by Americans. *(see Commoditize; Democratize, -ize; Herding cats; Locked into; Monetize)*

Dick-swinging: 1. Moving genitals from side to side. 2. Overbearingly macho, despite possessing rather small genitals; priapic posturing; peacock strutting; boasting. *(see Clout; Nero syndrome)*

Difference, make a: 1. Make a difference. 2. Pretend to make a difference without influencing anything at all; talk about 'making a difference' without actually making a difference.

Digital native: 1. Person, usually young, fully-versed in all matters relating to the internet and modern technology, having grown up with it. 2. Potentially pejorative, borderline racist term for a hairy bloke called Dean who skateboards dramatically into the office, and then sits in the corner with his headphones on all day furiously tapping on a keyboard; any person who knows more about the interweb than you do. *(see Baked in; Democratize; Drive traffic; Free-roaming experience; iGod; Monetize; On-rails experience; Productize ; User experience)*

DILLIGAF: 1. Do I look like I give a f**k? 2. Profane rhetorical question disguised as acronym and designed to humiliate the listener absolutely. *(see Enlighten me; FOFO; Follow me, do you; Lips, read my; Respect, with)*

Dinosaur: 1. Prehistoric animal. 2. Ancient or old-before-time member of staff who keeps referring to 'the good old days', or beginning sentences with *"Of course, in my day..."* *(see Jobsworth; Halcyon days; Rose-tinted)*

Direction, lack of; strategic: 1. Intended line of travel; vector; course. 2. Abstract and diffuse notion designed to suggest that everyone knows what they are doing, when they probably don't. *(see Aims; Grasping at fog; Strategize; Objectives)*

Disaster, total: 1. Mishap. 2. Meltdown; absolute failure; catastrophic collapse in capability. *(see Armageddon plan; Scorched earth policy)*

Disconnect: 1. To unplug an electric appliance. 2. Utter failure to connect; complete void in communication or understanding, as in: *"Do we have a disconnect here, Colin?"*

Disinvestment: 1. Removal of funds. 2. Annual removal of funds at exactly the same moment after the traditional three-month budget bidding round; 15 February, after only six weeks of financial support; pulling the plug. *(see Dog, this is a)*

Disruption: 1. Breaking things up. 2. Somewhat fatuous term for interrupting someone with a selling message – good for the advertiser and possibly bad for the recipient. *(see Abruption)*

Disseminate: 1. To distribute or scatter about. 2. To vaguely announce; fail to announce at all.

Diverse range: 1. Spectrum; options, hopefully varied. 2. Weasel word pairing usually denoting not much choice at all; sometimes referring to participants, as in: *"As you can see, we have a diverse range of attendees,"* uttered while pointing to an all-white middle-class audience. *(see Package; Raft of ideas, proposals; Tranche)*

Diversity: 1. Mixture of X and Y; varied mix. 2. Inability to hire anyone different to oneself; flagrant nepotism; refusal to accept findings of psychometric testing that suggests a broader blend in the team would be beneficial. *(see Broad church; Multicultural)*

DNA: 1. Deoxyribonucleic acid, the main constituent of chromosomes responsible for transmission of hereditary characteristics. 2. Intensely annoying shorthand to describe 'the character of a brand', as in: *"The brand's DNA is crucial here, guys."* *(see Baked in; Brand strategist; Mission critical)*

Doable: 1. It can be done. 2. Sometimes offered in a genuine way, as in: *"Yes, Steve, that's definitely doable."*; more commonly used when it can technically be done but it's neither advisable nor likely to be any good, as in: *"It's doable, Jane, but it'll be crap."* *(see Can do attitude)*

Dog, this is a: 1. Death knell for a product or brand after analysis using the Boston Consulting Group matrix deems it so. 2. It's rubbish, kill it now. *(see Disinvestment; Duck, lame)*

Dog food, eat your own: 1. Experience the (bad) result of something you initiated yourself. 2. Canine-influenced phrase suggestive of being on all fours in a humiliating posture, and consuming something pretty nasty. *(see Hoist with one's own petard)*

Dogs bark but the caravans move on, the: 1. Nothing really changes. 2. Amusing imagery of strays howling at a passing vehicle, as though it will make a difference; metaphor for the futility of much office work, as with: *"The flies change but the shit stays the same."*

Dog's bollocks: 1. Canine testicles. 2. Brilliant; superb; enviable, as in: *"Can you lick yours then?"* *(see Bee's knees, it's the; Mustard, cut the, that's ___ that is)*

Dolly back: 1. Of a wheeled support on which a camera can be mounted, to retreat or move backwards. 2. Hold on a minute; withdraw hastily; think again, as in: *"Whoa Gavin, I think we need to dolly back on this one!"*

(see Closer look, stand back and take a; Focus; Helicopter view; Telescope, we have to look at this from both ends of the ____)

Done deal: 1. A deal that has been done. 2. Pipe dream; pie in the sky; categorically not in the bag; classic overclaim of Terylene-suited sales managers when returning from a meeting without a signed contract. *(see Door, knocking on an open; In the bag; Paving the way; Pipeline, in the; Seals, left them clapping like; Slam dunk)*

Doomsday scenario: 1. Moment of reckoning. 2. Ultra-bleak possibility of everything going horribly wrong; crisis planning; strong likelihood of total nightmare; time to leave the office rapidly, or resign. *(see Armageddon plan: Scenario, best-case, nightmare, worst-case)*

Door, knocking on the, pushing at an open: 1. Attempting something that will certainly receive a positive response. 2. Pride before a fall; unwarranted hubris of the overconfident salesperson; not in the bag at all; only a distant possibility. *(see Done deal)*

Doorstepped: 1. Caught at one's front door or unexpectedly in the street without prior warning. 2. Unnervingly intercepted by Bernadette from accounts when you least expect it; confronted at one's desk by her ample midriff, disconcertingly at face level. *(see Cold-calling; Doorstopped; Heavyweight)*

Doorstopped: 1. Wedged a door open. 2. Comprehensively blocked by Bernadette from accounts outside the gents in a tight space; prevented from escaping an unwanted conversation about a spreadsheet; total eclipse of the corridor. *(see Cold-calling; Doorstepped)*

Dosser: 1. Lazy person; idler. 2. 99% of any workforce, including the post room, maintenance, IT helpdesk, accounts, 'human' resources, security staff, managing director, and your boss.

Dotted line: 1. Line broken into a series of dashes. 2. Seemingly innocuous device found on organizational charts that wreaks utter havoc by leaving all concerned totally confused about who reports to whom; source of hundreds of office brawls. *(see Hierarchy; Matrix; Non-hierarchical; Organogram; Pecking order; Pull rank; Snake's honeymoon)*

Double click on that issue (vb): 1. Concentrate, redouble efforts (assumed, true meaning unclear). 2. *"We have to double click on that issue Jane!"*; desperate cry of a bewildered executive suddenly realising that they have failed to get something done, and then passing the buck to someone else. *(see Buck, pass the; Double down)*

Double down: 1. To double one's wager. 2. Go full throttle; chuck in the kitchen sink; overcompensate; overdo it; flagrantly gamble with all resources, regardless of consequences. *(see Double click on that issue; Full-tilt boogie)*

Double-loop learning: 1. Management process coined by Harvard professor Chris Argyris in the 1970s in which executives continually question the policies within which their decision-making power is constrained. 2. Anarchy in which no one does what they are told; overwhelming feeling that the law is an ass, and that you are absolutely right; cocky, self-righteous attitude of new graduate who believes they know everything, and that the world owes them a living; privately-educated toff with similar beliefs.

Double whammy: 1. Negative impact, occurring twice. 2. Sucker punch; knockout blow; straight in the slats immediately after receiving a hit to the slats; one on each testicle; minimal chance of recovery; down and out for good; the end. *(see Sucker punch)*

Doughnut rather than the hole, it would be wise to concentrate on the: 1. Look at the relevant bit of the problem. 2. Slightly surreal, semi-culinary analogy to allude to the irrelevant part of an issue; stop talking about the stuff that doesn't matter and get to the point; this person is way off brief. *(see Waffle)*

Downside: 1. Disadvantage; the con to the pro; the bit where things go wrong. 2. Overwhelming reason why something should certainly not be done; pitfall; certainty of failure; long list of cons that heavily outweigh any suggested pro. *(see Upside)*

Downsize: 1. Reduce the size of, usually workforce. 2. Weasel word to disguise anything from mild reduction to total annihilation; dastardly retention of the word 'size' in the body of the new word allows macho managers to imply that scale remains part of the action, whereas in fact it doesn't. *(see Decruit; Lay off; Negative growth, profit; Quantitative easing)*

Draconian: 1. Harsh, severe (after the strict rules of Draco, Greek lawmaker). 2. All-encompassing; total and utter; everyone out; last one out turn the lights off; complete company or departmental meltdown; factory closure or punitive outsourcing decision, *(see Across the board, right; Armageddon plan; Scorched earth policy; Swingeing cuts)*

Draining the swamp: 1. Turning boggy area into dry land. 2. Purging company or department of horribly poisonous member of staff; weeding out constant moaners; working out weasels who smile obsequiously to members of management while slagging them off in private; purge; cleanse. *(see Bad apple)*

Drains up, have the: 1. Examine sewage system. 2. Find out what's really going on in a company; discover nasty truth of working reality; pay attention for the first time; annual review with unpleasant consequences. *(see Deep dive; Drains up, have the; Drill down; Flush out; Forensic, send it down to the boys in; Lift up a rock; No stone unturned; Root-and-branch review; Warts and all; Witch-hunt)*

Drawing board, back to the: 1. Return to the original design or blueprint. 2. Begin again, having got nowhere; complete rethink; start from scratch; write off millions of investment money having made the wrong choice; plaintive cry of new product development managers from Penzance to Preston, as in: *"Right guys, it's back to the drawing board!"* *(see Back to basics; Bugs, iron out the; Crafting, it needs a bit of; Evolving to meet customer demand; Optimal; Rebrand; Redesign; Sub-optimal)*

Dream team: 1. Assembly of the best possible people for the job. 2. Random ragbag of semi-qualified personnel; anyone who isn't on holiday or off sick; whoever is left after we fired everyone; two trainees and an overstretched director; the tea lady and the bloke on security; two people who know nothing whatsoever about the subject matter but are quite good at finding things on the web; interns being paid nothing; B, C, or any other lower grade team. *(see A Team, this calls for the)*

Dress to impress: 1. Put on clothes that will create a favourable impression. 2. Choose completely the wrong suit for a crucial meeting, such as pinstripe to meet a whizzy entrepreneur or a purple one with an eerie sheen for an investment bank; ill-advised selection of 'office jester' tie for annual pay review. *(see Casting; Minister for fun)*

Drill down: 1. Drill down. 2. Find out what's really happening; discover the awful reality; usually, the first time that the chief executive has realized the true nature of the business they are running; moment of reckoning; dawning of real understanding; find out that the business is fundamentally flawed, or dangerously teetering on the edge of bankruptcy. *(see Drains up, have the; Granular; Needs and wants; No stone unturned; Root-and-branch review)*

Drink the Kool-Aid: 1. To mindlessly adopt the dogma of a group or company without really understanding why or questioning intentions sufficiently. 2. Reference to an American fruit drink, purported to have been laced with cyanide and given to the followers of the Jim Jones cult at the

Jonestown massacre in 1978 (unverified and often disputed); intensely annoying capacity of enthralled staff to parrot the company line; typical examples include a rabid and irrational hatred of any competitive product, an unshaken belief that their product is always the best (despite persistent evidence to the contrary), and an inevitable adoption of all company jargon, even at home and with mates in the pub.

Drive: 1. Golf shot; to operate a car (vb); ambition. 2. Naked ambition; preparedness to tread on any colleague to win or be promoted; machismo; greed; selfishness; self-centred motivation at any price; undesirable quality in a colleague, but much-prized by macho sales directors, as in: *"Yes, Martin's figures are good, but has he got the drive to be regional manager?"* (see Ambition; Competitiveness; Driven)

Drive a coach and horses through: 1. Find many flaws in an argument. 2. Totally dismantle; humiliate a rival in an important meeting; tear to shreds, piece by piece; reduce subordinate to tears; savagely deploy superior intellect to undermine less bright colleague or customer; publicly execute.

Drive a stake into the ground: 1. Hammer a wooden or metal spike into terra firma; create an anchor point. 2. Another in the lexicon of pseudo-macho managers determined to define their territory, scent mark on lampposts, and generally hammer and forge in any way possible. *(see Groundbreaking; Ringfence; Stakeholder)*

Drive it home: 1. Transport unspecified object to its dwelling, probably in a car. 2. Repeat a point again and again, even though everyone else in the room knows precisely what you are saying; drone on; preach; incessantly say the same thing over and over after realizing that you only have one point and have run out of material. *(see Waffle; Word dump)*

Drive traffic: 1. Encourage quantity of customers to use or do something. 2. Pointless pseudo-automotive phrase usually associated with websites, as in: *"We need to drive traffic to our site, guys!"*; curious suggestion that we are somehow driving everyone else's cars, while presumably driving our own; odd implication that the collective effect of customers' buying decisions is akin to the flow of vehicles on a road; staple phrase of hairy computer coders throughout Shoreditch. *(see Digital native)*

Driven: 1. Taken somewhere, perhaps by a chauffeur or friend. 2. Possessed of 'drive' (qv); overtly ambitious, but only on behalf of oneself; adjective describing a total arsehole whom everyone universally despises; narcissistic; loathsome; riddled with self-perception problems; determined to own a Porsche by the age of 30; prone to celebrate sales achievements by spending thousands on champagne and cocktails; inclined to show off and humiliate as many other people as possible, including wife, children, and parents; twat-like. *(see Ambition; Competitiveness; Drive; Hungry, are they _____enough?)*

-driven: 1. Suffix denoting something that has been pushed in a certain direction, such as change-driven, or market-driven. 2. Egregiously bad bastardization of almost any word that requires macho turbo charging (qv); devious method for changing any verb into an adjective, as in needs-driven, consumer-driven, web-driven, and so on, ad infinitum; possible technique for retrieving some humour from a bad situation, as in idiot-driven, boss-driven, tosser-driven, etc. *(see -centred, -centric; -focused, people-, goal-; –oriented; Results-driven; Turbo charge)*

Drivers, key: 1. People operating vehicles, presumably in possession of an ignition key; important influences that make things happen. 2. Hideous catch-all phrase to describe anything and everything to do with how a market works; random hotchpotch of stuff to do with the matter in hand; lazy, default phrase for marketing director or advertising executive referring to things that may or may not make a difference; not drivers at all, and certainly not 'key'; passive constituent parts that have no bearing on anything at all. *(see Change drivers; Key criteria; KPIs)*

Drop a ricket: 1. Make a mistake. 2. Lose it completely; fail to live up to boss's expectations; fail to display any of the basic qualities claimed at interview. *(see Ball, take one's eye off the; Bazooka after a fly, we're not going to send a; Beans, spill the; CV; Drop the ball; Platform, eat one's own)*

Drop our trousers: 1. Take our pants off (USA). 2. Reduce price significantly; make a whopping loss; offer a loss leader in the hope of more profitable work to come; get comprehensively shafted. *(see BOHICA; Compliance; Flexible; Pants down, caught with our; Sprat to catch a mackerel)*

Drop the ball: 1. Relinquish control at a crucial moment. 2. Fail miserably; blow it; demand greater responsibility and then fail to deliver; be found in the pub when supposed to be in a crucial meeting; not turn up; struggle to cope with a delegated task. *(see Ball, take one's eye off the; Drop a ricket; Hospital pass; Pass the baton)*

Dropping grenades in fishponds: 1. Detonating hand-held incendiary devices in small aquatic environments; generating a dramatic outcome via use of excessive firepower. 2. Causing absolute chaos; destroying everything one touches; being a total liability; wreaking havoc in a department or company; slashing and burning; changing all the rules on first day in job;

acting before taking advice; executing decrees without considering the possible consequences; being a thoughtless prat. *(see Blue touch paper, light the; Bull in a china shop; Gung ho)*

Duck, lame: 1. Aquatic bird that has trouble walking. 2. Project that will never get off the ground; no-hoper; doomed case; non-starter; sudden real-ization that the company's star project or product is deficient; exasperated cry of chief executive on discovering that Project Dominatrix is a compre-hensive failure and has soaked up millions in investment money. *(see Dog, this is a; SNAFU)*

Ducking and diving: 1. Deploying a range of evasion techniques. 2. Bob-bing and weaving; hiding in the toilets so as not to bump into boss; refus-ing to answer the phone to suppliers needing to be paid; avoiding client interaction of any kind in case one is found wanting; nipping off to the pub rather than facing the music; throwing a sickie; wandering around the park trying to work out how not to be fired on returning to the office.

Ducks in a row, get our: 1. Take some aquatic birds (that we own) and arrange them neatly; make sure we know what we are doing. 2. Rush around in a blind panic trying to create some vague semblance of order; generate an illusion of organization where there is none; bluff; lie; pretend we know what we're doing when we patently don't; frantically draft an impressive looking chart that suggests structure, rigour and process. *(see Act together, getting our ___: Hymn sheet, singing from the same; Realign-ment; Wavelength, on the same, not on the same; Wildebeest in a row, has the lion got his)*

Dumbing down: 1. Making simpler. 2. Making simpler because we don't understand it; making simpler because our customers don't understand it; making simpler because no one understands it; make simplistic because everyone is too dim to get it when it's actually very simple: drawing a child-ish diagram because the words are just too much, frankly.

Dyke, finger in the: 1. Small intervention holding back what could be a massive flood. 2. Digit ill-advisedly inserted into lesbian; sticking plaster approach to business; problem about to explode; hopelessly ill-equipped solution to a problem; bomb waiting to go off. *(see Bombs, box of)*

Dynamic: 1. Concerned with energy. 2. Lacking in any form of dynamism whatsoever; listless; of a product or person, inert; the opposite of what is claimed on a CV, as in: *"Dynamic personality"*; Bernard from accounts, who likes to push the boat out with a half of bitter on pay day.

Ear to the ground: 1. Well informed. 2. Phenomenally nosey.

Earn-out period: 1. Time during which the price of a company sold will eventually be paid. 2. Shorter-than-expected passage of time during which the person who sold the company walks out in disgust at the antics of the new owners, and simultaneously loses more than half of what they agreed to sell it for.

Ease the throttle back: 1. Reduce speed. 2. Skive; neglect; take the piss; ignore; skim; cut corners in the hope of getting away with it.

Eastern front, this is like the ___ when the bullets didn't turn up: 1. Archaic military reference to Napoleonic or World War in which troops did not have the right equipment. 2. Any occasion on which the team is woefully under-equipped. *(see Paper cup, here's a ___ , there's a tidal wave coming; Pathologist's interest; Titanic, rearranging the deckchairs on the)*

Easy answers, there are no: 1. This is actually quite difficult. 2. I haven't got a clue what I'm talking about, but I don't want anyone to rumble it so I am using a broad platitude as a distraction. *(see Quick fix; Magic ingredient, there is no)*

Easy tiger: 1. Calm down. 2. I know we encourage blind enthusiasm round here but now you're getting on my nerves, so shut up. *(see Can do attitude)*

EBITDA: 1. Earnings before interest, taxes, depreciation and amortization. 2. Any fabricated figure that makes it look as though profits are healthy, regardless of a range of skeletons in cupboards. *(see Fiscal juggling; Skeletons in the cupboard)*

Ecosystem: 1. A system of interactions between living organisms (ecology). 2. Nasty, and usually wholly inappropriate, analogy stolen from the scientific world and applied to something such as interrelationships in media or a network of companies; suggestion that the commercial world emulates much of the elegance and wonder of the natural world – a highly unlikely state of affairs.

Educating consumers: 1. Letting customers know what we offer. 2. Patronizing the people who buy our products, because we are much more intelligent than they are.

EDLP: 1. Everyday low pricing. 2. Cheap tat. *(see Permanently reducing prices)*

Ego: 1. The self of an individual. 2. Massively over-inflated opinion of oneself, most commonly fuelled by status, power, money, perceived gonad size or the sycophancy of subordinates. *(see Brown-nosing)*

Effectiveness: 1. Degree to which something has an effect. 2. 'Professional' word much loved by creative industries desperately trying to prove that they are indeed professional; broad term that usually yields no quantification; pseudo-rigorous hint at return on investment when in all probability there is none. *(see ROI)*

Efficiency drive: 1. Concerted effort to be more efficient. 2. Massive purge of everything; decimation of anything within reach; sacking of entire workforce; disposal of all factories and real estate; cancelling of all contracts; screwing every supplier; pawning of desk lamps; selling of grandmother and office cat. *(see Armageddon plan; Efficiencies, finding; Scorched earth policy)*

Efficiencies, finding: 1. Discovering ways to run a business more efficiently. 2. Deviously seeking out more ways to cut costs to the bone; freezing all pay rises; refusing to sign expense forms; allowing dilapidation of offices; failing to replace broken sign over entrance to office; downgrading all international travel to economy class; insisting salesmen sleep in their cars rather than check in to a hotel; cancelling office party; giving oneself a pay rise and no one else. *(see Efficiency drive)*

80/20 rule: 1. The Pareto principle, named after the 19th century professor who spotted that the majority of activity in most markets was accounted for by a minority of operators. 2. Faux mathematical platitude that frequently bears no relation to the matter in hand at all; brilliant catch-all for innumerate sales people wishing to add a dash of quantification to a meeting, as in: *"Of course, this is the old 80-20 rule isn't it, guys?"*, when it's actually nothing of the sort. *(see Peter principle, the)*

Elasticity: 1. Stretchiness; flex. 2. Scope to wriggle out of almost anything; superb cover word for reneging on everything that was agreed last week; massive downgrading of forecast or target; weasel word to escape from any awkward situation, as in: *"Well naturally there's a certain amount of elasticity in those figures, Brian."* *(see Flexible, flexibility)*

Elephant in the room: 1. Big issue that is being ignored. 2. The main point of almost every meeting that is never discussed, such as catastrophic sales figures, or the fact that the chief executive is paid millions for doing sod all while everyone else works like a slave for a pittance. *(see Emperor's new clothes; Fat man in the canoe; White elephant)*

Eleventh hour, at the: 1. We have barely any time left. 2. I am pathologically incapable of doing anything until the very last minute. *(see A Team, this calls for the; Essay Crisis; Cavalry over the hill)*

Email: 1. Electronic communication. 2. Fantastic medium with which to delegate and abdicate all responsibility. *(see BCC; CC; Voice mail)*

Embedding: 1. To fix firmly in a surrounding solid mass. 2. Verb borrowed from the construction industry in a vain attempt to give solidity to ephemeral ideas such as culture and creativity, as in: *"We really need to embed these values, guys!"*

EMEA: 1. Shorthand for Europe, Middle East, and Africa. 2. Job title offering the broad excuse to fly round Europe and the Middle East hurling abuse at the locals and surreptitiously shagging well-stacked hookers, or drinking illicit booze in gambling dens. *(see APAC)*

Emotional intelligence: 1. Awareness of one's own emotions and those of others. 2. Curiously fluffy phrase much-loved of HR personnel from Land's End to John o' Groats; touchy-feely; technically incompetent but 'really good with people'; vague excuse for being nice and useless at the same time, as in: *"I know Jane has her weaknesses but she has high emotional intelligence."* *(see Empathy; Minister for fun; Touchy-feely)*

Empathy, empathetic: 1. The power of understanding someone else's feelings. 2. Strange connective quality, usually offered by Barbara from Human Resources; endless ability to have cups of tea and chat; adjective describing the broad phenomenon that is encapsulated by the phrase 'let's sit down and talk about it'; annoying ability to see everyone else's point of view; total inability to have a point of view; vicarious living of office life entirely through the actions of others; lack of originality and character; sympathetic but not really cut out for any particular job function. *(see Emotional intelligence; Minister for fun)*

Emperor's new clothes: 1. Short story by Hans Christian Andersen featuring a suit whose material is invisible to those unfit for their positions. 2. Hubris of many senior executives; inability to realize one is metaphorically naked in front of colleagues and clients; titanic self-delusion; failure to spot the blindingly obvious; flat refusal to confront the truth; delusional stupidity of the highest order. *(see Elephant in the room)*

Empire building: 1. Increasing power and land ownership on a large scale. 2. Nakedly trying to be in charge of as many people, and as much budget, as possible; obsessed with numbers, as in size of workforce who report to you; power crazy; prone to exaggeration at interview or on CV, as in: *"I have 10,000 direct reports." (see Dick-swinging; Nero syndrome)*

Empower: 1. Give someone the power or authority to do something. 2. Do nothing of the sort; suggest autonomy whilst constantly peering over someone's shoulder; offer power and simultaneously take it away; undermine; erode; flatter to deceive; deceive outright; overclaim; overstep one's brief; pass the buck. *(see Air cover; Buck, pass the; Enablement; Hospital pass; Micromanaging; Riot act, read the)*

Enablement: 1. Provision of the adequate means, opportunity or authority to do something. 2. Nothing of the sort; fail to back up or protect properly; permission to hang oneself; hoisting by petard, not usually one's own; opportunity to be ritually humiliated under the guise of new responsibility; poisoned chalice. *(see Air cover; Empower; Hoist with one's own petard; Poisoned chalice)*

End-end user: 1. User at the very end of the process. 2. Even more pointless modifier to a perfectly good word; no different from a 'beginning user' either; a user, full stop; additionally annoying trumped-up adjective to suggest that the user at the end is strangely not at the end at all, but some kind of false one, thereby requiring another end, called an end-end. *(see End user)*

End of play: 1. When a theatrical production has finished; after everyone has left the office. 2. At the very last minute; not today, tomorrow in fact; never; at some unspecified point in the future, maybe; broad cover-up for hoping that the requester will forget what they have asked for, as in: *"I'll get that over to you by the end of play, Steve." (see At the end of the day; At this moment in time; At this point in time; Put to bed)*

End-to-end: 1. From one end to the other. 2. Possessing significant gaps; patchy; hastily cobbled together; apparently comprehensive, but not really, as in an 'end-to-end user experience'. *(see Seamless)*

End user: 1. Someone who uses something. 2. Pointless modifier to a perfectly good word; no different from a 'beginning user'; a user, full stop. *(see End-end user)*

Enduring: 1. Lasting a long time. 2. Short-lived; ephemeral; fly by night; fair-weather; flaky; self-serving and fame-seeking, as in: *"What's our enduring legacy here, guys?"*

Enemy, sleeping with the: 1. Procreating, or possibly just dormant with, an adversary. 2. Utterly unscrupulous; happy to do business with anyone just to gain a sale or promotion; amoral; immoral; illegal; uncaring; doing anything for a legover. *(see Collars and cuffs; Get into bed with; Kimono, open the; Matching luggage, Scratch my back and I'll scratch yours)*

Energies: 1. Sum total of vigour or vitality. 2. Woeful Americanism that turns a perfectly good word, energy, into an unnecessary plural; peculiar office-based life force that bears no relation to one's home-based vim level; weirdly fluctuating indicator of output that vacillates between full throttle and can't be arsed, depending on a range of factors including hangovers, looming pay day, impending appraisal or resignation, day of week, time of day, or distraction by large-breasted new receptionist. *(see Geography, geographies)*

Engage, engaged, engagement: 1. To involve. 2. Straightforward verb now transmogrified into a grotesque bastard son of its original form; 'customer engagement' has nothing to do with an impending marriage, but simply refers to their paying attention; 'engaging the staff and stakeholders' simply means getting them to agree to something as opposed to rejecting it outright. *(see Stakeholder)*

Engender: 1. Bring about or give rise to. 2. Weasel word for bring about or give rise to, as in: *"We really need to engender customer loyalty, guys."*; start; begin; get on with; persuade; do something; get going; pull one's finger out. *(see Pull your finger out)*

Enhance, enhancement: 1. To intensify or increase in quality 2. Annoying verb or descriptor to suggest that something is somehow better or more 'premium' than it probably is; redundant modifier, as in 'enhanced outcomes' and 'product enhancements'; direct substitute for improve or improvement. *(see Premium)*

Enlighten me: 1. Increase my understanding. 2. Hugely patronizing imperative that aims to assert the intellectual superiority of the asker; shades of the enlightenment, or some higher power or deity; roughly translates as

"I am a lot cleverer than you but if you really must say something I suppose I'll have to indulge you, you dimwit." (see *Aha moment; Follow, do you; FMF; Lips, read my; Respect, with; Teach your grandmother to suck eggs, don't, would never, would you; Word dump*)

Ensuing: 1. Following. 2. Slightly more pompous and smug than simply following, as in: *"The ensuing carnage wasn't pretty"* when describing a nasty round of blood-letting; or the rather dreadful: *"What implications will be ensuing from this?"*

Entering a new plateau: 1. Flatlining again. 2. Stasis; nothing happening; business as usual; stagnant; lifeless; moribund business performance; near terminal. (see *Dead cat bounce; Flatline; Negative growth; SNAFU*)

Enterprise/Enterprisewide: 1. Catch-all descriptor for a company of indeterminate size. 2. Across all such companies, as in: *"I want Project Slug to revolutionize the way people think of us enterprisewide, Darren!"* (see *Across the piste*)

Entrepreneur, entrepreneurial: 1. A businessperson who takes risks, from the French *entreprendre*, to undertake. 2. Tremendously overused term to describe anyone who runs a small business, or who has made a staggering number of cockups before getting it right, if at all; smug and self-deluding personal introduction at networking meetings, as in: *"Pleased to meet you, I'm an entrepreneur!"*; ubiquitous descriptor for any perfectly ordinary person running a business from home. (see *Coming or going, he doesn't know if he's; Marketing guru; Multitasking; Pivot*)

Environment, business, challenging: 1. External conditions or surroundings. 2. Vastly overused word to describe the context in which business is being conducted; suggestion that the business is operating on a far greater scale than is truly the case; desperate attempt to imply that the company trades beyond Rochdale, or the panty pad market, as in: *"This is a really challenging environment."*; approximate translation: things are difficult at the moment. (see *Battleground; Jungle out there, it's a; Out there*)

Equity, brand: 1. What a brand might be worth. 2. Finger in the air guesstimate of value in order to inflate the worth of a company's intangible assets, having sold all tangible assets; comprehensive guesswork; shareholder ruse to fleece buyer for higher price; fabrication.

Ersatz traditionalism: 1. Pretending to be traditional. 2. Nasty tendency for so many modern brands to claim authenticity; imitation of the real thing; artificial background trumped up by company librarian who tracks down an ancient ancestor of the founder who once worked as a blacksmith; faux history generated in the vain hope that someone won't rumble it via thorough research online. *(see Authenticity; Back story; Provenance)*

Essay crisis: 1. Cramming too much work into too little time. 2. Continuing utterly flawed student cramming behaviour into (so-called) professional work life, working through the night fuelled only by a range of semi-legal substances. *(see Cavalry over the hill; Eleventh hour, at the; ETA; Maxed out; Pushing the envelope; Needle, pushing the)*

ETA: 1. Estimated time of arrival. 2. Whenever; when I get round to it; possibly never. *(see ASAP; Eleventh hour, at the; Essay crisis; PDQ)*

Ether, float into, lost in the: 1. Hypothetical medium formerly believed to fill all space and support the propagation of electromagnetic waves. 2. I have no f**king idea where it's gone; it was there seconds ago, honestly; disappeared without trace; total deletion of email inbox, generating initial panic, followed by all-embracing elation and a sweet feeling of release. *(see Smoke and mirrors job)*

Even less to this than meets the eye: 1. Genuinely of no substance. 2. Lovely reverse put-down, hinting that there might be something there, but verifying that actually there isn't; a classic for commenting on the vacuity of empty announcements, usually by CEOs or politicians. *(see Obvious, a firm grasp of the)*

Event: 1. A thing happening. 2. Word usually surrounded by dramatic (and usually untrue) hyperbole, such as launch, one-off, or once-in-a-lifetime; nothing much happening at all; trumped-up non-event hyped to within an inch of its life by overexcited public relations agency; pure fabrication, as in most news stories; almost the entire editorial 'content' of most news programmes. *(see Black swan)*

Evidence-based policy: 1. Policy based on evidence. 2. Deeply suspicious qualifier immediately suggesting that the proposal may actually be based on no evidence at all; instant alarm bell hinting at no basis whatsoever; evidence-free; without any justification; baseless; poorly informed; plain wrong; trumped-up; done on the fly; on a whim; in all probability, total bollocks.

Evolving to meet customer demand: 1. Changing, based on what customers have requested. 2. Radically departing from original intentions; overhauling; changing completely; ignoring customers and doing what we want to do, because the chief executive says so. *(see Coming or going,* *he doesn't know if he's; Drawing board, back to the; Pivot; Reverse gear; Tweak; U-turn)*

Exceptional: 1. Not ordinary; the exception. 2. Not extraordinary at all; total crap; euphemism for totally unexpected, as in: *"I was gobsmacked by Dave's exceptional performance."*

Executive: 1. Person or group responsible for the administration of a project. 2. Overpaid boss; underpaid underling; catch-all word for anyone unfortunate enough to work in an office; in its collective form, a toothless committee of time wasters intent on doing sod all other than eating biscuits on company time.

Executive retreat: 1. Time out of the office for management to contemplate long-term strategy. 2. Costly excuse to play golf, visit a posh hotel and demonstrate appalling taste in casual clothing; ill-advised chino and polo shirt wearing 'opportunity'; astonishingly high consumption of complimentary mints, chocolate rolls, and evil-looking lime cordial. *(see Away-day; Brainstorm; Off-site; Workshop)*

Exit interview: 1. Chat when leaving a company. 2. Pathetically earnest set of questions levelled at someone who has just been made redundant for no particular reason; annoying and pointless gathering of opinion to which no one will play a blind bit of notice; complete waste of time for all concerned; charade. *(see CSR)*

Exit strategy: 1. Plan to get out. 2. Plan to get out very fast indeed; rapid extrication from tricky situation; absolute removal from market when it becomes apparent your product or service has been found sadly wanting; scheme to leave building, painfully or otherwise. *(see Defenestrate, defenestration)*

Expect more: 1. Exhortation or statement based on level of expectation. 2. Odd incitement from company to prospective customer suggesting that they 'expect more', as though they expected anything in the first place; disappointment-tinged phrase familiar to anyone who has experienced an unsatisfactory appraisal, as in: *"I'm afraid to say, Anna, we expected more from you." (see Expectations, exceeding, failing to achieve, living up to, managing, meeting)*

Expectations, exceeding, failing to achieve, living up to, managing, meeting: 1. Doing more, less, or about as much as necessary for someone to think you are doing okay. 2. Debatable notion that customers give a shit about what a company does; diffuse set of things that consumers apparently 'expect' from a company; notional 'benchmark' much loved of

HR, as in: *"I'm afraid to say, Nigel, you failed to live up to expectations,"* when none have ever truly been articulated; thoroughly biased basket of attributes made up by your boss when he wants to fire you; even more biased set of attributes conjured up by sales director who wants to give a bonus to his favourite protégé for 'exceeding expectations'. *(see Always on; Constantly striving; Customer journey; Expect more; Go off half cock; Sun, the ___ never sets at; 24/7/365; Valued customer; Work-life balance)*

Experiential curve: 1. Learning through experience, intended to be on a metaphorical rising curve. 2. Regular repetition of exactly the same mistake, again and again, by a company or individual incapable of learning anything at all; harsh lesson; kick in the slats one may or may not forget, depending on brain power. *(see Learnings; Learning curve, steep, vertical)*

Experiential marketing: 1. Branch of marketing that gives potential customers a chance to experience the product for free in the hope that they become true customers. 2. Frantic mass giveaway of product in desperate hope that some interest is generated; brutal and random assault of unsuspecting commuters at busy railway termini offering them free yoghurt, toothpaste, or pile ointment when on the way to work; marauding gangs of scantily-clad, stick-thin blondes called Stacey let loose in shopping centres wearing promotional t-shirts. *(see Chuggers)*

Eyes and ears: 1. Visual and aural body parts. 2. Crucial components in the arsenal of industrial espionage; phrase much loved by secretive executives, as in: *"I want you to be my eyes and ears on this one, Brian.";* unnecessarily clandestine phraseology usually deployed by member of a researc and development team who mistakenly believes (a) that they are living in a Robert Ludlum novel, or (b) that anyone gives a shit about their new product.

Face the music: 1. Take the consequences. 2. Hope to get away with something dreadful but fail utterly. *(see Can, carry the; Team, take one for the)*

Face time: 1. Speak to someone in person. 2. Try to work out the time by staring at someone; use conventional time-honoured communication technique when all crap modern alternatives have failed completely. *(see Face-to-face; Heads up; Interface; One-to-one)*

Face-to-face: 1. Two people facing each other, possibly speaking, possibly not. 2. Nauseating phrase depicting two people meeting, and emphasizing, possibly inaccurately, that they are facing each other; failure to acknowledge that many people do not face each other when meeting, and sometimes deliberately so, as in embarrassing meetings. *(see B2B; Face time; Heads up; Interface; One-to-one)*

Facilitate, facilitation: 1. Make easier, assist the progress of. 2. Dominate proceedings in an all-day workshop, refuse to let anyone else speak their mind, and steamroller your view through regardless.

Facts, cold hard: 1. The untainted truth. 2. What's left after all the bullshit has been stripped away, most commonly exposed as nothing of substance at all.

Fag packet, back of a: 1. A quick summary or overview. 2. A hopelessly inadequate case – badly thought through, or not thought through at all.

Failure is not an option: 1. We must win at all costs. 2. If we lose I'll get fired, so I'm using a macho metaphor to put the pressure on everyone else. *(see Can do attitude; Face the music; Go the extra mile; Land, we need to ___this one; Unfair advantage; Unthinkable, think the)*

Fall on your sword: 1. Take the blame. 2. Take the blame for everyone else's incompetence. *(see Spear, fall on one's; Team, take one for the)*

Fallen over: 1. Finished; collapsed. 2. Slightly patronizing and glib phrase much loved by dealmakers in the City, as in: *"Okay Seb, so the deal has fallen over, but you need to get back into the ring and keep fighting,"* or some such rubbish.

Falling off a log: 1. Really simple. 2. Apparently easy, but probably horribly booby-trapped. *(see ABC, easy as; Art form, got it down to an; Cooking on gas; Halcyon days)*

Fallout, coping with the: 1. Handling the consequences (of something bad, such as a nuclear explosion). 2. Sweeping up the chaos after something has gone spectacularly wrong. *(see Team, take one for the)*

Fall short: 1. Fail completely. 2. Fail, but re-express the abject failure in relation to some spurious or non-existent target that everybody has long since forgotten. *(see Achieve learning outcomes)*

FAQs: 1. Frequently asked questions. 2. Fatuous checklist of trivia thinly disguised as patronizing advice for customers; kindergarten series of basic common sense. *(see Advisorial; Behavioural economics; Hints and tips; Practical advice)*

Fast track: 1. Vector of travel that gets you there quicker than another comparable one. 2. Claimed shortcut to promotion, pay rise and fame that has a strange habit of never arriving; *El Dorado, Shangri-La* or promised land. *(see CPD)*

Fat lady, it's not over until the ___ sings: 1. It's not necessarily a failure until we reach the very end. 2. It's a total failure – we just haven't got the humility to admit it even though we are now flogging a dead horse *(see All over bar the shouting; Horse, flogging a dead; Setback; Win or lose, we're in with a chance)*

Fat man in the canoe: 1. Obvious and out of place element. 2. Palpably inappropriate for the circumstances; ill-equipped; not remotely in control of one's situation or equipment. *(see Elephant in the room; Push the boat out; Rock the boat, don't; Rowing in the same boat, direction)*

F-Bomb, drop an: 1. To use the word f**k in a business meeting or encounter. 2. Profane outbursts spanning the two extremes of (a) persistent swearing as the norm, as in: *"This f**king product will never see the f**king* *light of day in a million f**king years"*, or (b) a totally unexpected ejaculation from someone who is normally polite, as in a one-hour presentation extolling the virtues of a premium brand followed by: *"Oh for f**k's sake Brian, that'll never bloody work, you f**king idiot!"*; both approaches usually result in a failure to secure the business, or disciplinary action for the perpetrator.

Fear: 1. Feeling of distress or apprehension. 2. Permanent state of affairs at work; horrible feeling that something, somewhere is going horribly wrong. *(see Blame culture; SNAFU)*

Feature creep: 1. Steady increase in the number of features on a product. 2. Steady increase in the number of features on a product, with no discernible benefit to the customer; excuse for product designers to show off what they can do, regardless of value.

Feedback: 1. Amplifier distortion much loved by Jimi Hendrix; comment from boss or customer. 2. Unwanted comment; litany of complaint; long list of moans and misgivings; chapter and verse on your personal deficiencies providing the company with every possible reason not to give you a pay rise; debrief from boss after a disastrous client meeting; ominous preface to a conversation you know you don't want to have, as in: *"May I give you some feedback, Kevin?" (see Bombs, box of; Pushback: Quality feedback)*

Feet, to dive in with both: 1. Rush into a situation rashly and clumsily; illegal football challenge liable to break an opponent's leg. 2. Thunder into a meeting without any prior briefing; accuse boss of malfeasance, having no evidence to prove it at all; blame colleague for an outcome before said outcome is even known; fly off the handle for no apparent reason; hurl punch at office party after one cocktail too many; hammer fist on meeting room table to emphasise a point, as in: *"Over my dead body will we have moist toilet paper in the gents!" (see Bazooka after a fly, we're not going to send a; Bull in a china shop; Nut, sledgehammer to crack a; Platform, eat one's own)*

Feet to the fire: 1. Pedal limb in flames. 2. Somewhat macabre form of staff torture loosely presented as an incentive, as in: *"I want to keep Nigel's feet to the fire on this one."* – as though he is likely to respond positively. *(see Failure is not an option)*

Fence mending: 1. Fixing a divider between two pieces of land. 2. Eating significant quantities of humble pie; apologizing profusely after jumping to conclusions and getting it all wrong; buy flowers for receptionist after inappropriate fumble in the lift. *(see Feet, to dive in with both)*

Ferret on amphetamines: 1. Feisty mammal made even feistier by stimulant drugs. 2. Irritating, over-zealous colleague; relentlessly enthusiastic member of staff whose energy levels expose the feckless nature of the rest of the workforce; goody-two-shoes universally loathed by all but slave-driving boss; Rottweiler puppy. *(see Rottweiler)*

Fertilize: 1. To provide sperm or pollen; to add nutrients to soil or water to aid growth. 2. Perfectly decent verb, often hijacked to suggest nurture or growth of an abstract construct, such as: *"We're just starting with a small seed, guys, so we really need to fertilize this idea!"* – a plaintive cry frequently heard in brainstorms when the facilitator is desperately trying to suggest that a crap idea has some potential. *(see Brainstorm; Putting lipstick on a pig; Turd, polishing a)*

FFS: 1. For f**k's sake. 2. Exasperated cry of any executive right in the thick of it, as in: *"FFS Brian, why can't we just get on with it??"*

FIFO (1): 1. First in first out, usually with reference to material in an in-tray or email inbox. 2. Ignored; left unattended; long forgotten; deleted; archived; passed over; junked; binned; trashed; delegated; filed. *(see Circular file; FIFO (2); LIFO)*

FIFO (2): 1. Fit in or fuck off. 2. Frank observation about one's current status by new boss; no-holds-barred assessment of immediate employment prospects, not necessarily to one's advantage; not to be confused with FIFO's alternative meaning, although if you are the first into the boss's office, you may well be the first out – of the company. *(see Align, aligned; Defenestrate, defenestration; FIFO (1); Hymn sheet, singing from the same; Realignment)*

FIMO: 1. Fuck it move on. 2. There's nothing to retrieve here; ditch it and get on with something else. *(see Park it; SUMO; STFU)*

Find your fabulous: 1. Work out what makes you appealing. 2. Nasty trend for the conversion of adjectives into nouns to suggest some sort of joyous development of personal awareness. *(see Find your happy)*

Find your happy: 1. Work out what you like. 2. More bad grammar with a utopian twist. *(see Find your fabulous)*

Fire hydrant, trying to drink from a: 1. Attempting to imbibe from a highly forceful source. 2. Attempting a genuinely impossible task; unable to cope; drowning; failing spectacularly; going down in flames, in full view of all colleagues. *(see Breathes through his arse; Human wind tunnel)*

Firing on all six, on all cylinders: 1. Fully operational; running smoothly; optimum performance. 2. Feeling rather self-satisfied after a supposedly 'stellar' performance in an important meeting; smug; pride before a fall, as in: *"We were awesome guys!"* – only to find the day after that you did not win the contract. *(see Great guns, going; Rubber hits the road, when the)*

First mover advantage: 1. Gains arising from being first in a market. 2. Management consultant's wank phrase asserting a colossal collapse in logic – that being first is always an advantage; subsequently discredited by hundreds of shrewder companies who have deliberately allowed rasher competitors to thunder into a market, make a stack of mistakes, and thus unwittingly equip all other entrants with the wherewithal to do better; macho concept based entirely on the obsession of business with speed. *(see First past the post; Pacesetter; Pre-emptive strike; Retaliation, get your ___ in first)*

First past the post: 1. Winner, originally in horse racing. 2. Whoever got there first, regardless of merit; first person in the meeting room gets all the biscuits; first one into the office gets to impress the boss. *(see Brown-nosing; First mover advantage; Pre-emptive strike; Retaliation, get your ___ in first)*

Fiscal juggling: 1. Moving money from one part of the financial year to another. 2. Incessant gerrymandering of spreadsheets to confuse anyone and everyone; legerdemain, literally lightness of hand; adding costs to reduce profit; removing costs to increase profit; changing financial years; shifting from quarters to tertials or vice versa; deliberately generating multi-sheet spreadsheets with hidden layers in order to obfuscate; pursuing opacity at all costs; using arcane financial language to disguise the working reality; all in all, a huge battery of techniques to prevent anyone understanding the monetary truth. *(see Above board; Aims; Balloon has gone up, the; Baseline; BHAG; Black arts; Bottom line; Calibrate; Cook the books; Crunch the numbers; Markers, put some ___ down; Massage the numbers; Numbers, the; Obfuscate; Quantitative easing; Quarter; Re-baselining; Tertial)*

Fish up a tree, he looks like a: 1. Not comfortable; out of context. 2. Horribly exposed; hugely miscast; patently in the wrong job; out on a limb; in for a fall, probably today; drowning, or possibly asphyxiating. *(see Casting)*

Fish where the ducks are: 1. Suggestion that the chances of catching a fish may be increased by the proximity of ducks. 2. Errant nonsense that fails to rumble that ducks are vegetarian and have no bearing on the presence of fish; car crash metaphor grabbed from the natural world at short notice; floundering grab for even the most crass analogy to add colour to a drab objective.

Flag up: 1. Mention; point out. 2. Alert; draw frantic attention to; state quite clearly that there will be shocking consequences of this decision; protest; object in the strongest possible terms; state one's case firmly but be overruled by boss who doesn't give a damn; fail to prevail with view; be blamed subsequently for not mentioning there was a problem. *(see Team, take one for the)*

Flagpole, run it up the ___ and see who salutes: 1. Raise a flag and establish whether anyone nearby is in the military, or is behaving as though they are; try something out and see if anyone reacts. 2. Another in a long line of military metaphors subverted for the cause of business; somewhat quaint suggestion that companies are akin to armies; vainglorious belief by chief executive that he is somehow a field general of some kind; miniburst of pomp and circumstance, likening the launch of a new flavour of crisps to a new government policy. *(see Battleground; Launch; Watch the boards light up)*

Flagship: 1. Ship flying a flag; most important item. 2. Best example of product or store as it really should be, when in fact all the others are crap or not up to scratch; isolated case; only asset that has received any support or investment for years; exception to the rule; worryingly exposed element carrying the full weight of the business on its shoulders, as in: *"OMG guys, our flagship store is flagging!"*

Flak, take the, dish out the: 1. Give out or take anti-aircraft fire, from the German acronym *Fl(ieger)a(bwehr)k(anone)*, literally: aircraft defence gun. 2. Hurl abuse or receive it; unseemly office ruck; corridor disagreement that can be heard at the other end of the department; final snapping of uneasy *entente* (not so) *cordiale*; blazing row with no holds barred; fist fight; bitchslapfest in the reception café, inappropriately occurring in front of visiting clients. *(see Soft area)*

Flatline: 1. To die or be so near death that vital sign monitoring equipment registers nothing. 2. Lifeless; beyond hope; bereft of any vitality; dead in the water; truly not happening, despite being on the status report for months. *(see Dead cat bounce; Entering a new plateau; Negative growth, profit; WIP)*

Flexible, flexibility: 1. Malleable, accommodating. 2. Prepared to do anything to win the business; having no principles or ethics at all; of any target, double what you can realistically achieve with current resources or time; inflexible; a direct order that cannot be challenged, as in: *"I need you to be flexible on this one, Tony."* (see BOHICA; Drop our trousers; Elasticity; Stretch target)

Flip chart: 1. Large sheet of paper on a stand for taking notes at meeting. 2. Seemingly inoffensive and inanimate object that can cause utter havoc for years to come; receptacle of some of the worst ideas in business history, ever; childish doodle pad allowing Barry from production to show everyone that he can draw; cartoonist's paradise; home to semi-offensive caricature of bald and chubby chief executive hidden on chart three, only revealed when Barry's group make their presentation. *(see Awayday; Bad idea, there's no such thing as a; Brainstorming; Off-site)*

Flight path: 1. Direction or vector taken by aircraft. 2. Unshakable course determined by over-zealous managing director on a mission; line of travel best avoided unless imminent trampling underfoot is the desired endgame; beeline taken by Marjorie from the legal department upon discovering a deal has been signed without her presence; resulting contrail leaving singed carpet and hingeless doors in its wake. *(see Bull in a china shop; Hell in a handcart, we're all going to)*

Flip side: 1. Another aspect of a person or thing. 2. Shocking, two-faced quality; total opposite of normal character; Jekyll to a person's Hyde; werewolf-like ability to transform in seconds from a perfectly nice colleague into a many-headed monster; Medusa in disguise; schizoid quality only revealed when under extreme pressure or sleep deprived from social overshooting. *(see Office party)*

Flounder: 1. European flatfish; to struggle. 2. Panic; flap; lose one's marbles; sweat profusely; do a runner; hide in the stationery cupboard until it's all over; throw a sickie; flee; jump; 'nip to the toilet' and never return, having legged it through the window; not cope.

Flush out: 1. To rouse wild game; expose. 2. Reveal the unpalatable truth; uncover shocking evidence of malpractice; root out someone to blame for unholy mess on your watch; find scapegoat; take evidence to chief executive, only to find that she authorized it. *(see Drains up, have the; Lift up a rock; No stone unturned; Witch-hunt)*

Fly by the seat of one's pants: 1. Operate an aircraft by instinct rather than knowledge or experience, presumably sitting down. 2. Make it up as one goes along; bluff; bluster; busk it; improvise; careen into a meeting breathless, clutching a set of charts you have never even looked at; take briefing in cab on way to pitch; have no proper grasp of the issues but start talking regardless; standard operating procedure in advertising and public relations. *(see Building the plane as we fly it; SOP; SNAFU; Woods, not out of the ___ yet)*

Fly in the face of: 1. To act in defiance of. 2. Ignore entirely; fly solo; go out on a limb despite all best advice from wiser colleagues; embark on glory trip; fly blind; gamble dangerously; disregard warning signs; crash and burn due to crass ignorance. *(see Come a cropper; Flying unstable)*

Flying unstable: 1. Pushing aeronautical tolerances to the limit in order to break speed records. 2. Reckless behaviour by any normal standards; lethal; hazardous to colleagues; stressed, prone to inappropriate decisions and actions; on the edge; about to blow; likely to crash at any moment; disconcertingly unreliable; utterly unpredictable; teetering crazily on the brink. *(see Building the plane as we fly it; Come a cropper; Fly by the seat of one's pants; Fly in the face of; Pushing the envelope; Wind, sailing close to the)*

FMF: 1. F**k me factor. 2. Supposed magic ingredient that impresses someone so much they shout *"f**k me!"* out loud; debatable idea that being shafted is somehow a good thing; unrealistic expectation that anything business related could invoke so much joy. *(see Aha moment; Wow factor)*

FNG: 1. F**king new guy. 2. New person who knows nothing because they haven't been briefed or trained properly; new person who can't do the job because they lied on their CV. *(see CV)*

Focus group: 1. Group of people, usually around eight of them, gathered to chat about a product or service in the name of market research. 2. Eclectic mix of individuals who may or may not have any interest in the subject matter; random selection of misfits picked up in the Arndale centre; people with nothing to do, enticed by the promise of free wine and crisps; unreliable collection of charlatans who have no intention of buying the product ever, despite claims to the contrary; friends and family of the recruiter using pseudonyms to make up the numbers; euphemism for one of the most unreliable research techniques ever invented. *(see Clapham omnibus, man on the; Consumer focused; Rebrand)*

Focus: 1. To see more clearly. 2. Comprehensively overused and abused word that used to be the sole preserve of opticians; effort to concentrate, a facet seemingly beyond many employees; opinion; point of view; also used as verb to exhort colleagues to wake up and pay attention; main staple of idiotic big picture/small picture discussions, as in: *"There's a focus here we can see beyond, Steven,"* and, *"we need to stand back and take a closer look."* *(see Clarity; Closer look, stand back and take a)*

-focused, people-, goal-: 1. Concerned with people, goals, etc. 2. Hideous, mutated suffix universally applied to any word that comes to mind, as in people/goal/target/market/consumer; pointless modifier that hints at comprehensive lack of focus in the normal course of events, or at least prior to 'focus' being mentioned; as redundant as 'going forward'; worst of all, frequently misspelled as focussed. *(See –centred, -centric; –driven; Going forward; Grounded; -oriented)*

FOFO: 1. F**k off and find out. 2. Stop asking stupid questions; exasperated cry of frustrated boss when faced with gormless subordinate; don't ask me; use your initiative for once; show some gumption. *(see DILLIGAF; RTFM)*

Fog, grasping at: 1. Trying to understand something that defies understanding. 2. Desperately floundering around in a futile attempt to rescue a lost cause, or comprehend a concept that exceeds one's brain capacity. *(see Jelly, nailing a ___ to the wall)*

Follow, do you: 1. Do you understand what I am saying? 2. Do you get it, you f**king idiot?; if you were any less intelligent I would have to water you; is this simple enough for you?; patronizing question to assert intellectual authority, especially when uncertain of subject matter. *(see Am I right or am I right?; DILLIGAF; Enlighten me; Intelligent, if you were any less ___, I'd have to water you; Lips, read my; Respect, with; Teach your grandmother to suck eggs, don't, would never, would you)*

FOMO: 1. Fear of missing out. 2. Inability to function without checking social media every minute or so; misguided belief that you are the epicentre of all that happens in the world. *(see Always on)*

Food chain, a long way down the, higher up the: 1. Hierarchy of which species eats, or is eaten by, another. 2. Unfortunate power pyramid topped by an apex predator, usually a chisel-jawed American called Doug or Todd; bad brief for the minnows at the bottom, liable to be corralled into a bait ball and swallowed whole for breakfast; failure to meet with appropriately senior level person in client company. *(see Apex predator; Casting)*

Foot, shoot oneself in the: 1. Inflict damage on oneself. 2. Score spectacular own goal; problem entirely of one's own making; personally generated cockup; no one else to blame but oneself; self-immolation; hoisted by own petard; chewing your own ear off. *(see Burning platform; Hoist with one's own petard; Kamikaze; Mountain to climb; Object, defeating the; Own goal, spectacular; Platform, eat one's own; Shafted down the river, yourself)*

Forces of darkness, deploy the: 1. Use every trick in the book to achieve your goal. 2. Enlist everybody and everything to win; rope in chief executive to ram the point home; sign up celebrity to endorse dubious brand or product; use dark arts and subterfuge, espionage and general skullduggery; cheat. *(see Air cover; Unfair advantage; Voodoo, corporate)*

Forensic, send it down to the boys in: 1. Have something properly analyzed in minute detail. 2. Crawl all over; send in the pathologists; scrutinize painfully; look for a scapegoat; find hidden reasons where none may exist; have the floorboards up; search high and low for a culprit; conduct post-mortem on failed pitch and conclude you 'came a close second'; discover sod all after a huge amount of wasted time and energy. *(see Drains up, have the; Drill down; Flush out; Lift up a rock; No stone unturned; Pathologist's interest; Pulse, check the, finger on the)*

Forward-looking: 1. Looking forward. 2. Paying attention, no more, no less; futile adjective stressing some sort of forward orientation, as though backward-looking is a serious alternative; often backward-looking, particularly in relation to competitive reviews and tedious historical data; not looking at anything at all, just staring blankly into space or out of the window; daydreaming; navel gazing. *(see Going forward; Moving forward; Navel gazing)*

Forth Road Bridge, like painting the: 1. Never-ending process or project. 2. Outdated analogy based on the old adage that by the time the painters of the famous bridge finish the job it needs doing again – longer-lasting paint has since been invented; dreary default phrase for anything taking a long time, usually uttered by the person doing the least work; world-weary bleating of middle manager in boozer while drinking half a pint of real ale, as in: *"Cor, dear me, it's typical isn't it, Project Hatstand has turned out to be like painting the Forth Road Bridge!"* *(see Jobsworth)*

Foundations, lay the, firm, shaky: 1. Structural underpinnings, solid or not. 2. Another piece of blether half-borrowed from the construction industry in a vain attempt to imply structure and solidity where there almost certainly is none; part of a suite of materials including concrete, bricks and mortar that lend spurious reassurance to otherwise completely nebulous concepts; suggestion of architectural rigour; likening of diffuse brand-related nonsense to physical structures such as pyramids; close ally of 'overarching'. *(see Architecture, brand ___, business___; Clicks and mortar; Concretize; Overarching; Penthouse, furnishing the)*

Framework, operating, overarching: 1. Parameters within which work is conducted. 2. Annoying chart with arbitrary boxes and clusters of words dumped inside them; incomprehensible flow diagram signifying nothing; semblance of system that fools client into believing there is a sequence to things; spider diagram where everything is inextricably linked to every-thing else; vacuous word much-loved of pedestrian politicians, as in: *"This is the overarching operating framework we will be concretizing going for-ward."* *(see Foundations, lay the; Snake's honeymoon)*

Frankenbrand: 1. A brand that has gone too far, frankly. 2. Hideous mutation of once perfectly normal product, now twisted beyond its original remit.

Frankly: 1. In all candour. 2. Not frank at all; I'm lying to you. *(see Absolutely, At the end of the day; Basically; Literally)*

Free lunch: 1. Midday meal, gratis. 2. Bonus with no strings attached; pleasant break from work; congratulatory repast; blowout gourmet inter-lude; phenomenal piss-up, with a tiny finger buffet; liquid lunch; sprint to the boozer at lunchtime with no prospect of ever returning to the office; evil-looking cling-filmed sandwiches, with side tray of nuts, olives and twiglets, sitting on plastic trays in a meeting room. *(see Free ride, there's no such thing as a)*

Free ride, there's no such thing as a: 1. Everything has a price. 2. Tedious platitude often trotted out by world-weary travelling sales managers; cynical world view spouted by hangdog bar stool preachers who have made little progress in life; resentful side swipe at anyone who has indeed experienced a free ride, thus disproving the statement altogether. *(see Free lunch)*

Free-riff idea ramp: 1. Launchpad for new thoughts. 2. Ludicrous example of Americans getting a little over-excited about generating what are most likely some perfectly ordinary ideas, as in: *"Our goal is to really blow it out on the free-riff idea ramp!"* Utter twaddle.

Free-roaming experience: 1. One where the user decides where to go next; something that happens when wandering about untethered. 2. Gibberish jargon from the world of so-called digital devices, where everything is 'experiential' or linked to the 'user experience'; shades of organic claim, as in 'free range eggs'; visions of feral gangs of digital natives roaming the country 'having an experience', possibly induced by mind-bending drugs. *(see Digital native; On-rails experience; User experience)*

Frictionless: 1. Without friction; moving smoothly. 2. Annoying modern adjective denoting two possibilities – proceeding without incident, or joining together without hiccups. *(see Seamless)*

Fromage, grand: 1. Big cheese (French version); very senior person. 2. Heavy-weight visiting dignitary; chairperson; client with ability to hire and fire; pompous and overweight man in pinstripe suit; windbag; perennial bore. *(see Big cheese; Head honcho; Heavy hitter; Human wind tunnel; Player, big)*

Front burner, let's bring that onto the: 1. Make this a priority now. 2. We've flagrantly ignored this for far too long and now it's even worse, so reme-dial action is required immediately. *(see Back burner, we'll have to put that on the)*

Front end: 1. The bit at the beginning of a project. 2. The start of the proj-ect where no one gives a toss because the deadline is so far away. *(See Back end architecture)*

Frontline: 1. First line of attack, or defence; line of military or sporting deployment. 2. Coalface; sharp end; metaphorical place where hapless executives do the work and take all the pressure; woefully under-re-sourced 'thin blue line'; first port of call for customer complaints and, in many cases, downright abuse. *(see Backroom; Coalface; Ground, on the)*

Front of mind: 1. Being thought about right now. 2. Irritating advertising and media phrase to suggest a consumer is thinking about your product every second of the day; curious division of the brain into front and back; inference that back of mind is somehow undesirable; blind faith that front of mind is the best place to be, when any presence of mind would be a start. *(See Frontofmindness)*

Frontofmindness: 1. State of being 'front of mind'. 2. Hideously mutated noun-cum-adjective suggesting a state of actively thinking about some-thing; four syllable car crash much loved by designers and self-styled 'brand strategists'. *(see Brand strategist; Front of mind; Here-and-now-ness; Worklessness)*

Front stabbing: 1. Blaming someone to their face. 2. Deliberately blam-ing someone in front of the boss to avoid personal criticism, regardless of the truth of the matter. *(see Back stabbing; Blitz; Rowing in the same boat, direction)*

FUBAR: 1. F**ked up beyond all recognition. 2. Truly unrecognizable from the original; utterly destroyed; annihilated; blown to smithereens. *(see FUBB; SNAFU)*

FUBB: 1. F**ked up beyond belief. 2. Horrible mutated version; concep-tually ruined; twisted poor relation of what was intended; massive own goal; spectacular cockup when doing it well would have been easier. *(see FUBAR; SNAFU)*

FUCT: 1. Failed under continuous testing. 2. Not up to it; deficient; kaput; below standard; same meaning if the T is replaced by KED. *(see FUBAR; FUBB)*

FUF: 1. F**k up factor. 2. Likelihood of going spectacularly wrong, always high.

Full Monty, the: 1. Everything; the lot; the whole shooting match. 2. Make it look as if we've covered everything by putting on a great show. *(see A-Z, Chapter and verse; Death by PowerPoint; Jazz hands; Kitchen sink)*

Full-on: 1. Busy; on all the time. 2. Stacked; swamped; overloaded; not coping; overworked; doing the work of three people. *(see Arse in alligators, up to my; Stacked, completely)*

Full-tilt boogie: 1. All out; 100%; full-throttle, possibly of dancing to heavy rock music. 2. Ill-advised diving in with both feet; little or no preparation, followed by a no-holds-barred assault; thundering into a meeting blind, firing off a range of deeply-held prejudices, only to discover that you are woefully under-briefed. *(see Bull in a china shop; Come a cropper)*

FYI: 1. For your information. 2. Just so you know; to remind you I'm doing this, not you; to prove I've done this, so you can't point the finger later; to cover my arse. *(see Arse covering; BCC; CC)*

FULLAB: 1. Fat, ugly, looks like a boy. 2. Appalling, sexist, chauvinistic, non-politically correct acronym to describe woman not blessed in the looks department; last bastion of sweaty fat salesmen in Beckenham who desperately want sex but can't get any; after work pub 'badinage' run amok after two small Martinis. *(see Collars and cuffs, I bet the ___ don't match; Kimono, open the; Matching luggage)*

Future-facing: 1. In the future; from now on. 2. Abstract concept strangely pointing to a time yet to come, as though past-facing is helpful to anyone other than a historian. *(see Futureproof; Going forward)*

Futureproof: 1. Protecting against future developments. 2. Self-deluding notion that forthcoming events can be predicted accurately; soothsaying; crystal ball gazing; navel gazing; pure guesswork; placing finger in the air and whistling Dixie. *(see Black swan; Crystal ball; Navel gazing)*

Game-changing: 1. New, revolutionary. 2. Extraordinarily perverse piece of logic that suggests that if you can't win the game you are playing, you should move on to another game entirely; quite how this helps anyone in business is a total mystery. *(see Break the mould; Groundbreaking)*

Game plan: 1. What you have decided to do. 2. Rambling document full of half-truths and guesses; so-called 'five-year plan' that flies in the face of all modern business development such as pace of technological advance and a series of worldwide financial crashes; supreme work of fiction whose contents never come to pass. *(see Black swan; Strategy)*

Game is up, the: 1. We've been rumbled. 2. And we've been fired. *(see Black hole, disappeared into a; Blood bath, on the walls)*

Gangbusters, it's going: 1. Things are going very well. 2. We're all on a caffeine-fuelled rollercoaster that we can't get off, usually headed by a narcissistic chief executive desperate for a knighthood. *(see Mega; Meta; Monster, it's a; Net net)*

Gap analysis: 1. Identifying where the gaps are, usually in a market. 2. Desperately flailing around with a flipchart and an overly simplistic diagram trying to convince all present that you've spotted something that no one else has; last refuge of crap facilitators the world over.

GEIGE: 1. Good enough is good enough. 2. A version of corporate beige, where okay will do; little attempt at excellence; relentlessly average. *(see Best is the enemy of better; Great, good is the enemy of)*

Gene pool, swimming in the shallow end of the: 1. Not intelligent. 2. Wry notion that the gene pool is akin to a real life swimming pool, with a shallow and deep end. *(see Box of frogs, mad as a; Bundle, one stick short of a; Mid-life crisis; Picnic, one sandwich short of a; Postal, go)*

Geography, geographies: 1. The study of the natural features of the earth. 2. Any region in which Americans do business and attempt world domination, as in: *"As you know, Todd, we operate in a number of geographies"*; pointless plural of the word geography. *(see Energies)*

Get ink: 1. Persuade a journalist to write something (preferably favourable) about your product or service. 2. Get a hack so paralytic that they write a good review, or slip them cash to achieve the same end.

Get into bed with: 1. Sleep together, often sexually. 2. Embark on a sleazy and incestuous business relationship for mutual benefit or status. *(see Collars and cuffs, I bet the ___ don't match; Enemy, sleeping with the; Kimono, open the; Matching luggage, Scratch my back and I'll scratch yours; Playtex strategy)*

GIGO: 1. Garbage in garbage out. 2. If the original data are rubbish, then any subsequent conclusion drawn from analyzing them will be too; much loved of computer programmers, often heard exclaiming mournfully: *"This is GIGO – all we're doing here is polishing a turd!"* *(see Putting lipstick on a pig; RIRO; SISO; Turd, polishing a)*

Glass ceiling: 1. State of affairs in which progress or promotion appears to be possible but restrictions or discrimination create a barrier that prevents it; silicon based roofing material, not always advisable. 2. Abhorrent two-faced working reality in many companies that pretend to promote the cause of women, ethnic groups and non-graduates while in truth making it very difficult for them to get anywhere; colonial era status quo perpetuated by flabby, white men wearing club ties and ill-fitting blazers.

Global, globalization, globally: 1. All over the world. 2. Croydon borders; a bit further than most hard-pressed executives have been: somewhere really scary where the food is different and they talk funny. *(see Sun, the ____ never sets at)*

Glocal: 1. Attempting to reflect worldly and local characteristics at the same time. 2. Wince-inducing elision of 'global' and 'local'; abject failure to comprehend that world domination is a rather different thing than a homespun approach; classic desire to have cake and eat it; impossible brief, as in 'target teenagers but don't alienate pensioners'; consummate twaddle.

Aa
Bb
Cc
Dd
Ee
Ff
Gg
Hh
Ii
Jj
Kk
Ll
Mm
Nn
Oo
Pp
Qq
Rr
Ss
Tt
Uu
Vv
Ww
Xx
Yy
Zz

Gloss over: 1. Add shiny coat of paint; skim fast to avoid detail. 2. Avoid the point at all costs; circumnavigate; duck; dive; dodge; evade; flim; flam; embark on extended analogy to detract from main theme; have no working knowledge of any main theme; filibuster. *(see Broad brush; Chairman; Keep it dark; Mum, keep; Strategy)*

Goal-oriented, -driven: 1. Someone who concentrates on, or is motivated by, what they are trying to achieve. 2. Self-evident piece of nonsense that adds nothing to a person's understanding of the job in hand, ever; close contender for the worst piece of business bullshit ever, coming a close second to 'Going forward'; complete waste of a rainforest every time it is written down; energy sapping and depressing when spoken; absolute drivel. *(see Action; Aims; –driven; Going forward; Objectives; -oriented)*

Goal posts, move the: 1. Move football target to a different place. 2. Change objective entirely; ask for one thing then expect another; fail to brief accurately; have no idea what is wanted in the first place; mislead; dupe. *(see Wild-goose chase)*

Gobbledegook: 1. Pretentious or unintelligible jargon, such as used by officials; bullshit. 2. Nonsense; piffle; static; hot air; tripe; codswallop.

Going forward: 1. The opposite of backwards. 2. Truly a king among kings; the undisputed champion of utter bullshit, with the possible exception of 'proactive'; entirely pointless modifier somehow designed to suggest a forward-looking demeanour, when any fool knows that a backward one would be detrimental for everybody, except possibly historians who should indeed adopt a backward-looking approach; selfish waste of time perpetrated by anyone using these two utterly redundant words – those subjected to them could probably increase their life expectancy by removing themselves from the room immediately whenever they are spoken, thus saving years of meeting time. *(see –focused; Forward-looking; Future-facing; Futureproof; Goal-oriented; Here-and-now-ness; Momentum; Moving forward; Proactive)*

Going linear: 1. Moving straight towards something. 2. Sudden realization that all efforts so far have been meandering and directionless.

Golden goose, bite the hand of the, milking the: 1. Take advantage, or ruin, a decent opportunity. 2. Bizarre bestial car crash with extremely confusing anatomical reference points; a goose is made of gold, apparently; it has at least one hand; it has breasts that can be milked; all very confusing.

Golden handcuffs, handshake, hello, goodbye: 1. Money handed over to stay or go. 2. Strange two-faced expression with variations; cash provided to stay at a company (presumably good, but not necessarily if you have sold your soul to Mammon); cash provided to go away (possibly bad if you liked the job, or good if you couldn't stand it); money on arrival (great); money on departure (even better).

Gold-plated: 1. Covered with a layer of gold. 2. Suggestion of quality but without going all the way; a level down from pure gold; runner up; highish quality, but not the very highest; pretty good but not the best. *(see Premium)*

Good to great: 1. Classic management book by Jim Collins in 2001, selling over 1 million copies and adorning the bookshelves of most CEOs. 2. Rallying cry of Terylene-suited sales managers across the country, as in: *"We have to move this from good to great, guys!"*; diffuse and arbitrary reference point for the quality of any project, none of which anybody truly understands. *(see Built to last; Great, good is the enemy of)*

Go off half cock: 1. Embark on a task when not fully prepared. 2. Damp squib; half-baked effort; wet firework; non-dramatic fizzle rather than spectacular launch; crash and burn; suffer significant humiliation in presentation when proposal is found to be seriously wanting; return to office with tail between legs; fall well below expectations. *(see Expectations, exceeding, failing to achieve, living up to, managing, meeting; Launch)*

Goose it up: 1. Liven it up a bit; put finger up someone's bottom. 2. Once again anthropomorphic observations prove irresistible to all and sundry; unusual inference that geese are somehow full of energy and pep.

Go round the houses: 1. Circumnavigate a number of dwellings. 2. Comprehensively fail to take the direct route; faff about unnecessarily; sod around when doing some work would be the easier option; procrastinate; prevaricate; search for, and always find, displacement activity; do absolutely anything other than the task in hand; stare out of the window; daydream; navel gaze; pick fluff from navel. *(see Navel gazing; Research)*

Go the extra mile: 1. Travel one mile further than necessary to reach required destination, presumably overshooting it in the process. 2. Pathetic distance-related *cri de coeur* from management determined to pump one last bit of sweat out of already beleaguered workforce; fantastically eclectic mantra hinting at sport, warfare, marches to conquer the pole etc. in the vain hope of attaching some sort of macho endurance theme to the otherwise workaday nature of business; annoying yet somewhat hilarious 'if you do this you'll be as revered as Captain Scott' implication; comprehensive failure to spot that anyone genuinely going the extra mile will not have arrived at the intended destination, but in fact somewhere entirely different. *(see Failure is not an option; Go the whole hog; Push the boat out)*

Go the whole hog: 1. Meaning obscure; to go all the way, or perhaps eat an entire pig. 2. Do it all, for better or worse, depending on the context; finish the job comprehensively (good); shag Darren from accounts after office party (bad). *(see Go the extra mile; Office party; Pull out all the stops; Push the boat out)*

Granular, let's get: 1. Let's study grains intensely; let's get into detail. 2. Rather vexing idea that looking at sand intently is an interesting thing to do; probably sourced from geology or mining world; yet another attempt by business to appear more credible when dealing with elusive, ethereal or conceptual material. *(see Concretize; Deep dive; Drains up, have the; Drill down; Unbundling)*

Grasp the nettle: 1. Take a firm hold of a plant in the full knowledge that it will sting you; tackle an unpleasant problem. 2. Strangely foolhardy piece of advice; go ahead, hurt yourself; dive right in, regardless of the consequences; self-harm. *(see Kamikaze)*

Grasping at fog: 1. Attempting an impossible task. 2. Brilliant undoable metaphor for grappling with an intangible item. *(see Banana, stabbing a seal with a; Behavioural economics; Nailing a jelly to the wall, trying to)*

Gravitas: 1. Heaviness; weight; import. 2. Nebulous idea that certain people have more weight than others, irrespective of their physical mass; implication that this has some bearing on the outcome of important decisions, as in: *"I think Nigel has the sort of gravitas that we need for this business."*

Great, good is the enemy of: 1. Settling for good may prevent the achievement of greatness. 2. Trite mantra trotted out in all creative industries, with the sole intention of suggesting the highest possible standards, whether they exist or not; platitudinous deflection technique to gain more time when no idea has been generated at all, be it good, great or piss-poor; suggestion of quality through apparent 'company philosophy' where none may exist. *(see Best is the enemy of better; GEIGE; Good to great)*

Great guns, going: 1. Going well. 2. Feeling rather macho; pretending that selling bathroom fittings is akin to being Billy the Kid; gunslinger; packing a punch. *(see Dick-swinging; Firing on all six, on all cylinders)*

Greatest Imaginable Challenge: 1. The most ambitious thing you can do. 2. Testosterone-fuelled ambition finely crafted by chisel-jawed chief executive and self-styled 'brand strategists', hired at great expense; over ambitious target that will never be achieved. *(see BHAG; Dick-swinging; Impossible, nothing is; Unthinkable, think the)*

Green flag, that's a ____ at this stage: 1. Go ahead; originally based on the waving of such a flag at the beginning or resumption of a motor race. 2. Rather annoying use of Grand Prix vocabulary to imbue humdrum business approvals with a touch of Formula One glamour; implication that everything is a fuel-injected race of some kind; as ever, propagated by plump salesmen who spent far too much of their youth playing with toy cars, but not learning how to drive them very well. *(see Green light; Greenlit)*

Green light: 1. Signal to go. 2. Annoyingly flip, semi-automotive, word pairing to indicate approval, as in: *"That's a green light on Project Pilchard, Barry."*; worse, deployment as an active verb, as in: *"I'm prepared to green light Project Centipede now, Monica." (see Buy-in; Greenlit; Issues , I have ___ with that; Problem, I don't have a ___ with that; Redlit; Unhappy, I'm not ___ with)*

Greenlit: 1. Past tense of giving something a green light. 2. Horrible application of past tense of the word 'light' added to a colour to generate a mutant child; further mutation into a verb, as in: *"I've greenlit Project Cummerbund, Steve."*; still disastrous as an adjective, as in: *"This is a greenlit project, as you well know, Richard." (see Buy-in; Greenlit; Issues , I have ___ with that; Problem, I don't have a ___ with that; Redlit; Unhappy, I'm not ___ with)*

Ground, on the: 1. Not in the air, or underground. 2. Doing the work rather than just talking about it; much-loved phrase of those who haven't a clue what is really going on, as in: *"We need to talk to the troops on the ground, Gemma."*; further overuse of the military metaphor. *(see Coalface; Frontline)*

Groundbreaking: 1. Destroying terra firma; genuinely new or pioneering. 2. Macho imagery of rock breaking, chain gangs, construction, pick axe-wielding, drilling and digging to imbue lightweight project with semblance of authority; not remotely heavy duty; flimsy, but with a hard-sounding adjective attached for ballast. *(see Break the mould; Game-changing)*

Grounded, people-, theory-, strategy-: 1. People, theory or strategy at ground level; level-headed; anchored in. 2. People, theory or strategy; meaningless modifier. *(see –focused)*

Grow a pair: 1. Miraculously develop testicles; get a backbone. 2. Applicable to either male or female, toughen up, as in: *"For God's sake Colin, grow a pair." (see Man up)*

Grown-ups: 1. Mature people. 2. Immature people who happen to run the company; anyone paid more than you; anyone credible, unlike most of the hapless jokers at our disposal; court jesters, but in more expensive suits.

Growth accretive: 1. Gradually getting larger. 2. Cumbersome way of suggesting gradual growth, much loved by pompous consultants who only feel happy when things are getting bigger.

Growth hacking: 1. Having a think about how to grow a company or brand. 2. Ridiculously pseudo-hip phrase for doing what any sane businessperson should be doing anyway, i.e. working out how to promote the best interests of their product or service; most likely invented by someone with a beard.

Growth trajectory, personal, explosive: 1. Direction of travel, individual or otherwise. 2. Pseudo-scientific term to suggest physics and quantification of personal or company direction; introduction of some pyrotechnics to imply quantum progress. *(see Launch; Learning curve, steep, vertical)*

Grunt work: 1. The workaday, practical stuff. 2. Activity comprehensively avoided by all board members.

Guardian, brand: 1. Person or company in charge of a brand's direction or reputation. 2. Self-appointed overseer of 'brand health'; prone to outbursts of rules and regulations surrounding brand trivia such as size of logo or minute pantone shade difference; 'brand guru', apparently possessing an alchemist's touch when it comes to simple decisions such as how to phrase a voiceover; author of impenetrable diagrams purporting to explain what the brand stands for. *(see Brand onion, pillars, pyramid, values; Brand strategist; Custodian; Monitoring)*

GUGOI: 1. Get up get over it. 2. Rallying cry for those desperately trying to encourage colleagues to regroup and go again. *(see SUMO)*

Guidelines, brand, corporate: 1. Guidance manual that explains how a brand or corporation should be portrayed. 2. Chapter and verse on every arcane detail that makes the Bible look like a short read; mindless, seemingly infinite portrayals of logos, typefaces, colour swatches, and letterhead examples; tedious examples of 'how we do it round here', as though anyone cares; trite diagrams covering every possible eventuality; gravy train for design agencies and self-appointed 'brand strategists'.

(see Brand onion, pillars, pyramid, values; Brand strategist; Guardian, brand; Tramlines)

Gung ho: 1. Extremely enthusiastic, sometimes to excess; keen to participate in military combat; pidgin English from Mandarin Chinese *Gung* work and *ho* together. 2. Completely over the top; unsubtle; careening into meetings without due care and attention; blunderbuss; liability; liable to cause intense damage to proposals, plans and, on occasion, property. *(see Bath, take a; Bull in a china shop; Catch a cold; Dropping grenades in fish ponds; Pull out all the stops; Ton of bricks, subtle as a)*

Gut feel: 1. Instinct about what to do, not necessarily rational. 2. Whim; madcap notion; unexplainable desire; pure guess; strange belief that decisions should be based on the state of one's intestines; visceral decision. *(Must, this is a; Pants, fly by the seat of our; Pull rank)*

Gynocracy: 1. Company run by, or consisting entirely of, women. 2. Extremely scary place for men; male no-go zone; sorority; sisterhood; lesbian enclave. *(see Ballbreaker; Mediocracy; Nutcracker)*

H2H: 1. Human to human. 2. Truly awful acronym-cum-digital mnemonic used to describe interacting with someone, as though this were somehow unusual or distinctive. *(see B2B, C2C, B2C)*

Halcyon days: 1. Happy and carefree days symbolized by the fabulous winter solstice bird from the Greek myth. 2. Piss-easy phase, probably somewhere in the eighties, when doing business was as easy as making one phone call and then going smartly to the pub. *(see Falling off a log; Marriage made in heaven; Rose-tinted)*

Halo effect: 1. Reflected glory from someone else's efforts. 2. Disastrous feedback loop in which everything gets progressively worse following an ill-advised decision.

Hamster is dead, the wheel is turning but the ___: 1. This burrowing rodent has ceased to be, although its plaything continues to rotate. 2. It may look as though something is happening, but this person or initiative stopped working long ago. *(see Lights are on, but nobody is home; OCD)*

Hand over fist: 1. A hand over a fist (self-evident this, no dictionary required). 2. We are losing money at an alarming rate and can't do a damn thing about it.

Handrails, hold the: 1. Brace yourself – things are about to get rough. 2. Everything's shot to bits as usual and we have no sensible coping strategies; we're understaffed and overstretched due to years of mismanagement and a succession of executives siphoning off funds for their personal benefit. *(see Coals, walk on hot; Ride, bumpy, along for the, roughshod over; Riding the razor blade)*

Hands-off: 1. Happy to delegate and let trusted staff get on with it. 2. Conspicuously absent; utterly disinterested in anything or anybody other than myself; providing no air cover or back-up whatsoever.

Hands-on: 1. Thoroughly involved in every aspect of a project. 2. Anal, obsessive, infuriating micro-manager; permanently convinced that they are the only person on the planet competent enough to do anything; purveyors of the time-honoured phrase 'if you want something done, do it yourself', usually accompanied by a large sigh or raising of the eyebrows to the heavens.

Handbags, dancing around the: 1. Not getting to the point. 2. Consistently dodging the issue to the point of blind ignorance; refusal to accept the facts; flagrant self-denial.

Hard decisions: 1. Decisions. 2. Easy decisions a child could make, made pathetically complex by politics, incompetence and self-aggrandizement.

Hard stop: 1. Coming to a halt. 2. Overly dramatic way of saying that there's a deadline and we really need to stick to it, as in: *"I've got a hard stop on Project Termite on Friday, Brian."*

Hard-wired: 1. Permanently wired into a computer. 2. Preternaturally inclined to do precisely what the boss says, regardless of common sense, personal safety or the more balanced opinion of colleagues. *(see Brown-nosing)*

Harnessing synergies: 1. Making several things work together properly. 2. A futile attempt to post-rationalize a ragbag of initiatives as having some kind of coherent rationale; cynical ploy to charge customers over the odds, or more than once for the same product or service. *(see Synergy)*

Hatchet, bury the: 1. Agree to stop arguing. 2. Pretend to stop arguing, while simultaneously continuing to bad-mouth and discredit a rival. *(see Back stabbing)*

Hate sponge: 1. Source, or subject of, all negative comment. 2. Lightning conductor for everything bad in a company; rotten apple; invidious presence; spiteful gossip; weasel; goblin; troll; poison-penned anonymous contributor to online feedback forums; ne'er-do-well; vituperative venom source; bad penny; single-handedly responsible for low company morale; force of darkness; constant subject of amazement due to uncanny ability to escape the chop whenever there is a round of redundancies, probably down to possessing incriminatory evidence about the chief executive.

Headcount: 1. Number of people in room, department or company. 2. Highly volatile statistic that could change in an instant; random number; seemingly ever-decreasing quantity; number of staff that the finance director can instantly compute as a payroll cost; target list of people to be fired. *(see ABC session; Axe, face the; Phone list, go down the)*

Head honcho: 1. Person in charge; top dog. 2. Curiously Hispanic-tinged seniority reference; shades of drug baron hierarchy with mildly sinister overtones; Spaniard running organization, as is increasingly common in Britain. *(see Big cheese; Fromage, grand; Heavy hitter; Player, big)*

Headline benediction: 1. Short summary of a theme. 2. Curiously religious reference, rather suggesting that the Pope or some other church dignitary has blessed the findings of a business meeting; shades of divine intervention, possibly hoping that approval from on high will improve one's mortal business chances of success. *(see Beneficiate)*

Head of the valley syndrome: 1. Phenomenon to do with source of a river, perhaps; source of something generally. 2. Vague sweeping reference to something somewhere else (origin obscure); irrelevant and meaningless geographical observation inappropriately applied in a business context. *(see Blue yonder)*

Head off at the pass: 1. Stop before it goes wrong, or happens at all. 2. Nostalgic Cowboys and Indians reference, usually drawn from a childhood spent watching too many John Wayne films; mild military analogy invoked when it would be easier simply to say, *"I'm going to stop that."* *(see Nip in the bud; Rabbit, cutting the legs off the ___ to fit it in the hutch; Roots, take the plant up by the; Wagon, the Indians have surrounded the)*

Head office, I'm from ___ and I'm here to help: 1. *"I'm in charge – can I help at all?"* 2. *"I'm in charge – what the f**k are you playing at?"*; head office is deeply concerned about your performance: I'm a power-wielding xenophobe and I've jetted in to sort this out. *(see Big cheese; Black swan; Conference call; Management by walking about; Paper cup, here's a ___, there's a tidal wave coming; Stick that, some American is going to jet in and tell you exactly where to)*

Heads down: 1. Several crania crouched low; concentrate hard on desk work; avoid eye contact. 2. Hide from all possible blame or responsibility; pretend to be hard at work when in fact nothing is happening, as in: *"We need to keep our heads down on this one, Steve."* *(see Heads up)*

Heads up: 1. Update; collective lifting of crania. 2. Vital information, as in: *"Thanks for the heads up on this one, Brian"*; curious reference to head position as indicator of ability to assimilate news or pay attention; dire warning, as in: *"I need to give you a heads up on tomorrow's meeting, Jane."* *(see Beans, spill the; Face time; face-to-face; Heads down; Help and guidance; Interface; Loop, out of the, keep in the; One-to-one)*

Hearts and minds, winning: 1. Appealing both to feelings and logic, or limbic brain and neocortex. 2. Horribly overused phrase to describe anyone paying attention at all; suggestion of linkage between brain and coronary apparatus. *(see Gut feel; Information needs; Look and feel; Needs and wants)*

Heat, take the: 1. Be blamed and receive the appropriate punishment; warm up. 2. Get it right in the neck; full frontal assault, mental or physical; massive bawling out, often in front of colleagues; humiliation; be dismissed. *(see High jump, in for the; Scapegoat, make a ___ out of)*

Heavy hitter: 1. Powerful striker of a baseball; senior person. 2. Senior person hired at great expense, as in: *"We need to invest in a heavy hitter like Jenkins."*; lightweight hitter with over-inflated reputation; puffball; narcissist; show off; physically overweight board member, having overindulged on company expense account. *(see Big cheese; Chairman; Fromage, grand; Head honcho; Player, big)*

Heavy lifting, do the: 1. Difficult work, by crane or person. 2. Assertion that the hard work has already been done, as in: *"We've already done the heavy lifting on this one, Nigel"*; sudden realization that no one has done any work at all on a project, as in: *"Why the f**k hasn't anyone done the heavy lifting on this project??!"* *(see Shift, put in a)*

Heavyweight: 1. Weighty; senior. 2. Obese; fat; overly large; obsessed with biscuits, especially in meetings; constantly eating; focal point of all office cake consumption; Bernadette from accounts. *(see Doorstepped)*

Hedge our bets: 1. Back both sides; refuse to commit. 2. Fudge; obfuscate; be vague; refuse to recommend or take a position; mealy-mouthed non-committal; obsequious fawning in two directions at once; act like a civil servant. *(see Brown-nosing; Obfuscation; Play the percentages)*

Helicopter view: 1. Bird's-eye view; overview; full picture. 2. Another in the significant lexicon of the visually confused; constantly fluctuating between far away and close up; delusions of aeronautical prowess; boyhood aspirations of becoming a pilot; utterly bereft of any understanding about what the view is indeed like from a helicopter; phrase usually used by someone who has never been in such a craft. *(see Big picture; Closer look, stand back and take a; Deep dive; Holistic; No stone unturned; Witch-hunt)*

Hell in a handcart, we're all going to: 1. It's all going wrong; we're about to be found out. 2. Awful sensation of 'oh shit, they're on to us'; sweeping declaration about state of the nation or company, as in: *"Project Ballbag is a complete shambles – we're all going to hell in a handcart." (see Flight path)*

Help and guidance: 1. Assistance or training. 2. Hindrance and obstruction; tiresome micromanagement; under observation in case someone cocks it up, as in: *"I want you to give Veronica some help and guidance on this one"*; direct instruction with no deviation allowed; mandatory; order on pain of death. *(see Heads up)*

Herding cats: 1. Gathering together of felines. 2. Unfeasible metaphorical task; something that cannot be done, or is nigh-on impossible; exasperated cry of person trying to organize a large meeting, as in: *"Getting the board together is like herding cats!" (see Diarize; Locked into)*

Here-and-now-ness: 1. Immediacy; contemporaneity. 2. Nasty pseudonoun twisted into an adjective; arbitrary addition of –ness suffix to any word or phrase in sight; desperate realization that now is all that matters, having spent far too long staring blankly at the future without actually doing anything. *(see Frontofmindness; Going forward; Must-have; Worklessness)*

Herring, chasing a different: 1. Pursuing a fish of a different kind. 2. Aquatic analogy gone AWOL; loose grasp of piscatorial basics; extraordinary ability to distinguish between two different types of soft-finned teleost fish – a skill beyond most of us. *(see AWOL, go; Bark into the wind, up the wrong tree; Fish up a tree, he looks like a; Sprat to catch a mackerel)*

Herringbone principle, this is a clear example of the: 1. There truly is no definition for this, because I invented it. In order to test a client who always repeated what was said in the previous meeting, I introduced this fictitious phrase, and, sure enough, he repeated it without knowing what it meant. Truly staggering.

Hierarchy: 1. System of people or things in a graded order. 2. Ability to pull rank; nasty seniority ladder often leading to competent staff being summarily overruled by less competent bosses. *(see Dotted line; Matrix; Non-hierarchical; Organogram; Pecking order; Pull rank; Viper's nest)*

High flier: 1. Overachieving executive. 2. Yet another pseudo-military aero-nautical term; inference that humble office workers somehow have the skill and bravery of jet pilots; hints of altitude and speed, much loved by land-based slow people; low flier; slowcoach; laggard; slothful individual who tries something racy only to crash and burn horribly.

High ground; take the moral ___: 1. Superior position. 2. Hugely arrogant stance; intrinsic self-belief; hubris; 'cock of the roost' mentality; engage in intense bout of narcissism; thumb nose at plebs. *(see Premium; Rise above it)*

High jump, in for the: 1. Athletic contestant specializing in levitation. 2. In deep trouble; due for a massive bollocking; liable to be fired imminently; being set up as a scapegoat; done up like a kipper by devious colleague. *(see Heat, take the; Scapegoat, make a ___out of; Team, take one for the)*

High profile: 1. Very visible; noteworthy. 2. Horribly exposed; destined to take one for the team; project or person constantly talked about, with variable consequences; not high profile at all, but described as such. *(see Parapet, heads above the, keep our head below the; Team, take one for the; Hype)*

High risk: 1. Very likely to go wrong. 2. To be avoided at all costs; foolhardy; very dangerous indeed, for both individual and company; disastrous; only one possible outcome: failure. *(see Crash and burn; Wheels coming off)*

Hints and tips: 1. Advice and suggestions on how to do something. 2. Patronizing 'how-to' ideas designed for children; so-called 'step-by-step' guides claiming to be with you 'every step of the way'; selling techniques disguised as impartial advice; nudges to purchase; inspired by the pseudo-science of behavioural economics. *(see Advisorial; Behavioural economics; FAQs; Practical advice; Shell-like, a word in your)*

Histogram: 1. Pictorial representation of data. 2. Work of graphic fiction; Lego-like series of tower blocks depicting the square root of nothing; impenetrable skyscraper-style skyline of sales figures; irreversible sales decline shown in stark relief. *(see Bar chart)*

Hit the ground running: 1. Strike terra firma while on the move. 2. Macho military phrase redolent of paratroopers landing and breaking into a sprint in one uninterrupted movement; apparent ability to begin some-thing immediately, without any training or direction; vain attempt to plug gaps in staffing or service, as in: *"Dave will hit the ground running as soon as he arrives."* *(see Rubber hits the road, when the; Seamless)*

Holding our nerve: 1. Sticking to a decision when it looks like a bad one. 2. Unpleasant sinking feeling denoting a very bad move; knowledge of imminent disaster; flying in the face of all sensible advice; stubbornness; pig-headedness.

Honours even: 1. Equal on both sides. 2. We got our revenge.

Hoist with one's own petard: 1. Undone by one's own actions, from the old French word for explosives used to breach walls or doors. 2. So stupid as to destroy one's own prospects of success without any assistance from a third party; monumentally dim; incapable of knowing when to stop; prone to self-immolation. *(see Enablement; Foot, shoot oneself in the; Kamikaze; Mountain to climb; Own goal, spectacular; Platform, eat one's own)*

Holistic: 1. Working as one. 2. Overworked adjective suggesting that the sum is greater than the parts, as offered up by Gestalt theory; thinly-veiled effort to claim that this sub-standard piece of crap will be absolutely fine when viewed 'in the round'; pretence at understanding the complete picture. *(see Big picture; Helicopter view)*

Holy Grail: 1. Chalice, supposedly used by Jesus. 2. Chimeric outcome, never to be achieved; ideal; nirvana; dream situation; job you will never get; woman you will never sleep with, such as Julia on reception.

Hook to hang our hat on: 1. Useful repository for headgear. 2. Reflected glory from something far superior to ours; vicarious benefit; so-called 'piggyback' effort to improve poor position. *(see Piggyback)*

Hoops, jump through: 1. Have to prove a series of points. 2. Humiliating initiation process for new recruits; pointless sequence of redrafts of presentation or document only to end up making exactly the same point; tiresome approval process; endless round of budget justifications.

Hopper, pour into the: 1. Fuel, feed or otherwise top up supply. 2. Agricultural metaphor much loved by new business executives, as in: *"We need to pour more leads into the new business hopper, guys!"*; spurious grain-related theme, redolent of hour glasses, funnels and other tapering sales prospect diagrams. *(see Baseline; Leaky bucket; Pipeline, in the)*

Horizon, above the, change the, below the, small ripple on the: 1. Place where sky appears to meet land or sea. 2. Imaginary baseline; ever-shifting basis; semblance of vanishing point where none truly exists; God-like claim to be able to defy physics, as in: *"Guys, we need to change the horizon on this one."* *(see Baseline; Blue yonder)*

Horse, flogging a dead: 1. Continuing to hit equine after vital signs have stopped. 2. Persisting with a lost cause; insisting on carrying on with same approach even though it isn't working; failure to learn from new information; beating up hapless colleague; trying to secure pay rise for umpteenth time. *(see All over bar the shouting; Fat lady, it's not over till the ___ sings; Seal, stabbing a ___ with a banana)*

Hospital pass: 1. Receiving handover (of ball or project) resulting in need for medical attention. 2. Appalling and cowardly act of delegation; classic enactment of blame culture; slick manoeuvre to avoid all responsibility; project handover or apparently comprehensive briefing that singularly fails to reveal any of the associated pitfalls. *(see Ask, big; Blame culture; Bombs, box of; Buck, pass the; Catching a falling knife; Drop the ball; Micro-managing; Out of office message; Poisoned chalice; Riot act, read the; Wash our hands of it)*

Hot button topic: 1. Subject that is currently fashionable or relevant. 2. Rather aggravating pseudo-technological idea that a discussion theme can somehow be summoned by the press of a button, perhaps as on a game show; even more annoying when applied to a person, as in: *"I think this is definitely going to press Virginia's hot button,"* a notion that could certainly be open to misinterpretation.

Hot desking: 1. Being able to work at any desk, any time. 2. Abject failure of company to provide enough desks; total absence of appropriate office furniture; loose aggregation of bean bags and second-hand chairs bought in a car boot sale; kitchen table powwow. *(see Powwow; Soft area)*

Hot lead: 1. Contact very likely to result in business. 2. Dead end; random phone number; clapped out data provided by a direct marketing agency, including many so-called 'deads and gone aways'; bloke the managing director met in a bar last night; lap dancer called Suki, who might know the chairman of a potential customer as reliable as Enron. *(see Chuggers; Cold calling)*

Hot potato: 1. High temperature vegetable; tricky-to-handle issue. 2. Subject that must never, ever be raised; CEO's ex-wife; CEO's mistress; CEO's sexual proclivities; mysterious item found in company kitchen microwave.

Howler, strategic: 1. Dreadful error of judgment in business planning. 2. Horrible logic disconnect; abject failure to connect A to B intellectually; synapse jump from A to H with no apparent explanation; eccentric ramblings of so-called 'brand strategist'; blatant lie; patently incorrect approach dressed up as a firm recommendation; utter f**k up.

Huddle: 1. Small team gathering. 2. Embarrassing man cuddle; so-called team meeting; gay 'metrosexual' hug, usually causing intense mental discomfort, and often requiring subsequent therapy; ill-advised clinch with Sylvia over the photocopier, usually resulting in disciplinary action. *(see Soft area)*

Human resources: 1. People, viewed as a commodity; department in charge of same. 2. Retirement department for people fed up with doing the front-line job; roving gang of ladies called Veronica and Beverley who are good at the touchy-feely stuff; ferocious hit squad fronted by Bernadette, equipped with an all-encompassing brief to 'decruit'; brown-nosing mouthpiece of CEO, whose remit is to fire anyone or everyone on demand; curious, dusty function located somewhere in the basement, next to maintenance; non-existent department, usurped by power-crazy managing director who hires and fires at will. *(see Decruit; Touchy-feely)*

Human wind tunnel: 1. Person unable to stop talking. 2. Individual inordinately keen on the sound of their own voice; chairman; sales director; Jeanette from the legal department; crashing bore; incessant monologue of inane drivel; person delivering same; perpetual word dumper; consummate purveyor of verbal diarrhoea. *(see Breathes through his arse; Chairman; Dialogue; Fire hydrant, trying to drink from a; Word dump)*

Humanegement: 1. Hideous elision of humane and management. 2. Pioneered by UK local government, a word that in most cases presages precisely the opposite, as in: *"Our humanegement policy has concluded that 500 staff will be fired and the services outsourced to Mumbai."*

Hundred Day Plan: 1. The first 100 days of a project, or the tenure of a new chief executive. 2. An excuse to buy time after appointment to a top job, under the guise of 'getting to know the business', after which the newcomer realizes it's all far too complicated, is rumbled by the chairman and unceremoniously booted out. *(see Six-Week Sprint; Spin Cycle, Twenty-Mile March)*

Hungry, are they ___ enough: 1. Has this individual eaten recently?; Is this individual sufficiently keen? 2. Can I work this employee like a dog?; can this person be pushed to within an inch of their life? *(see Driven)*

Hymn sheet, singing from the same: 1. Intoning the same song as someone else; doing the same thing; seeing eye to eye. 2. Doing utterly different things; disagreeing entirely; not remotely in line with policy or view of company or colleague; categorically not aligned; off brief; out of sync; out of tune; in fundamental disagreement. *(see Align, aligned; Ducks in a row,* *get our; FIFO (2); Loose cannon; Off message; Off-piste; Realignment; Same page; Wavelength, on the same, not on the same; Wildebeest in a row, has the lion got his)*

Hype: 1. Exaggerated publicity or sales promotion. 2. Excessive hysteria about humdrum product; unjustified hoo-ha; so-called 'buzz', noise, clutter or general static; PR brouhaha; here today, gone tomorrow; song and dance; bells and whistles. *(see All-singing, all-dancing; Bells and whistles; Buzz; High profile; Pull out all the stops; Push the boat out)*

Hyperbundled: 1. Lumped together to an excessive degree. 2. Truly ridiculous vocabulary describing clusters of apparently related skills linked together in some dubious way; impenetrable bollocks by any other name.

Iconic: 1. Like an icon; highly distinctive and memorable. 2. Fractionally better than all the other dross surrounding it; not that impressive at all really, but good for morale. *(see Idea, big)*

Idea, big: 1. An idea. 2. A small, perfectly ordinary idea described as a big one to make the originator feel more important. *(see Bad idea, there's no such thing as a; Iconic; Initiatives; Innovation, innovative, innovatively)*

Idiot in search of a village: 1. A total fool, usually found out of context. 2. A total fool indeed, annoyingly present in the workplace; someone whose inane drivel causes more problems than if they were not there at all; major hindrance, capable of doubling the length of any meeting or project; dunderhead; dunce.

If you can't beat 'em, join 'em: 1. If you are losing, join forces with whoever is winning. 2. If you are being outmanoeuvred by lowdown, dirty tactics, then start using them yourself.

Ignoral, I'm going to treat that to a total: 1. I'm going to ignore that. 2. Classic Americanism turning a verb into a noun that doesn't exist. *(see Look through)*

iGod: 1. Self-appointed technological guru who believes they are omniscient. 2. Tiresome IT bod who condescends all other staff on the grounds that they 'don't get the internet'; skateboarding, bobble hat-wearing scruff ball called Mike, who commands an extortionate salary because no one understands what he does, including the people who hired him. *(see Digital native)*

IMHO: 1. In my humble opinion. 2. Seemingly innocent four-letter acronym that usually precedes a splenetic burst of invective in an overlong email. *(see Enlighten me; TBH)*

Immersion: 1. A form of baptism in which part or whole of the body is submerged in water. 2. Thorough investigation or familiarization process, usually from a standing start; much loved by communications agencies and management consultancies desperate to (a) work out what on earth the project is all about, and (b) string the whole thing out so as to charge more money. *(see Deep dive; Drains up; Drill down)*

Impact (vb), impacting: 1. To have an impact or bearing on. 2. An unforeseen domino effect, in which one seemingly trivial action brings down the whole pack of cards with unpleasant consequences.

Impact, high, low: 1. High impact means somebody noticed. 2. Low impact means nobody did, so you wasted your time. *(see Plug-in impact)*

Impactful: 1. Having impact. 2. Vastly overused faux-adjective to suggest making any sort of impression, as though making little or no impression would be preferable. *(see Choiceful; Insightful; Meaningful)*

Implement: 1. To carry out. 2. To take orders blindly from an uncaring boss without having a clue as to why.

Implementation, strategic: 1. Doing things. 2. A futile attempt to make doing things sound more important than it actually is.

Impossible, nothing is: 1. We genuinely believe we can do anything. 2. Patently untrue mantra given that time travel, unaided flight, the firing of mind bullets, and a vast array of other dreams clearly remain out of the reach of humans; massively patronizing *cri de coeur* much loved by motivational therapists and desperate call centre managers, as in: *"Impossible is two letters too long guys!"* (see Asking a duck to bark; BHAG; Can do attitude; Failure is not an option; Greatest Imaginable Challenge; Unthinkable, think the)

In a nutshell: 1. In just a few words. 2. In many words, typically a twenty-minute corridor verbal download that you weren't expecting.

In cahoots: 1. In collusion. 2. Horribly intertwined in a shady way, via nepotism, favouritism or outright bribery.

Incentive, staff: 1. Potential prize for a job well done. 2. Suggestion of a potential prize that will never be forthcoming; chimera; wishful thinking. *(see Carrot, big, ___ and stick)*

Incentivize: 1. Provide an incentive. 2. Repulsive Americanism once again needlessly turning a noun into a verb, a process doubtless referred to as 'verbizing'. *(see Carrot, big, ___ and stick; –ize)*

Influencer, influence the: 1. Affect the opinion of someone influential. 2. Phrase much loved in the PR industry; hopeful notion that a celebrity or opinion-former can be swayed, usually with cash; repetitive statement that is a staple of self-styled 'brand strategists', as in: *"Of course, what we need to do here to champion brand success is influence the influencer."* ; sage nods typically follow such a remark even though nobody has a clue what to do as a result.

Information mountain: 1. Large amount of data. 2. Rather over-dramatic way of observing that there's a lot to take in; tired trope usually uttered by a swamped marketing executive who can't make sense of anything, possibly on account of having too small a brain; sometimes called a data mountain. *(see Data dump; Wood, can't see the ___ for the trees)*

Information needs: 1. What must be known. 2. Strange suggestion that people somehow 'need' data. *(see Hearts and minds, winning; Needs and wants)*

In for the long haul: 1. Around for the long term. 2. Earnest pledge of commitment suggesting constancy where there is none, as in: *"Don't worry Roger, you have my personal word we're in for the long haul."*; immediate withdrawal at the first sign of trouble; short-termist; fly-by-night; churn and burn. *(see Churn and burn; Leaky bucket; Long-term; Marathon not a sprint, it's a)*

In front of the game: 1. Ahead. 2. Spatially baffling reference suggesting that someone can be playing a game and also be in front of it, wherever that may be.

Initiatives: 1. Ideas or actions showing some enterprise. 2. What decent employees should be doing all day as a matter of course; standard behaviour dressed up as somehow special; sub-standard behaviour treated the same way; lame ideas; below par tat. *(see Idea, big; Innovation)*

In it to win it: 1. Necessity of being present in order to stand a chance of succeeding. 2. Trite, nursery rhyme-like aphorism that is tiresomely self-evident; patronizing exhortation to overworked sales staff, as in: *"Come on guys, you've got to be in it to win it!"*; annoying statement of the bleeding obvious, pointing out that a competitor needs to compete in order to achieve something, which even the dimmest person already knows. *(see Milestones)*

Innovation, innovative, innovatively: 1. Something new. 2. Nastily over-used word to describe any half-baked idea; one half of the classic tauto-logical howler 'new innovation' (literal meaning: 'new new thing'); old idea hastily pulled out of a dusty bottom drawer; random thought in the shower; re-hash of previously-rejected proposal. *(see Collaborvation; Idea, big; Initiatives; Mission statement; Values)*

Input, inputs: 1. Something put into something else; suggestion; data entry. 2. Pseudo-technical twaddle referring to anyone saying anything at all, as in: *"I'd really value your input on this one, Wayne."*; baffling sugges-tion of scientific rigour where there is none, as in: *"Once we've got all the inputs we'll make a decision, guys."* *(see Insights; Obvious, a firm grasp of the; Outputs)*

In respect of: 1. Relating to. 2. Thoroughly pointless modifier. *(see In terms of; In the context of)*

Insights: 1. Things we have learned, or now understand. 2. Massive unex-pected developments; things we had no knowledge of before at all; Road-to-Damascus-style revelations; blinding flashes of the patently obvious; patronizing summing up of extended awayday diatribe, as in: *"I'd like to thank Keith for his valuable insights there."* *(see Input, inputs; Obvious, a firm grasp of the; Valuable)*

Insightful: 1. Full of insight. 2. Horrible bastard son of insight; another in a long line of words with –ful placed at the end to generate a lazy adjec-tive that invariably adds nothing to understanding, as in: *"Thanks for your highly insightful comment, Bernard."* *(see Choiceful; Impactful; Meaningful)*

Insperience: 1. Experience happening indoors. 2. Dreadful elision of the words 'inside' and 'experience', coined by trite futurologists to point out that many people these days are quite capable of enjoying themselves in their own home, as though this were a major surprise.

Inspirational: 1. Full of inspiration. 2. Not remotely inspiring; monumentally dull; dreary and predictable, as in: *"Thanks for that inspirational address, Mr Chairman."*

Institutionalize: 1. Ensure that the whole company does something as a matter of course. 2. Horrible abuse of the −ize suffix to suggest universal approval for an idea, or the blanket imposition of one; vain hope that any employee at all will do what the management suggest, as in: *"Once we've socialized our strategy and have achieved buy-in from our sponsors, let's make sure it gets institutionalized throughout the organization, Brad."*; another example of American nonsense. *(see Baked in; Diarize; Incentivize; Internalize; -ize; Maximize; Optimize; Prioritize; Productize; Professionalize; Utilize)*

Integrate, integral, integration: 1. Join together; absorb. 2. Desperate attempt to join the unjoinable; ragbag of disparate junk that will never fit together in a million years; not remotely integral. *(see Merger; Mix, the right, the wrong; Vertical market, ___ integration)*

Intelligent, if you were any less ____, I'd have to water you once a day: 1. You are as stupid as a plant. 2. You are too dim to work here; horticultural insult reserved for the most mentally challenged employees. *(see Bandwidth, he doesn't have the; Follow, do you; Mental furniture; Obvious, a firm grasp of the; Psychic RAM; Shilling, not the full)*

Interconnectedness: 1. Stuff joined together. 2. Rather silly and unnecessarily long word denoting some form of union. *(see Frictionless; Intertwingled; Seamless)*

Interface: 1. Point where two things come together or interact. 2. Literally, 'between the face'; chronically overused way to describe even the most basic of interactions, as in user interface; at its worst as a verb, as in: *"We need to interface with Malcolm on Project Stepladder."* *(see Face time; Face-to-face; Heads up; One-to-one)*

Internal communications: 1. Informing one's own staff. 2. Total radio silence; smokescreen; complete absence of any information whatsoever; pack of lies; set of diversionary tactics; propaganda; earnest announcement, as in: *"As the new CEO I can categorically confirm that there will be no redundancies"*, followed immediately by a swingeing round of redundancies. *(see Motivational posters; Swingeing cuts)*

Internalize: 1. Consider from a personal perspective. 2. Take personally; resent entirely; stew over; rake over in one's mind again and again; generate a personal head of steam; fume; quietly smoulder, then erupt the following day with unseemly outburst to boss; fester on an issue and subsequently overstate the case in public, usually leading to disciplinary action, or outright dismissal.

122

Internecine warfare: 1. Mutually destructive battle, maiming both sides in the process. 2. Vicious fights between companies or departments; no survivors permitted; carnage; bloody slaughter. *(see Blood bath, on the walls; Smarketing; Turf wars)*

Interpersonal skills: 1. Ability to deal successfully with others. 2. Abject failure to deal successfully with others, as in: *"With respect, Dave, you're a f**king idiot."*

Interrogatives: 1. Questions. 2. Unnecessarily pompous word for questions, as in: *"Thank you for those enlightening remarks, Mr Chairman, and now – does anyone have any interrogatives?"*

Intertwingled: 1. A portmanteau of intertwined and intermingled, coined by Ted Nelson to describe the way information is presented on the web. 2. Usable in pretty much any situation, as in: *"Bollocks, the cables under my desk are totally intertwingled."*

In terms of: 1. Relating to. 2. Utterly pointless modifier that merely confirms that the person speaking has not made it clear what they are referring to in the first place; mindless repetition of something already known, as in: *"This is the best phone on the market, in terms of phones."* *(see In respect of; In the context of)*

In the bag: 1. Agreed; signed and sealed. 2. Not a certainty at all; absolutely not in the bag; wishful thinking; pie in the sky; evidence of testosterone-fuelled hubris on return from new business meeting, as in: *"Great news, guys, it's in the bag!"* *(see Done deal; Pipeline, in the; Seals, left them clapping like)*

In the context of: 1. Relating to. 2. Thoroughly pointless modifier. *(see In respect of; In terms of)*

In the same boat: 1. Experiencing similar circumstances. 2. Misleading nautical reference with two entirely different meanings: (a) I'll succeed or fail with you because we are genuine equals, (b) I'm making it sound as though we're in this together because it's good for morale but at the first hint of trouble I'll be off; patently untrue matey reference, as in: *"We're all in the same boat on this one, Steve."* *(see Blame culture; Rock the boat, don't; Rowing in the same boat, direction)*

Intrapreneurs: 1. So-called entrepreneurs on the payroll, as in internal entrepreneurs. 2. Horrible car crash of ideas, vainly hoping that normally paid employees will be as motivated as desperate (and usually poor) unemployed individuals who have little choice but to come up with smart ideas. *(see Entrepreneur; Inventrepreneur; Olderpreneur; Wantrepreneur)*

Inventrepreneur: 1. An entrepreneur-inventor hybrid that makes and markets their own creation. 2. Another nasty elision designed to capture the mood of modern multitaskers; shock horror, someone who can do more than one thing; someone with both an idea and the ability to see it through – a rare breed indeed. *(see Entrepreneur; Intrapreneur; Wantrepreneur)*

-ize: 1. Action-based suffix. 2. One of the most pervasive and undisputed kings of the bullshit world; near-omnipresent in almost any business meeting or document; disgraceful weapon in gradual erosion of English language. *(see Diarize, Incentivize, Internalize, Maximize, Optimize, Prioritize, Productize; Professionalize; Utilize; -wise)*

Issue, key: 1. Important matter. 2. Totally unimportant matter; trivia; part of a tiresome long list, as in: *"There are seventeen key issues here."*; quite unrelated to keys in any way. *(see Key criteria; Key learnings)*

Issues, I have ___ with that: 1. I don't agree with you. 2. That's utter bollocks and you know it; if you try to enact that I'll have you fired/resign on principle; I don't agree, but I haven't a clue why; I am too stupid to articulate my reservations with your proposal; I have issues with myself. *(see Buy-in; Green light; Greenlit; Problem, I don't have a ___ with that; Redlit; Unhappy, I'm not ___ with)*

It is what it is: 1. This object or state of affairs is precisely what it appears to be. 2. Pointless platitude that merely states the obvious, offering no discernible benefit to anyone present; mindless statement of what everyone knows already; much loved by jobsworths and panjandrums. *(see Jobsworth; Obvious, a firm grasp of the; Panjandrum; We are where we are)*

Jacking: 1. A shortened version of hijack. 2. Attached to various types of agenda – newsjacking, trendjacking, crisisjacking, etc. – this suffix injects a sense of ambush, commando raid or military authority to subjects that are invariably nothing of the sort.

Jargon: 1. Specialized vocabulary concerned with a particular subject or industry. 2. Pretentious twaddle intentionally designed to confuse, obfuscate, and make the speaker seem more intelligent, usually with precisely the opposite effect.

Jargoned: 1. Riddled with jargon. 2. Meeting or document that is dominated by same, rather like this volume; observation on working practice, as in: *"I fear that Reg may suffer in their overly-jargoned environment."*

Jazz Hands: 1. All style and no content. 2. Soup this presentation up immediately because it is essentially content-free. *(see Zee, we've covered everything from A to; Full Monty, the; Turd, polishing a; Wow factor)*

JFDI: 1. Just f**king do it. 2. I am a power-crazed autocrat who will brook no discussion and is undoubtedly in the right.

Jigsaw, final piece of the: 1. The last piece of the puzzle. 2. Final recruit to a team, meaning that the boss won't have to do a stroke of work from now on.

Jobsworth: 1. Someone who invokes the precise letter of the law to do the absolute minimum amount of work without being summarily dismissed. 2. The entire civil service workforce of the United Kingdom, France, Spain and Italy. *(see Adminsitrivia; Bread and butter; Bureaucracy; Closure; Forth Road Bridge, like painting the; Panjandrum; Process; Risk-averse; Spaghetti junction; Target manager; Vin ordinaire; Viper's nest)*

Joined-up thinking: 1. A selection of ideas that make sense together. 2. Trite phrase to hoodwink anyone who will listen into believing that a random set of thoughts have some coherence, when they patently don't. *(see Connectivity; Seamless; Segue)*

Joining the dots: 1. Working out the relationship between several facts. 2. Extended bout of head scratching in a vain attempt to make sense of some impenetrable waffle uttered by the chief executive, who is doubtless convinced that he has found *El Dorado, Shangri-La,* or the Promised Land.

Journey, customer: 1. Sales or service process experienced by the customer in which the brand purports to 'delight them every step of the way'. 2. Infuriating sequence of hard-sell encounters, cross-selling attempts, failed deliveries, automated call centre frustrations, surly staff conversations, and ball-breakingly annoying set of interactions leading to increased medical bills and, on occasion, suicide. *(see Customer experience, -centric, -facing, -focused, journey, satisfaction, value)*

Jump start: 1. Effort to get something underway. 2. Last-ditch attempt to resuscitate a hopeless case. *(see Horse, flogging a dead; Kickstart; Last chance saloon, drinking at the)*

Jump through the hoops: 1. Meet all necessary requirements to reach the standard needed. 2. Frantically scrabble around for justification, evidence of skill or capability in the vain hope of convincing someone that you or your company are up to the job.

Jumped the shark: 1. No longer cool; now going downhill (after the TV series *Happy Days,* in which the scriptwriters were widely believed to have run out of ideas when making Fonzie jump over a shark on water skis). 2. Proof of the pervasive power of the American entertainment industry, if any were needed; proof of the insanity of the very same. *(see Jump start; Shark, keep moving like a, waiting for the sharks to circle)*

Jungle out there, it's a: 1. Our market is rather nasty. 2. It's certainly not a jungle out there, unless stated by a Brazilian in the Amazon – more likely it is a car park in Basingstoke filled with identical silver saloons, or a bleak industrial estate capable of draining all sense of hope from even the most optimistic of salesmen. *(see Battleground; Environment, business, challenging; Out there)*

Kamikaze: 1. Suicidal Japanese pilot. 2. Crazed executive with a not dissimilar death wish; hellbent on destruction, of company, self, or colleagues, in no particular order; a dangerous idiot, to be avoided at all costs. *(see Crash and burn; Foot, shoot oneself in the; Grasp the nettle; Hoist with one's own petard; Pacesetter; Platform, eat one's own; Right arm, give your ___ for:)*

Keeling over like flies: 1. Almost everyone is off sick. 2. The boss has driven them like a pack of dogs for months, and they can't take it any more.

Keep it dark: 1. Don't tell a soul. 2. Bury it immediately – it's illegal and we'll go to prison if we're caught. *(see Broad brush; Gloss over; Mum, keep; Ps and Qs, mind your)*

Key learnings: There is no definition for this – learning is knowledge gained by study. There is no such thing as a key learning, nor several of them, unless it means learning how to use a key. *(see Criteria, key)*

Keynoted (vb): 1. Delivered a keynote speech. 2. Wince-inducing past tense of keynote as a verb, as in: *"Yes Tarquin, I was a triumph when I keynoted the annual conference in Tahiti."*

Kickstart: 1. Prompt immediate action. 2. Realize with horror that a critical project has been thoroughly mismanaged, and you are in for the chop; immediately start scanning the corridors for someone to take the fall. *(see Blame culture, Jump start)*

Kidology: 1. The art of bluffing or deception, usually in harmless jest. 2. Blatant lies to hurt, deceive or commit a full-blown crime. *(see Fiscal juggling)*

Killer whale: 1. Orca; large aquatic mammal. 2. Ludicrous expression referring to online offers that generate large volumes – a whale is large, and a killer whale even bigger. *(see Off the scale; Whaling)*

Kill the competition: 1. Be a commercial success, at the expense of competitors. 2. Macho exhortation designed to motivate sales force; ever-recurring use of the military metaphor; suggestion that death is somehow acceptable in the normal course of business; ridiculous notion that annihilation of all other companies in the category will be beneficial; blinkered hatred of rival company, only to defect to said competitor only a few months later for a higher salary.

Kimono, open the: 1. Reveal a little of the inner workings. 2. Disgracefully sexist remark perpetrated by sweaty businessmen in Terylene suits to imply that business is somehow like sex. *(see Collars and cuffs, I bet the ___ don't match; Get into bed with; Matching luggage; Playtex strategy)*

KISS: 1. Keep it simple stupid, a term originally coined by designer Kelly Johnson at the Lockheed Skunk Works. 2. Trite acronym trotted out by poorly educated sales directors who are usually both simple and stupid; rapid attempt to clarify something one doesn't understand, but without wishing to admit it; failure to comprehend, followed by offensive-defensive tactic, as in: *"Enough of the technical mumbo-jumbo, Robert, it's clearly a case of KISS here."*

Kitchen sink: 1. Water-bearing receptacle in culinary area. 2. The full works; everything; the lot; the whole shoot, with absolutely no editing, as in: *"They've really thrown the kitchen sink at this."* *(see Death by PowerPoint; Full Monty; the; Pull out all the stops; Up the ante)*

Kitchen sinking: 1. Revealing all the bad news at the same time, as in throwing in the kitchen sink. 2. Technique much loved by the PR industry and politicians: when rumbled on one issue, you might as well admit to all the dirty laundry and get it over with in one go; in financial reporting, to declare all losses in one hit to get it over and done with.

Knee-jerk reaction: 1. Involuntary reflex action of knee joint, usually generated by neurologists testing muscular responses. 2. Tit-for-tat return strike; petty eye-for-an-eye act of revenge; puerile determination to get one's own back; vicious counter strike when spited. *(see Knock-on effect; Tent, standing outside the ___ pissing in)*

Knitting, stick to the: 1. Continue to do what one is best at, coined by Peters and Waterman in their 1982 book *In Search of Excellence*.

2. Plangent plea to resist temptation to diversify, as in: *"For f**k's sake stop fiddling about at the margins!"*; counterintuitive idea that doing what you've always done is just fine – an alien concept for all macho CEOs. *(see Competencies, core; Core; Loose-tight properties)*

Knock spots off: 1. Win emphatically. 2. Curious nose-thumbing statement often enjoyed by gloating winners, as in: *"We knocked spots off the competition, guys!"*; of unclear origin, possibly suggesting a leopard or cheetah being reduced to a neutral hue, as though that were some sort of benefit.

Knock-on effect: 1. Thing happening as a result of something else. 2. Nasty unexpected reaction; totally unforeseen consequence; abject failure to anticipate (usually entirely predictable) sequence of events. *(see Knee-jerk reaction)*

Know-how: 1. Knowledge; expertise. 2. Inference that knowledge or experience can take on the cachet of voodoo or black magic; suggestion of mysterious intangible mojo. *(see Knowledge management, transfer; Talent, war on)*

Know it when I see it, I don't know what I want but I'll ___ : 1. I don't know what I want but can you help me work it out? 2. I don't know what I want and I never will, even when I do see it; frustrating stance that is the bane of all exasperated advertising executives trying to work out what their clients really want. *(see Needs and wants; Open-ended; Straw man)*

Knowledge management, transfer: 1. Control, or handing over of, wisdom. 2. Catastrophic inability to control or hand over any wisdom at all; brain drain; complete loss of expertise when one intelligent person leaves the company; collapse of all IT functions when Dave leaves; haphazard filing system that passes on no knowledge whatsoever. *(see Know-how; Talent, war on)*

KOL: 1. Key opinion leader. 2. Person with a view, possibly not 'key' at all; windbag who can't stop expressing an opinion; media tart; self-publicist; loudmouth; show off. *(see Key criteria)*

KPIs: 1. Key performance indicators, usually poor. 2. Trumped up metrics rolled out either to demonstrate that a target has been hit and thus a self-satisfying bonus triggered, or to prove that a member of staff should be fired for incompetence; almost never key. *(see Benchmarking, category, industry; Markers, put some ___ down; Metrics; Milestones: Success, what does ___ look like?)*

Ladder it up: 1. Make it look bigger and more impressive. 2. Take something distinctly average and try to make it seem bigger and impressive, to no avail. *(see Putting lipstick on a pig; Ramp up; Ratchet up; Turd, polishing a)*

Lamb, sacrificial: 1. Scapegoat. 2. Hapless individual who takes the blame for an entire department or company when there has been a colossal cockup, even if they were clearly nothing to do with it, on holiday, or on secondment at the time. *(see Fall on your sword: Spear, fall on one's; Team, take one for the)*

Land, we need to ___ this one: 1. We need to win this contract. 2. For once, can we please win? Our new business track record is woeful. *(see Failure is not an option)*

Landmark: 1. A recognizable feature. 2. Any port in a storm that will give us our bearings, since we don't have a clue what we are doing. *(see Grasping at fog; Milestones)*

Large, giving it: 1. Boasting. 2. Indulging in braggadocious behaviour to disguise basic lack of talent and competence. *(see Braggadocious behaviour)*

Last chance saloon, drinking at the: 1. On a final warning. 2. About to be fired, probably this afternoon. *(see Coals, walk on hot; Line in the sand, draw a; Riding the razor blade)*

Late breaking gay: 1. Person who changes sexual preference later in life, usually male. 2. Mid-forties man, commonly of suspiciously louche disposition, who announces unexpectedly that he prefers Martin; colleague demonstrating unnerving wardrobe relaunch after sabbatical in

Costa Rica; Rupert on reception, recently seen sporting a newly-acquired 5 o'clock shadow look. *(see Mid-life crisis)*

Lateral thinking: 1. A way of solving problems by unorthodox and apparently illogical means. 2. Idiotic and foolhardy random thought that bears no relation to the matter in hand and has absolutely no chance of helping. *(see Bad idea, there's no such thing as a; Conceptual thinking)*

Launch: 1. The bit at the beginning; take off. 2. Damp squib; flop; embarrassing failure; best-kept secret. *(see Flagpole, run it up the ___ and see who salutes; Growth trajectory, personal, explosive)*

Lay off: 1. Fire. 2. Dismiss. *(see Decruit; Dejob; Downsize)*

Lead from the front: 1. Set a good example and take total responsibility. 2. Set a dreadful example based on hubris and an inflated sense of self-importance. *(see A Team, this calls for the; Cavalry over the hill; Eleventh hour, at the)*

Leader, category, market, thought: 1. The product or service that sells the most. 2. The product or service that doesn't sell the most, but would desperately love to; persistent 'reframing' of leadership concept in order to make it appear as though you are number one, such as 'brand leader, premium category', when it is only in fact a small brand; so-called 'thought leader' being the spurious idea that if you are not the leader you can think like one, as though that might help. *(see Thought leadership)*

Leading: 1. In front; ahead. 2. Invariably used to describe something that is not leading, but would like to be.

Leading edge: 1. Sharp corner of blade or surface such as a table; advanced. 2. Hackneyed catch-all term for any old crap that needs pepping up, as in: *"Our leading edge products are the envy of our competitors."* *(see Bleeding edge; Cutting edge; Next-generation; Pioneering)*

Leaky bucket: 1. Sub-standard water receptacle. 2. Woeful ability to retain customers; condemning evidence of sustained appalling customer service; losing business as fast as it can be won; incessant turnover of customer base; lamentably low quality performance. *(see Black hole, disappeared into a; Churn and burn; Hopper, pour into the; In for the long haul; Pipeline, in the)*

Leap of faith: 1. Pledge or decision based on little or no evidence. 2. Absolute shot in the dark; pure guesswork; finger in the air stuff; whim; blind optimism; foolhardy decision making; flying in the face of all known information; commercial insanity.

Learn the ropes: 1. To gain a thorough understanding of a sphere of activity. 2. Work out what on earth one's job involves; receive no brief at all; endure hopelessly inadequate farce of a 'handover'; sit through painful induction programme; learn on the job, aka make it up as you go along; fly by the seat of one's pants.

Learning curve, steep, vertical: 1. Amount of increased understanding, of variable speed and quantity. 2. Disastrous geometrical collision of straight and curved lines wreaking havoc in the business world, as in: *"We have a steep learning curve on that one, Stephanie.";* euphemism for *"we f**ked it up completely but don't tell anyone". (see Experiential curve; Growth trajectory, personal, explosive)*

Learning opportunity: 1. Chance to find out something. 2. Abject failure to listen; head-in-sand approach to paying attention; faux-humble word pairing suggesting some form of progress or improvement; panic-stricken scramble to acquire even the most basic of starter information; ABC approach to new subject; widespread ignorance, with little hope of enlightenment, ever. *(see AFLO; Learnings; Lessons)*

Learnings: 1. More than one piece of knowledge acquired. 2. Grim plural of active verb, suggesting intellectual progress on all fronts where usually there is precious little, as in: *"It's time we accumulated our learnings on Project Earwig, everybody." (see Experiential curve; Learning opportunity, setback)*

Left field, from: 1. Out of nowhere; emanating from a grassy area not on one's right hand side. 2. Another in the seemingly ubiquitous baseball lexicon; totally unexpected; a real turn up for the books; unnerving development leading to dismissal. *(see Sucker punch)*

Left hand, not knowing what the right is for, ___ and second left hand: 1. Lack of coordination between departments or individuals. 2. Total chaos; Armageddon; anarchy; risible failure to communicate even the simplest of information; uncoordinated; random; haphazard; fundamentally disorganized. *(see Reinventing the wheel; Right arm, give your ___ for)*

Legs, it's got: 1. This animal or person has the ability to stand up or walk; this project has long-term potential. 2. There's an outside chance this idea might work; it's rubbish – it'll never work; it's the best we've got even though it's a no-hoper; flimsy attempt to introduce the athletic metaphor to business; vague allusion to sprint versus marathon aphorism; hint of endurance, where normally none is warranted; pat putdown when confronted with lame idea, as in: *"It's a decent enough idea, Patrick, but has it got legs?"* *(see Bench, has this got; Real estate, how much ___ does this have; Success, what does ___ look like?)*

Lessons: 1. Teaching occasions. 2. Often hard-learned; utter cockups; fundamental failure in product or service delivery; nightmare scenarios; abject collapse of infrastructure; closure of company; outright shutdown. *(see Learning opportunity)*

Let go: 1. Allow to leave; force to leave. 2. Deceitful five letters designed to make dismissal sound acceptable, as in: *"We had to let Doug go."* *(see Metrics)*

Let me just say this: 1. I am trying to get a word in edgeways. 2. I haven't a clue what I am about to say, so I am stalling for time with a holding phrase. *(see Lie to you, I'm not going to; Respect, with)*

Let's not go there: 1. Let's not discuss it. 2. We can discuss it, but you won't like it; if you insist on pursuing this I'm going to humiliate you in front of everyone that matters, or blame you outright. *(see Blame culture; Scapegoat, make a ___ of)*

Level playing field: 1. Non-sloping sports venue; a fair chance for all contestants. 2. Quaint notion that many sports venues are on a hill, thus providing an advantage to the side playing downhill; failure to spot that all sports involve a change of ends precisely to make matters fair; pathetic use of sporting metaphor to allude to bias or lack of fair play, as in: *"We didn't win the business but it wasn't a level playing field."*; basic sour grapes. *(see Failure is not an option; Unfair advantage)*

Leverage: 1. Ability to move something with a lever. 2. Horrible and near-omnipresent noun or verb; false notion that business is anything whatsoever to do with physics; suggestion of power and influence; last bastion of cliché-ridden presenter in full bullshit mode, as in: *"We really need to leverage our assets on this one, Steve."* *(see Competitive advantage, edge)*

Lie to you, I'm not going to: 1. I'm going to give you the unvarnished truth; I am going to lie to you. 2. Highly deceptive opening line, usually presaging something nasty. *(see Let me just say this; Respect, with)*

Lifestyle: 1. Way of life to which one aspires or is accustomed. 2. Lazy catch-all for anything remotely aspirational, as in: *"This is clearly a lifestyle brand."*; overused and quite pointless word.

LIFO: 1. Last in, first out, usually applied to tasks in in-tray or email in-box. 2. Swift and clinical firing policy in which the most recently hired are the first to go; failure to cope with in-box, dealing only with most recent requests and ignoring the rest. *(see ABC session; FIFO; Phone list, go down the)*

Lift up a rock: 1. Raise geological specimen to see what is underneath; investigate. 2. Find out what is really going on, almost always with unpleasant consequences; recoil in horror on discovering the unadulterated truth; unveil corruption on an unprecedented scale. *(see Drains up, have the; Flush out; Look, take a long hard; Root-and-branch review; Witch-hunt)*

Light bulb experience: 1. Moment when inspiration strikes. 2. Complete failure to generate any decent thoughts at all; bereft of initiative; false suggestion at brainstorm that a breakthrough has been achieved, when none has. *(see Aha moment; Brainstorm; FMF)*

Lights are on, but nobody is home: 1. It appears as though a person is engaged, or even intelligent, but they are not. 2. This metaphorical house looks as though it is brimming with life, but in reality it is empty; person demonstrating similar characteristics; deceptively displaying all the traits of activity where none are truly present; flattering to deceive; all talk and no trousers; not bright at all, in fact quite dim. *(see Hamster is dead, the wheel is turning but the ___; Jazz hands)*

Line in the sand, draw a: 1. Beach-related message or artwork; agree not to mention something uncomfortable again. 2. Final warning; uneasy truce after significant bust up; last chance; pretence at moving on, usually followed by a trail of vindictive bullying. *(see Last chance saloon, drinking at the; Mum, keep)*

Line manager: 1. Person to whom you report. 2. Person who has no clue who you are or what you do, but is nevertheless in charge of your career development. *(see Appraisal, one degree; Appraisal 360 degree; Performance review)*

Line of sight: 1. Ability to spot something; unimpeded view. 2. Pseudo-military reference with semi-macho hints of being some sort of sniper in the undergrowth, as though that had anything to do with humdrum office affairs on a business park in Aldershot; often used when someone is clearly withholding information or playing politics, as in: *"Clive, I need a clear line of sight here before I can present to the board."*

Lingua franca: 1. Language used for communication among people of different mother tongues; any such system allowing mutual understanding. 2. Feeble attempt by drab and formulaic executives to add a dash of exotic flair to proceedings, as in: *"Of course on the web, English is our lingua franca, Steve." (see Segue; Tranche; Vis-à-vis)*

Lips, read my: 1. Pay careful attention to what I am saying. 2. I'm going to say this only once: if you cock things up again, you'll be fired; favourite staple of hectoring sales directors, as in: *"Read my lips, Mervin, Project Puddle will never see the light of day while I'm around." (see DILLIGAF; Enlighten me; Follow, do you; Respect, with)*

Literally: 1. In a literal manner. 2. Pointless and inaccurate hyperbole as in: *"It was literally an eye-opener." (see Absolutely, At the end of the day; Basically; Frankly; Real teeth, our campaign needs to have ___)*

Lock and load, let's: 1. Get ready for action. 2. Tired military metaphor borrowed from a range of overly macho Hollywood war films; ludicrous idea that preparing for a business meeting is somehow akin to going into battle; even worse if the expression is accompanied by a hand action mimicking a cocked gun or slotting an imaginary bullet into the breach. *(see Rock and roll, let's)*

Locked into: 1. Immovable; fixed. 2. Something that simply cannot be shifted from the diary of an important person, as in: *"Brian's locked into 11.30, but 1 o'clock is when we're hitting it." (see Diarize; Herding cats)*

Log on to: 1. Access an online site, usually with a password. 2. Modern internet phrase that has strangely morphed into deciding whether you agree with someone, as in: *"Well now you've explained it, we can all log on to that, Malcolm."*

Long tail, the: 1. Extended set of niches or small components of a market, rather than the big volume hits, coined by Chris Anderson in the book of the same name. 2. Poorly understood and often misused term referring to anything that's rather longer than expected; often deployed by so-called 'brand strategists' with a knowing nod, as in: *"Of course, Veronica, this is a classic example of a long tail"*, without really knowing what one involves. *(see Contiguous niches; Coterminous; Niche, carve out a, market ___)*

Long-term: 1. Consistently committed for a long period of time. 2. Nowhere to be found; gone; absent; not there; done a runner; vamoosed; pulled out; scarpered; reneged comprehensively; naffed off; set in train and then moved jobs; bailed out completely. *(see In for the long haul)*

Long time no see: 1. I haven't seen you for ages. 2. I have been too lazy or disorganized to get in touch; I haven't bothered because I don't like you very much; glib phrase delivered by over-familiar salespeople, usually accompanied by a patronizing pat on the shoulder and a wan smile.

Look, take a long hard: 1. Comprehensive search or analysis. 2. Unwelcome post-mortem; thorough interrogation, usually unearthing something rotten; inquest; uncomfortable period of soul searching, normally after a spectacular cockup, such as a disastrous product launch. *(see Lift up a rock; Pathologist's interest; Root-and-branch review; Witch-hunt)*

Look and feel: 1. How something appears or comes across. 2. Omnipresent pat phrase deployed by clichéd designers everywhere, as in: *"Guys, we need to make the look and feel consistent across all consumer touchpoints."* *(see Hearts and minds, winning; Rebrand; Touchpoints)*

Look through: 1. Look through a window or transparent substance, such as glass. 2. Ignore completely, as in: *"That issue is not relevant to us Nigel, so we'll just have to look through it."* *(see Ignoral, I'm going to treat that to a total)*

Loop, out of the, keep in the: 1. Informed, or not. 2. Weird idea that information is circular, thereby generating some kind of circuit; misinformation; gossip; deliberate exclusion from same in order to disadvantage or humiliate; covert operations-style lingo, as in: *"Thanks for keeping me in the loop there, Gordon."* *(see Beans, spill the; Chinese whispers; Heads up)*

Loose cannon: 1. Dangerously unsecured armament. 2. Appallingly indiscreet member of staff; chairman after two glasses of claret; complete liability; inclined to say something completely inappropriate at precisely the wrong moment. *(see Arse, up your own; Bull in a china shop; Off message; Off-piste)*

Loose-tight properties: 1. Seemingly contradictory characteristics of a successful company, first propounded by Peters and Waterman in their 1982 book *In Search of Excellence*. 2. Improbable and very-hard-to-pull-off blend of not giving a damn on the one hand and constantly meddling on the other. *(see Closer look, stand back and take a; Competencies; Control freak; Knitting, stick to the; Micromanaging)*

Lose-lose: 1. Whatever we do we'll fail. 2. Mindless repetition of the word lose, with no increase in meaning; most commonly deployed as a 'situation', as in: *"As far as I can see, Mary, this is a lose-lose situation."*; statement of the blindingly obvious. *(see SNAFU; Win-win)*

Low-hanging fruit, go for the: 1. Do the easy stuff. 2. Do the easy stuff first and see if you can get away with it; avoid hard work at all costs; skive; take path of least resistance; cut corners; exploit. *(see Wins, quick, easy, there are no easy)*

Low risk: 1. Not dangerous. 2. Highly dangerous, but not packaged as such, as with almost all financial investments.

Loyalty, beyond reason, customer, staff, team: 1. Sustained patronage or goodwill. 2. Self-deluding nonsense suggesting that staff or customers are truly enthralled with every aspect of management or product range; messianic, cult-like qualities attributed to workaday items such as cleaning products or the mundane business of just turning up at the office. *(see Delighting customers)*

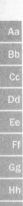
Machiavellian: 1. Cunning, amoral and opportunist. 2. Acting like an utter shit with no regard for others – it's me, me, me and the rest can go hang. *(Shit creek, up ___ without a paddle)*

Magic ingredient, there is no: 1. This is quite difficult. 2. We haven't got a bloody clue how to sort this out. *(see Easy answers, there are no; Quick fix, there is no; Silver bullet, there is no; X factor)*

Make a difference: 1. Make a significant contribution. 2. Make no difference whatsoever, as in: *"Steve, I want you to really make a difference on Project Woodlouse."*

Make it happen: 1. Make it happen. 2. Fail to make it happen after being blocked at every turn by obstructive colleagues, unreliable suppliers and a fundamental lack of skill and charisma.

Manager: 1. Someone who manages. 2. Someone who utterly fails to manage anything whatsoever; incompetent bureaucrat. *(see Administrivia; Bread and butter; Bureaucracy; Jobsworth; Panjandrum; Target manager)*

Management by walking about: 1. Inclusive management style based on regular interaction with staff. 2. Chief executive with a massively annoying tendency to turn up unannounced, make some unhelpful observations, derail a project, and then disappear just as quickly. *(see Head office, I'm from ___ and I'm here to help)*

Management by wishful thinking: 1. The erroneous belief that one's wishes are in accordance with reality, as is so often the case when managing a company. 2. Fanciful view that everything will be alright, despite overwhelming evidence to the contrary; wing-and-a-prayer style; hit-and-hope approach;

use of sticking plaster to make do and mend; laissez-faire attitude; board of directors demonstrating no rigour or competence at all.

Managing change, expectations: 1. Reassuring colleagues when things are changing so that they don't get any nasty surprises. 2. Deliberately introducing a package full of said nasty surprises in order to increase status and pay.

Managing downwards, upwards, sideways: 1. Managing a subordinate, boss or equal-ranking colleague. 2. Floundering around in all directions, bullying direct reports, fawning to management and knifing rivals at every opportunity. *(see Back stabbing; Blame culture; Brown-nosing)*

Man up: 1. Increase virility or masculinity levels; mature; grow up. 2. Take some responsibility for the first time in your life; make a decision for once; get on with it; ditch metrosexual wishy-washy stance and deliver to required level at last; knuckle down. *(see Grow a pair)*

Map, on the: 1. Recognized by anyone who needs to know. 2. Totally obscure and unheard of, as in: *"It's time to get this brand on the map"*, precisely because at the moment it's nowhere; peculiar cartographical reference implying sense of direction where usually there is none; vocabulary loosely lifted from Outward Bound course or distant Boy Scout memories; not registered at all; totally unnoticed by anyone except the most zealous devotee.

Marathon not a sprint, it's a: 1. This will take a long time so don't rush it. 2. Exasperated plea from managing director to try a more thoughtful approach, even though he probably set the punitive monthly targets himself; delusion by same that he is somehow similar to the best Olympic coaches; athletics metaphor misapplied; thinly-disguised attempt to appear 'strategic' in a meeting by proposing a more orderly method to solving the problem. *(see Closer look, stand back and take a; In for the long haul; Methodology)*

Marching orders, get your: 1. Be fired. 2. Be fired emphatically, on the spot; be escorted from building by security; be defenestrated (advertising industry in particular). *(see Bombshell; Bullet, get the; Defenestrate, defenestration; Dejob; Destaff; Out, I want him/her; Swingeing cuts)*

Marker buoy, let's stick a ___ on that: 1. Let's come back to that point. 2. Bizarre faux-nautical observation attributing marine qualities to a point made in conversation; possible overuse of drugs by the person saying this; hints of some kind of fantastic hallucination in which all conversations are oceans, and the comments made are represented by life buoys; maritime mash-up of massive proportions. *(see Mental lay-by; Ring fence; Tangent, returning to the)*

Markers, put some ___ down: 1. Outline clearly. 2. Wreak trail of havoc; enumerate erratic history of financial performance; recalibrate; change criteria to create semblance of improved position; fabricate previous targets to imply success; plot points on a graph to invent a shape where none exists. *(see Benchmarking; Fiscal juggling; KPIs; Metrics; Milestones)*

Marketing: 1. Publicity and communication designed to increase sales. 2. Strange alchemy purporting to increase sales, but frequently unproven; advertising puffery; ability to talk theoretically about 'the brand' without taking any practical responsibility for the tangible aspects of a business; smoke and mirrors; snake oil salesman's favourite preserve. *(see Architecture, brand ___, business ___; Brand onion, pillars, pyramid, values; Marketing; Positioning; Smoke and mirrors job)*

Marketing guru: 1. Expert in communication. 2. Self-styled expert in communication, in order to procure publishing contract or public speaking fees; hints of Indian mysticism, or request to visit one's own personal ashram; occasionally mistyped as the embarrassing 'marketing gnu', suggesting a particularly savvy wildebeest; at its worst when uttered by a person describing themselves, as in: *"Pleased to meet you, I'm a marketing guru."* *(see Brand strategist; Entrepreneur; Positioning)*

Market-leading: 1. The number one product or service. 2. Delusional catch-all rarely used by true market leaders; aspirational hot air spouted by all market followers; also-ran; has-been; piss-poor; dog; generic wibble desperately grasping for quality. *(see Challenger brand; Thought leadership; World class)*

Market share: 1. Proportion of sales in relation to competitors. 2. Ever-shifting percentage that can be recast in multiple ways to suit the ends of the owner of the data; market share is very low = *"I need more budget."*; market share is very high = *"I want a pay rise."*

Mark-up: 1. Surcharge on base price in order to generate a profit. 2. Near-infinite additional charge in order to fleece customer; favourite domain of so-called 'luxury goods', safe in the knowledge that their clients are loaded and indiscriminate; strange notion that paying more is actually better – a phenomenon only true of vainglorious show-offs.

Marriage made in heaven: 1. Perfect match. 2. Doomed to failure, like many marriages; divorce fodder; victims of relationship fatigue; awkward pairing; glib referral to rosy relations in honeymoon phase, followed by acrimonious dust-up. *(see Halcyon days; Rose-tinted)*

Massage (vb): 1. Administer rubdown to a range of body parts. 2. Soft soap a colleague, usually with the spoken word; butter up; prepare for tricky negotiation, as in: *"I do think that politically we'll have to massage Michael on this one."* *(see Brown-nosing)*

Massage the numbers: 1. Rearrange finances or statistics to create a different conclusion. 2. Deceptive, often downright illegal, alteration of financial reporting information in order to generate an entirely different outcome, usually favourable; sleight of hand; legerdemain; malfeasance; contemptible twisting of reporting line to create a better picture, often resulting in company closure or personal imprisonment. *(see Bottom line; Cook the books; Crunch the numbers; Fiscal juggling; Negative growth, profit; Obfuscation; Smoke and mirrors job)*

Masstige: 1. Mass prestige. 2. Revolting elision dreamt up by supercilious trends experts to suggest that a lot of people can now buy premium products, which of course we already knew. *(see Prosumer)*

Match fit: 1. Ready for action; in good condition. 2. Sporting metaphor applied to anything from a person to a team, division, presentation or a whole company; training analogy run rampant, suggesting that knackered and overworked staff are in some way finely-tuned athletes, when a quick glance at their physical condition would suggest otherwise; shades of winning the cup or playing in the Premier League; usually applied to thoroughly corpulent and out of shape executives. *(see Purpose, fit for; Rock and roll, let's)*

Matching luggage: 1. Items looking, or appearing to be, the same; part of a set. 2. Frantic appeal for a ragbag of ideas or products to look as though they are part of the same suite or range, when they are categorically not; dissimilar, unrelated thoughts; *cri de coeur* from enthusiastic product manager, as in: *"We need to make sure we have matching luggage on this one, guys!"*; sexist speculation about whether a woman's bra and panties are of the same material. *(see Collars and cuffs, I bet the ___ don't match; FULLAB; Kimono, open the; Playtex strategy)*

Matrix: 1. Latticework; enclosed environment; connective tissue. 2. Hazardous labyrinth of working relationships that requires impeccable navigation in order to avoid humiliation or dismissal; viper's nest; snake's honeymoon; bear trap; minefield of politics and hierarchy. *(see Dotted line; Hierarchy; Organogram; Non-hierarchical; Pecking order; Pull rank; Snakepit; Snake's Honeymoon; Viper's nest)*

Maxed out: 1. At full speed or capacity. 2. US air force lingo hijacked by oppressed executives usually working in far less glamorous fields such as baby food, pharmaceuticals or feminine hygiene; attempt to fob request to take on extra work, as in: *"I'd love to help, Marion, but I'm all maxed out this week as it is."* *(see Crash and burn; Essay crisis; Needle, moving the; Needle, pushing the; Participation; Pushing the envelope; Pyramided out; Wheels coming off)*

Maximize: 1. Make the most of. 2. Squeeze even more juice out of an already empty vessel; invariably referring to potential, as in: *"We need to maximize the potential of Project Dog Bowl, Bernard."* *(see –ize; Potential)*

MAYA: 1. Most advanced yet acceptable. 2. Term coined by designer Raymond Loewy, based on the belief that the public is often not ready to accept wild departures from what they currently find familiar; nothing to do with the Mesoamerican civilization whatsoever, many of whom may well have been more advanced than some people today. *(see MVP)*

MBA: 1. Master of business administration. 2. Dreary, time-consuming and very costly learning programme; last-ditch effort by mature businessman to make up for abject squandering of university years; near-endless stream of semi-fictitious case studies that can rarely be applied to the real world; excuse to avoid the monotony of the day job. *(see Sabbatical)*

Meaningful: 1. Full of meaning. 2. Utterly bereft of meaning, as in: *"We need a meaningful solution here, Veronica."* *(see Choiceful; Dialogue; Impactful; Insightful)*

Mechanics: 1. People who fix machines; the nuts and bolts of a programme. 2. Crass attempt to liken the flabby and diffuse world of business with precision engineering; much loved in wishy-washy areas such as marketing and advertising, as in: *"Gemma is now going to walk us through the mechanics of the campaign."* *(see Vehicle)*

Mediocracy: 1. Organization in which mediocrity is the norm. 2. Relentlessly average as standard; bland; ordinary; humdrum; workaday; quite unremarkable; qualities often displayed by companies claiming to have lots of 'drive' and 'passion'. *(see Challenger brand; Drive; Gynocracy; Passion, passionate; Run-of-the-mill; Vin ordinaire)*

Meetings: 1. Gatherings, ostensibly with the purpose of discussing or deciding something important. 2. Gargantuan waste of time; superb smokescreen for appearing busy when in fact the participants are merely holding court, eating biscuits, falling asleep or pretending to listen when in fact checking their personal emails. *(see BlackBerry prayer; Death by PowerPoint; Moi presentation; Open door policy)*

Mega: 1. Really big. 2. Claimed to be really big in order to make the claimer appear to be so; not that big really; unrealistic aspiration or plain exaggeration, as in: *"Project Bugbear is going to be really mega, guys!"* (see Gangbusters, it's going; Meta; Monster, it's a)

Mental furniture: 1. Brainpower; intelligence. 2. Near-complete lack of gumption, as in: *"Darren just hasn't got the mental furniture for this.";* partial DIY component to thought-processing capability; common sense; straightforward expertise or competence. *(see Bandwidth, he doesn't have the; Intelligent, if you were any less ___, I'd have to water you once a day; Obvious, a firm grasp of the; Psychic RAM; Shilling, not the full)*

Mental lay-by: 1. Daydream; thought cul-de-sac. 2. Near-permanent frame of mind in meetings; off with the fairies; looking out of the window; hypnagogic dream state; half asleep; fantasizing about Julie from accounts; reverie, often broken by an unwanted question from other meeting attendee. *(see Marker buoy, Let's stick a ___ on that; Meetings; Tangent, returning to the)*

Merger: 1. Joining of two companies or departments. 2. Unsuccessful joining of same; coming together of disparate parties resulting in no discernible benefit; warfare; bitter hatred between rivals; takeover; triumphant, self-serving manoeuvre orchestrated by board keen to realize their share options. *(see Apples with apples, not comparing; Assimilation; Integrate, integral, integration; Mix, the right, the wrong; Pay through the nose)*

Merit, not wholly without: 1. Not bad, but not that good either. 2. Mildly dismissive observation from the damned-by-faint-praise school; a close cousin of the double negative: *"I'm not unhappy with that."* (see Issues, I have ___ with that; Problem, I don't have a ___ with that; Unhappy, I'm not ___ with that)

Messenger, don't shoot the: 1. Don't blame the person who delivers the bad news. 2. On the contrary, blame the person comprehensively; emphatically attach news to bearer; shout *"oh my God!"* and run to the toilet in tears; nasty precursor to appalling revelation, as in: *"Don't shoot the messenger, but Stephanie says they're shutting the whole department down."*

Meta: 1. Vast; overarching. 2. Four letters cunningly deployed to make something sound unfathomably large; much loved by data planners, as in: *"I propose we do a meta analysis of this data set, Roger."* (see Mega)

Methodology: 1. Method. 2. Transparent attempt to lend intellectual credence to something far less important by adding the suffix –ology; way of doing something; approach; how it is going to get done; pseudo-academic line of enquiry, as in: *"What's our methodology on Project Earwax, Sebastian?" (see Marathon not a sprint, it's a; Strategy, strategize)*

Metrics: 1. Measurement criteria. 2. Futile and time-consuming effort at measuring the immeasurable; pointless data set that will never be looked at again; amorphous headings used to fire staff for apparently poor performance, as in: *"I'm sorry, Doug, but the management metrics clearly show that your work is below par, so regretfully we have to let you go." (see Benchmarking; KPIs; Landmark; Let go; Markers, put some ___ down)*

Micromanaging: 1. Checking every tiny detail; breathing down a subordinate's neck. 2. Infuriating inability to allow perfectly competent executive to get on with a task; misguided belief that only you can do something properly; characteristic consistent with control freaks unhappy leaving their 'comfort zone'; meddling; fiddling unnecessarily; making pointless tweaks to the work of others that have no bearing at all on the content or outcome; hovering; loitering at a colleague's desk; constantly asking whether the report requested for Friday will indeed be ready on time, to which the reply is invariably: *"Yes it will be, so long as you f**k off and let me get on with it." (see Autonomy; Buck, pass the; Comfort zone, out of one's; Control freak; Loose-tight properties; Non-judgemental)*

Mid-life crisis: 1. Near-total breakdown in confidence, usually experienced in one's forties. 2. Bizarre hormonal change leading to erratic and frankly embarrassing behaviour traits; ill-judged series of 'personal relaunch' decisions, which may include injudicious new haircut, a complete wardrobe change, purchase of sports car, motorbike or skateboard; appearance at highly unsuitable events such as office rave only for the secretaries; change of sexuality; purchase of ear stud or sudden sporting of inappropriate tattoo; wholesale introduction of gymnasium-based routine, complete with Day-Glo Lycra ensemble; utter loss of respect and integrity; loss of wife; gain of pitying looks from own children; all the above, often leading to dismissal for being too weird after a string of unfavourable staff complaints. *(see Ballistic, go; Bandwagoneering; Basket case; Box of frogs, mad as a; Bundle, one stick short of a; Late breaking gay; Picnic, one sandwich short of a; Postal, go; Pram, to throw one's toys out of)*

Milestones: 1. Road markers indicating mile-length distances; moment or recognition of a significant achievement. 2. Serious attempt to herald progress where usually there is precious little; suggestion of forward motion; triumphant production of tangible but invariably cheap memento of success, such as a plaque, hastily printed certificate, or plastic trophy emblazoned with 'Drain Surgeon of the Month', or 'Waxer of the Year'; misty-eyed intonation much loved by chairmen, as in: *"I am convinced we will look back on Project*

Jellybean as a significant milestone in the company's history." (see Benchmarking; In it to win it; KPIs; Landmark; Markers, put some ___ down; Metrics)

Minefield, complete, tiptoeing through a: 1. Area of ground strewn with lethal explosives. 2. Political nightmare, best avoided. *(see Bombs, box of)*

Minergy: 1. Use of minimal energy to get the task accomplished. 2. The elisions keep coming, in this case referring to a slacker who is determined to get away with as little work as possible; unnerving sonic cousin of synergy, as in: *"I am looking for a minergistic approach to this, Vernon." (see Synergy)*

Minister for fun: 1. Member of staff charged with keeping morale high. 2. Self-appointed office wag; wearer of bad ties and purveyor of unfunny jokes and non-PC remarks; twat; court jester; organizer of frequently unpopular social events, such as karaoke; horrible job description devised by companies with lousy products and low pay, along with either non-existent or inhumane HR policy; brief to keep staff happy with no budget or resources other than an arsenal of cheap knob gags. *(see Catalyst; Dress to impress; Emotional intelligence; Empathy; Poisoned chalice)*

Mission critical: 1. Vital to the task. 2. Not at all vital, merely claiming to be so; suggesting that the task in hand is somehow as important as a space rocket flight. *(see DNA)*

Mission statement: 1. Declaration of what a company does, or intends to do, or stands for. 2. Hackneyed bundle of weasel words and cliché; wishful thinking checklist of desired characteristics, most of which will never materialize; formulaic tick box of attributes usually including 'world class', 'exceeding customer expectations', 'innovative', 'passionate', and other such drivel, none of it accurate. *(see Expectations, exceeding, failing to achieve, living up to, managing, meeting; Innovation, innovative, innovatively; Passion, passionate; Values; Vision, visioning; Voodoo, corporate; World-beating, -changing; World class)*

Mix, the right, the wrong: 1. Blend, hopefully correct. 2. Oil and water; nasty clash of interests, usually due to inappropriate casting. *(see Apples with apples, not comparing; Assimilation; Casting; Integrate, integral, integration; Merger)*

Mode: 1. Style; way of doing. 2. Rather annoying word merely specifying what someone is up to, as in: *"He's in new business mode at the moment,"* or *"Jenny's in presentation mode this week.";* invariably unnecessary.

Module: 1. Component part; capsule or piece. 2. Strange way to denote the elements of a training programme, such as: *"Derek's just completing module two of our People's Champion Induction Course."*

Moi presentation: 1. Speech or presentation entirely for the benefit of the person making it. 2. Colossal showboating; pointless tirade whose sole purpose is to make the speaker appear rather brilliant; grandstand bravura performance, but with no tangible outcome or application; hot air; piffle; expedient drivel where silence would have been more productive. *(see BlackBerry prayer; Death by PowerPoint; Meetings)*

Momentum: 1. Impetus. 2. Manifestation of the business world's obsession with pace; effort; forward motion suddenly requested on seemingly already dead tasks, as in: *"We need some serious momentum on Project Birdbath, Brian." (see Going forward)*

Mondayize: 1. Contrived verb for moving a statutory holiday to the nearest Monday in order to secure a long weekend, originated in New Zealand. 2. Push to next week in the hope something will have changed; start the week in style, probably with a formulaic and depressing status meeting. *(see –ize)*

Monetize: 1. Make money from. 2. Repugnant financial verb coined by so-called digital natives, as in: *"We need to work out how to monetize content here, Alex.";* statement of something monumentally self-evident – that business activities should indeed make some money, unlike most social media, hence the urgent request to 'monetize'. *(see Democratize; Digital native; -ize; Productize)*

Money for old rope: 1. Easy cash. 2. Stacks of income for doing sod all; outrageous margins on premium products just because rich show-offs don't know the true value of anything; fleece; swindle; hoodwink; con; embezzle. *(see Pay through the nose; Premium)*

Monitoring: 1. Keeping an eye on. 2. Posher word for basic research, allowing self-appointed 'monitoring' company to charge a great deal more. *(see Guardian, brand)*

Monster, it's a: 1. It's big and/or very scary. 2. This presentation is far too long; this project is so unwieldy it will never succeed; this sales director is horribly overweight; this budget is bloated because the CEO thinks it's a winner. *(see Gangbusters, it's going; Mega; Meta)*

MOOC: 1: Massive online open course. 2. Bizarre educational product that has turned some very average teachers into multi-millionaire pseudo rock stars, by turning their tutorials into commodities and simultaneously undermining or bypassing real teachers everywhere.

Moofing: 1. Mobile out of the office working. 2. Multi-angled car crash of the words mobile, out of office, and working on the hoof; echoes of goofing and spoofing; possibly not working at all.

Moon, barking at the, over the, through the: 1. Mad, elated, or both simultaneously. 2. Baffling lunar reference, possibly rooted in lunacy itself; not the full shilling. *(see AWOL, go; Ballistic, go; Box of frogs, mad as a; Plot, lose the; Postal, go; Pram, to throw one's toys out of; Rails, gone off the; Sandwich, one ___ short of a picnic; Shilling, not the full)*

More than one way to skin a cat, there's: 1. There are a number of techniques for removing the epidermis of a feline. 2. We can approach this a number of ways, and frankly I haven't a clue which is the best, despite being in charge; redundant throwaway line much loved by dim sales managers in idea sessions.

Motivation, lack of, team: 1. Desire to do something, individual or collective. 2. Lack of desire to do something, individual or collective; boredom; ennui; listlessness; depression; oh what's the bloody point?; word only used when motivation is an issue, such as in badly-run companies with no money and a bad staff record, as in: *"Come on guys, we need something motivational for the troops!"* *(see Team, there's no I in; Troops, the)*

Motivational posters: 1. Notices on company wall designed to enthuse workforce. 2. Pat half-jokes that are in themselves the butt of much staff cynicism and, in some cases, outright abuse; homespun versions include the hardy perennial: *"You don't have to be mad to work here but it helps!"*; company-generated efforts invariably depict Lord Kitchener doctored to feature the managing director's face declaring: *"Your company needs you!"*, or a highly contrived mantra that no one understands, such as *"Aptitude + Attitude = Altitude!"*; typically found taped to the wall next to a furred up old kettle or in the wash and scrub up area next to the fire evacuation procedure; best avoided. *(see Internal communications)*

Mountain out of a molehill, make a: 1. Generate a big issue out of nothing much. 2. Completely overdo it; brew up vast head of steam; lose the plot; fail to cope; stack problem upon problem until the task is apparently insurmountable, when in fact it is perfectly straightforward; delay simple task and thereby make worse, such as fail to do expenses or timesheets for a year and then complain it will take the whole weekend.

Mountain to climb: 1. Large rock structure that needs ascending; difficult task. 2. Often part two of a project or series of presentations, such as the second half of a football match; usually preceded by sorry underperformance and, therefore, almost always of one's own making, as in: *"Since we shot our-selves in the foot in round one now we have a mountain to climb."* *(see Foot, shoot oneself in the; Hoist with one's own petard; Own goal, spectacular)*

Movers and shakers: 1. People with power and influence, possibly from a 19th century poem by Arthur O'Shaughnessy. 2. All board directors; cus-tomers in significant purchasing positions; members of procurement function; young buck on the up; chief executive's personal assistant, often referred to as 'the gatekeeper'; chairman's wife, often the one genuinely in charge of strategic direction; receptionist or security guard, who usu-ally know more about the company than all the rest put together. *(see Chairman's wife)*

Moving forward: 1. Heading in a direction other than backward, sideways, or any other point on the compass. 2. Intensely annoying and completely redundant word pairing signifying the square root of cock-all; as ever, based on the erroneous idea that moving backward might provide a viable alternative, although outright retreat may indeed be advisable for those who insist on using the phrase. *(see Forward-looking; Going forward)*

MRDA: 1. An abbreviation of Mandy Rice-Davies applies. 2. Slang used to indicate cynicism of a statement of fact due to the obvious bias of the per-son stating it. From the 1963 Profumo trial, in which Rice-Davies (18 at the time) responded to the prosecuting counsel pointing out that Lord Astor denied an affair or having even met her, by saying: *"He would, wouldn't he?"*

MTBL: 1. Memo to be leaked. 2. Disgraceful acronym deployed when an internal piece of information is intentionally to be given a wider audience; Machiavellian method used by those whose *raison d'etre* involves a con-stant cycle of brief and counter brief. *(see Machiavellian)*

Multicultural: 1. Relating to, or involving, several cultures. 2. Lazy adjective used to suggest diversity of any kind, as in: *"As you can see we're a pretty multicultural bunch here, Victoria"*, usually pointing to an all-Caucasian work force. *(see Broad church; Diversity)*

Multitasking: 1. Doing many things, usually at the same time. 2. Claiming to do many things at once, and failing to complete any of them; making a grandiose start on all fronts, with no discernible delivery of anything in particular; taking on far too much and underachieving as a result; making the schoolboy error of claiming to be good at multitasking, as in: *"Hi, I'm a brilliant multitasker!"*, and then being given far too much to do. *(see Entre-preneneur; Paper cup, here's a ___, there's a tidal wave coming)*

Multiskill: 1. To train employees to do a number of different tasks. 2. To claim to train employees to do a number of different tasks, not do so, and yet still ask them to do a number of different tasks; to woefully under-equip; to leave high and dry; to work like a dog with no relevant training. *(see Paper cup, here's a ___, there's a tidal wave coming)*

Mum, keep: 1. Say nothing, as in mum's the word (14th century, believed to be suggestive of closed lips). 2. Say nothing on pain of death; under no circumstances mention what's gone on or you'll be fired; deploy utmost secrecy; obfuscate; cover up; throw a veil over; refuse to reveal inner workings, especially of true pricing; demonstrate opacity; refuse to be transparent, normally while claiming to be so. *(see Gloss over; Keep it dark; Line in the sand, draw a; Obfuscation; Ps and Qs, mind your)*

Musical chairs: 1. Party game; any situation involving a number of people in a series of interrelated changes. 2. Similarly childish manoeuvres at the top of any company, such as putting the production director in charge of marketing when he knows absolutely nothing about it; arbitrary shuffling of sales force to create the illusion of improvement; bizarre merry-go-round of CEOs in which a failure from one company is suddenly hailed as the saviour of another, despite widespread knowledge of their incompetence; job swap; career carousel; March madness.

Must, this is a: 1. We have to do it, or have it. 2. I'd like to prevail with my bias immediately, albeit in the absence of any sensible knowledge of the subject; instinct and opinion must win out over the facts; my hunch is better than yours; forget time-consuming research and investigation, let's just crack on with it. *(see Gut feel; Must-have; Pants, fly by the seat of our)*

Must-have: 1. Vital; absolutely required. 2. Irritating adjective originally pioneered by style magazine journalists intent on telling people what they 'must have', as though it's any of their concern; absolutely not needed at all; frou-frou; flash in the pan; ephemeral; here today, gone tomorrow. *(see Here-and-now-ness; Must, this is a; Tipping point, the)*

Mustard, cut the, that's ___ that is: 1. (It has) come up to expectations. 2. That's really clinched it; we're on fire; we're brilliant; that's great; triumphant expression of apparent achievement, often before calamitous fall. *(see Bee's knees, it's the; Dog's bollocks)*

MVP: 1. Minimum viable product; idea invented by Al Ries representing the least amount of effort needed to run an experiment with a prototype. 2. What technology companies often launch with – sub-standard tat. *(see Always in beta; MAYA)*

Nail it: 1. Hammer a nail into something; get it right, usually first time. 2. Generate a trite sound bite that creates the impression of clarity and decisive action, while in truth there is none whatsoever; much loved by politicians, but also true of shyster chief executives.

Nailing a jelly to the wall, trying to: 1. Attempting an impossible task. 2. Using jelly to do something for which it was not intended; trying to use tools that will never do the job, however insane the job is; hammering away with an inappropriate approach, too dim to realize that pausing for reflection could be more productive. *(see Banana, stabbing a seal with a; Grasping at fog)*

Name and shame: 1. Find the culprit and let everybody know who they are. 2. Realize it's actually your fault, and then frantically generate a trumped-up case to incriminate someone else. *(see Backlash; Back stabbing; Blame culture; Front stabbing; Witch-hunt)*

Nationwide: 1. All over the country. 2. London plus a bit, but we couldn't afford anything else and we don't want to be accused of being southern softies. *(see Pan-global; -European)*

Natural order of things, don't upset the: 1. Don't do anything disruptive. 2. I love the status quo because it means I am in charge, so don't change a thing or you'll be fired. *(see Apple cart, don't upset the)*

Navel gazing: 1. Looking distractedly at one's belly button; being overly introspective. 2. Obsessively inward-looking; blindly hell-bent on one's own category, as in narrow-minded recruitment ads that demand previous experience of the sector, without realizing this will simply perpetuate the current stasis. *(see Black swan; Forward-looking; Futureproof; Go round the houses; Natural order of things, don't upset the; Planning; Research)*

Nearshore (vb): 1. Sourcing services from a country near your own, but not your own. 2. Nasty new take on outsourcing – still making full use of cheaper labour elsewhere, but somehow suggesting it's all a bit more friendly. *(see Offshoring; Right shoring)*

Neck of the woods: 1. A particular part of the woods, and certainly nothing to do with the neck. 2. Arcane and highly specific area that you are not supposed to know about, usually shrouded in cringeworthy jargon in order to obfuscate. *(see Jargon; Need to know; Obfuscation)*

Need to know basis: 1. Literal meaning: you or I need to know something. 2. We are treating this on a 'need to know' basis, and you don't need to know because we are covering up something very nasty indeed. *(see Access to information)*

Needle, moving the: 1. Making something happen; going faster than before. 2. Full-throttle, balls-to-wall, cock-of-roost, unadulterated machismo; this expression has everything that testosterone-fuelled sales directors require, including suggestions of fighter pilots, racing cars, speed and power; a veritable classic for pumping up the troops, as in: *"We really need to move the needle on this one, guys!" (see Crash and burn; Maxed out: Needle, pushing the; Pushing the envelope; Troops; Wheels coming off)*

Needle, pushing the: 1. Moving at excessive speed; about to explode. 2. An even heavier duty version of moving the needle, in this example it has been pushed as far as it can go, with dangerous consequences; running hot; overheating; about to blow a gasket; massively overdoing it, usually due to hubris or too much coffee; losing it on the chicane; careening perilously close to edge; crashing imminently. *(see Crash and burn; Maxed out; Needle, moving the; Pushing the envelope; Wheels coming off)*

Needs and wants: 1. What someone wants or needs. 2. Fairly mindless distinction between what someone needs and what they want; rather arrogant assumption that you know better, as in: *"Aha – that's what they say they want, but is it what they really need?"*; lazy and condescending catchall phrase to describe hypothetical mood of a target audience, much loved by so-called 'brand strategists', as in: *"Now Michael, let's drill down into the sub-segments to look in detail at their needs and wants." (see Brand strategist; Drill down; Hearts and minds, winning; Know it when I see it, I don't know what I want but I'll ___; Open-ended)*

Negative growth, profit: 1. No profit or growth; decline in same. 2. Egregious weasel phrase for attempting to disguise backward motion, significant failure or outright loss; abject inability to use plain language; hubristic assumption that no one else is smart enough to spot the pathetic attempt at a cover-up. *(see Dead cat bounce; Downsize; Entering a new plateau; Flatline; Massage the numbers; Quantitative easing; SNAFU; Worklessness)*

Negative momentum: 1. Stasis. 2. No movement at all; dead in the water; possibly even going backwards; a classic case of deceptively attaching an unfavourable modifier to an otherwise positive word in order to suggest that all is well, when it patently isn't. *(see Negative growth, profit; Nought percent)*

Nero syndrome: 1. Failure to acknowledge the unpleasant truth, named after the Roman emperor who played the fiddle while watching Rome burn. 2. Ego-driven refusal to face the facts; head-in-sand attitude to bad news; Enron-like denial; outright lying; blinkered obduracy, much evidenced by sales director who simply will not accept that it's all going wrong. *(see Coffee, wake up and smell the; Dick-swinging; Empire building; Wheels coming off)*

Nested choice cascades: 1. Steps of a strategic programme viewed at different levels, such as corporate, strategic group and individual business levels. 2. Utter bollocks invented by a top executive that shall not be named here.

Net net: 1. Remaining after everything is considered; conclusive. 2. Truly exasperating six letters in which three are quite obviously redundant; phrase much loved by pompous management consultants, as in: *"Of course, net net this will go gangbusters at the end of the day."*; flip line usually delivered after a long and drawn out debate, while leaning back in one's chair and assuming the air of a business sage; confirmatory flourish offered by finance people after intense scrutiny from a colleague who doesn't trust the numbers, as in: *"Yes Colin, net net, when all is considered, that is indeed the margin."* *(see At the end of the day; Gangbusters, it's going; Net out)*

Net out: 1. Conclude; arrive; decide. 2. Variation on 'net net', morphed into an active verb, as in: *"Where do you net out on this one Luke?"*; mealy-mouthed alternative for asking or telling someone straight, perhaps along the lines of: *"What do you think?"* *(see Net net)*

Network: 1. Make social or business connection with people; series of online connections. 2. Overused word for meeting lots of people, often for exploitative purposes, but without admitting as such; similarly overused in an online context, as in: *"Mary has a network to die for – she has 2,000 LinkedIn connections, 10,000 followers on Twitter and a highly popular blog."*

Next-generation: 1. New. 2. Silly word-pairing that does little to inform; curious idea that business ideas or products give birth to the 'next generation' in the way that humans and animals do; hints of evolution and Darwinism; suggestion that the latest product is *de facto* better than the one before – a notion not supported by history. *(see Bleeding edge; Cutting edge; Leading edge; Pioneering)*

Next level, take it to the: 1. Improve; make better; up the ante. 2. Crass piece of machismo perpetrated mainly by males who have spent far too long playing computer games; suggestion that increasing effort or productivity in business is something like playing *Tomb Raider*; weird idea that business has 'levels' at all; euphemism for pulling one's finger out, as in: *"We really need to take this to the next level, Steve."*

NFI: 1. Not f**king invited. 2. Petulant acronym that works in two distinct directions – with reference to a colleague or contact who is childishly excluded from a meeting for some tit-for-tat reason, or an equally immature perspective from someone who desperately wants to be involved but has deliberately been left out. *(see TLA)*

Niche, carve out a, market ___: 1. Find a gap in the market; relating to or aimed at a small specialized group. 2. Tired way of describing who is likely to buy your product or service; use of 'niche' to suggest premium; use of niche to suggest significantly big; general confusion all around with regard to how large a niche actually is; occasional suggestion that many niches can be linked together to create something altogether bigger and, therefore, presumably mass market; as such, not niche at all. *(see Across the board, right; Contiguous niches; Coterminous; Long tail, the)*

Nightmare, utter: 1. Terrifying or deeply distressing dream. 2. Something going badly wrong in waking hours; meltdown; chronic failure of everything that matters; career-threatening development. *(see Crash and burn; Ongoing; Wheels coming off)*

Nip in the bud: 1. Check or destroy the growth of. 2. Chop off at the knees; head off at the pass; stop forthwith; cease; desist; prevent from developing; identify as dangerous and take immediate and evasive action; intervene early, as in: *"I think we need to nip this one in the bud, Jeremy."* *(see Head off at the pass; Rabbit, cutting the legs off the ___ to fit it in the hutch; Roots, take the plant up by the)*

No-brainer: 1. Decision that is a foregone conclusion; requiring no thought. 2. Decision that probably does require more thought; hasty default for small-minded executives who may indeed have no brain; impetuous decision, often regretted later, as in: *"It's a no-brainer, guys!"*, followed by spectacular failure of product or service.

Non-core: 1. Not related to the main point; irrelevant. 2. Superfluous piffle; all the stuff that people and companies do all day when really they shouldn't be; displacement tactics; prevarication; nothing to do with the main point; peripheral in the extreme; marginal; fundamentally off brief; absolutely not the crucial issue; chairman's speech. *(see Core; Knitting, stick to the; NPD; Principle, core)*

Non-exec: 1. Non-executive director. 2. Old bloke who used to work in the industry and is fairly out of touch; primary duties include swanning into quarterly meetings, failing to grasp the working reality, dispensing a few *bon mots*, failing to write anything down, then buggering off, leaving the business in precisely the same position it was in beforehand. *(see Consigliere; Consultant)*

Non-hierarchical: 1. Everyone on the same level; not prone to issuing orders or pulling rank. 2. Deceptive modern concept to describe ultra-hip new ways of working, much loved by executives favouring a 'casual' working environment; excuse to wear relaxed office attire badly; contradictory management style suggesting involvement of staff opinion, only to overrule it comprehensively when it doesn't tally with the views of the board; faux-consultative stance, as in: *"We're all partners in this, Gordon – it's totally non-hierarchical"*, followed by an autocratic and unilateral decision. *(see Dotted line; Hierarchy; Matrix; Organogram; Pecking order; Pull rank)*

Non-issue: 1. It's not an issue. 2. Weasel reverse negative way of dismissing something, especially when used as a noun, as in: *"With respect Steve, that's a non-issue." (see Issue, key; Issues, I have _____ with that; Non-core)*

Non-judgmental: 1. Not inclined to take a view on other people. 2. Very inclined to take a view on other people; insidious criticism; constantly sniping; convinced that the other person isn't as good as you; nitpicking, as in: *"I'm non-judgmental, Adrian, but this work is substandard." (see Micromanaging)*

Non-verbal: 1. Not using words. 2. Truly baffling phrase usually married with communication, as in: *"His non-verbal communication skills are sub-optimal."*; bizarre idea that non-verbal communication is indeed a possibility in the world, sign language excluded; failure to acknowledge that both speech and writing include verbs; source of general confusion, as in: *"He came into my office and congratulated me verbally." (see Communication, lack of; Sub-optimal; Talking out loud)*

No-quibble guarantee: 1. Customer protection charter with no loopholes. 2. Lengthy treatise purporting to provide same, but with no intention of doing so; significant latitude in which to wriggle out of paying refund or compensation; document the length of *War and Peace*, riddled with ambiguity and room for manoeuvre; chapter and verse full of escape clauses; comprehensive attempt to abdicate or avoid responsibility of any kind. *(see Chapter and verse)*

None and f**k all, there are two chances of that happening: 1. It'll never happen. 2. Profane way of appearing to offer two possibilities, when in fact there is only one likely outcome; the idea is a dead loss, and we might as well acknowledge it now.

No stone unturned: 1. Every rock now facing upward; nothing left uninvestigated. 2. Phrase much loved by politicians and business people desperate to suggest that their efforts will be comprehensive; most commonly used when things have gone spectacularly wrong and someone has been rumbled, as in: *"Our investigation will leave no stone unturned."* *(see Drains up, have the; Flush out; Lift up a rock; Root-and-branch review; Witch-hunt)*

Nought percent: 1. Nothing. 2. Outrageous attempt to imply quantity where there is none at all; spurious introduction of percentage element when everyone knows that nought percent of nothing is nothing; often used to forge a desperate connection with growth, as in: *"Growth will be nought percent next year."*

NPD: 1. New product development. 2. All-embracing descriptor for people fiddling about aimlessly; last bastion of fruitless brainstorming sessions; increasingly frantic attempt to generate more sales when all existing products have stalled. *(see Brainstorm; Non-core)*

Nuclear, go: 1. Adopt fission-based energy approach. 2. Explode in a fit of rage; lose it completely; bawl out colleague; fail to see the funny side of things; defenestrate pot plant, or employee. *(see AWOL, go: Ballistic, go; Defenestrate, defenestration; Midlife crisis; Moon, barking at the, over the, through the; Plot, lose the; Postal, go; Radar, off; Rails, gone off the)*

Number, do a ___ on: 1. Convince someone of your point of view. 2. Do up like a kipper; stitch up; prevail over; lean on; bully; overwhelm; send the boys in; beat up.

Numbers, the: 1. Statistics. 2. Any spreadsheet with figures on it; entire set of company accounts; profit and loss estimate; annual budget. *(see Cook the books; Crunch the numbers; Fiscal juggling; Massage the numbers)*

Nut, sledgehammer to crack a: 1. Excessive power for the job in hand. 2. Completely over the top; machismo gone mad; testosterone flowing over; totally unnecessary resources for the task; overkill; too much firepower; display of force. *(see Bazooka after a fly, we're not going to send a; Feet, to dive in with both)*

Nutcracker: 1. Implement used to break open nuts. 2. Vicious female boss determined to 'crack nuts'; verbal cousin of, but completely unrelated to, the Nutcracker Suite; neither suite nor sweet, in fact, downright bitter. *(see Ballbreaker; Gynocracy; Rottweiler)*

Obfuscation: 1. Deliberately making something obscure or difficult to understand. 2. An egregious lie or cover-up; frantic fudging of the truth to disguise incompetence or outright crime. *(see Access to information; Bollocks, talking; Broad brush; Bullshit; Keep it dark; Hedge our bets; Mum, keep; Off the top of my head; Prevaricate; Talking out loud; Techno-babble; Waffle; Word dump)*

Object, defeating the: 1. Having the opposite of the desired effect; negating what you set out to do. 2. Suicidal act of self-destruction; woeful ability to set out to do one thing, and then immediately do the other. *(see Foot, shoot oneself in the; Platform, eat one's own)*

Objectives: 1. Things you want to do. 2. Appalling ragbag of poorly thought-through stuff, usually cut and paste without thought into a so-called brief and handed to someone else to unravel. *(see Aims; BHAG; Buck, pass the; Target, hit the___, miss the point, miss the ___left, right and centre, moving)*

Obvious, a firm grasp of the: 1. Ability to understand something quite simple. 2. Utterly thick, as in: *"Simon has a firm grasp of the obvious,"* usually meaning that he doesn't, or that it's the only thing he will ever grasp. *(see Bandwidth, he doesn't have the; Input, inputs; Insights; Intelligent, if you were any less ___, I'd have to water you once a day; Mental furniture; Psychic RAM; Shilling, not the full)*

OCD: 1. Abbreviation for obsessive-compulsive disorder, an anxiety disorder in which patients are driven to repeat the same act over and over again. 2. Business as usual for businesspeople lacking enterprise and woefully short on ideas and initiative; overused acronym to describe any colleague who is prone to repeat themselves regularly, either in word or action; rat in a trap, pacing around repeatedly; hamster on a wheel *(see Again; As I say; Hamster is dead, the wheel is turning but the ___)*

Office, the: 1. A place of work. 2. A place that in truth performs a social function, where hungover employees gather to discuss football results and *Coronation Street*. *(see Water cooler conversation)*

Office bike: 1. Environmentally-friendly mode of transport thoughtfully provided by one's employer. 2. Emma from accounts who will shag anyone for a small Martini. *(see Office party; Soft area)*

Office party: 1. Grand annual celebration of the year's achievements, including a triumphant speech by the chairman. 2. Rampant bacchanalian orgy at which everyone calls their boss an arsehole, tries it on with Emma from accounts (regardless of whether they are male or female), and throws up on the way home, usually in some form of public transport. *(see Autopilot; Chairman; Christmas party; Compatible, not; Go the whole hog; Office bike; Snakepit)*

Office politics: 1. Rational discourse between colleagues concerning the relative merits of the country's politicians. 2. Naked posturing and allocation of blame. *(see Back stabbing; Blame culture; Front stabbing)*

Offline, take it: 1. Something not done online. 2. I refuse to discuss this now because I can't think of a decent response on the spot, so I am resorting to the first awful Americanism I can think of to buy some time. *(see Clicks and mortar; Obfuscation; Ringfence)*

Off message: 1. Saying the incorrect thing, or not what was originally intended. 2. Saying what you really mean, despite clear instructions from the boss to toe the party line, usually resulting in dismissal. *(see Decruit; Dejob; Off-piste; On message; Realignment)*

Off-piste: 1. Relating to skiing on virgin snow outside the regular runs. 2. Horribly off brief; out of line; touting unauthorized view; a liability. *(see Across the piste; Ducks in a row, get our; Hymn sheet, singing from the same; Loose cannon; Off message; Realignment; Wildebeest in a row, has the lion got his)*

Off ramps: 1. Gone wrong. 2. Bizarre automotive analogy suggestive of a daredevil attempt or circus act; notion that something was going up a ramp, and has now fallen off. *(see On-rails experience; On ramps; Wheels coming off)*

Offshoring: 1. Moving the generation or purchase of goods and services to another country. 2. Getting everything done much more cheaply than at home, and avoiding tax in the process. *(see Right shoring)*

Off-site: 1. A meeting happening somewhere other than the office. 2. Usually unsuccessful effort to change the mood by leaving the stifling environment of the office; posh hotel hired in vain attempt to lift morale; golf venue favoured by chairman; opportunity to wear disastrous 'casual' clothes in front of colleagues; location of horrendous piss-up in hotel bar, leading to a series of indiscretions; Room 27, scene of Malcolm being caught *in flagrante delicto* with Sylvia from HR; origin of a series of staff dismissals. *(see Autopilot; Awayday; Bad idea, there's no such thing as a; Brainstorm; Executive retreat; Flip chart; Workshop)*

Off the scale: 1. Much better, or possibly much worse, than anticipated. 2. I have no language at all to describe what I am witnessing; unprecedented; unexpected; beyond all current experience. *(see Killer whale; Whaling)*

Off the top of my head: 1. Something has just fallen from my cranium, such as a hat, or my wig. 2. I haven't a clue what I'm talking about, so I'll just spout any twaddle I can think of and hope that nobody notices because they are all doing the same thing. *(see Bullshit; Talking out loud; Waffle; Word dump)*

Olderpreneurs: 1. Entrepreneurs that are getting on a bit. 2. Asinine and ageist notion that only young people can have a decent idea. *(see Entrepreneur; Intrapreneur; Inventrepreneur; Wantrepreneur)*

Omnishambles: 1. Cockup on all fronts, originally from Armando Iannucci's TV series *The Thick of It*; word migrated into mainstream government to ridicule persistent inconsistencies in policies and taxes. 2. Ragbag of misguided notions and poor execution; random set of initiatives with no coherence and crap delivery.

On a roll: 1. In a good flow of work; so excited that I just can't stop. 2. I am in the staff canteen and I truly have just sat on a cheese roll.

Onboarding: 1. Getting someone on board. 2. Nasty expression for explaining to a new recruit what on earth their job involves, by which time it is usually too late to decline.

Ongoing: 1. Happening now. 2. An appalling saga that simply won't end; endless nightmare; incapable of finishing a project or meeting due to lack of skill or decisiveness. *(see Meetings; Nightmare, utter)*

On message: 1. Saying the correct thing, or what was originally intended. 2. Parroting the company line by rote, while simultaneously failing to say what you really mean. *(see Off message; Yes man)*

On-rails experience: 1. Interface on a mobile device that is easy to use in a clear and linear way. 2. Piece of utter gobbledegook from the online world, spouted by self-appointed digital natives; curious train-based notion somehow likening the orientation of rolling stock with fiddling about with a mobile phone; as close as it comes to defying definition. *(see Digital native; Free-roaming experience; Off ramps; On ramps; User experience)*

On ramps: 1. Going according to plan. 2. Still on a ramp, as originally initiated, for reasons unknown. *(see Off ramps; On-rails experience; Wheels coming off)*

One fell swoop, in: 1. Done in a single action. 2. Hastily; rashly; in a Draconian fashion, often referring to the sacking of large swathes of the work force. *(see At a stroke; Dejob)*

One-stop shop: 1. Venue where you can buy everything you want in one place. 2. Rather glib phrase now in common parlance when companies are trying to suggest that they can cater for your every need; flagrant attempt to hoover up as much income as possible for the least amount of effort; thinly-veiled effort to have just one place of work, thus saving on any other premises; pretence at jack-of-all-trades capability, where usually none exists.

One-to-many: 1. One person or company addressing many people. 2. Dreadful bastard son of 'one-to-one'; needless distinction between an individual and their likelihood of communicating with more than one person; unhelpful jargon often found in communications briefs, as in: *"This is essentially a one-to-many communications challenge."* *(see B2B; B2C; One-to-one)*

One-to-one: 1. In person, two people talking to each other. 2. Quite baffling expression of two people having a conversation, as though that were a complicated concept to grasp; reinvented as a 'one-to-one', presumably in the hope that the re-expression clarifies the numbers involved, for those of us too dim to understand. *(see B2B; B2C; Cherry pick; Face time; Face-to-face; Heads up; Interface)*

One-upmanship: 1. The art of achieving advantage over others, often by slightly unscrupulous means. 2. Naked ambition; legerdemain; sleight of hand; deviousness; preparedness to throw all colleagues to the lions in order to advance one's own position; complete lack of morals; selfishness; desire to win at all costs; propensity to gloat uncontrollably when winning or getting one's own way; smugness.

Ooh and aah: 1. Make ecstatic noises about something. 2. Thoroughly improbable notion that anything in business will be sufficiently amazing as to illicit the response ooh! or aah!; fanciful overclaim, as in: *"Let me send you Melanie's CV so that you can ooh and aah over experience."* (see FMF; Wow factor)

OOO: 1. Out of office. 2. Automatic email response meaning: *"I'm not here"*; thinly-veiled euphemism for still being in a restaurant, or having buggered off to the pub. *(see WFH)*

Open: 1. Receptive to new ideas; unprejudiced. 2. Part of a modern suite of words aimed at conveying transparency, particularly in matters of finance; suggestion that the business is not 'closed' or secretive, when it usually is; up for grabs; up for anything; relaxed about revealing inner workings, as in: *"We are open to suggestions,"* aka we have no ideas at all so do please come up with something. *(see Open door policy; Openness; Transparency)*

Open door policy: 1. You can drop by any time; we have removed all the doors from the office. 2. Phrase much loved by touchy-feely bosses, as in: *"Come and see me with your issues any time, Justin – I operate an open door policy."*; closed door policy in which any attempt to 'drop by' unannounced will be met with fierce resistance from a Rottweiler of a personal assistant; comprehensive blocking out of the diary; perpetual unavailability on account of 'being in a meeting' all the time. *(see Open; Openness; Meetings; Rottweiler; Touchy-feely; Transparency)*

Open-ended: 1. Without definite limits. 2. Infinite; truly never-ending; disastrously over-running; something urgently requiring clarity, as in: *"Of course this is an open-ended brief, Ralph."*; hopelessly unclear; beyond vague; near-impossible to get a handle on. *(see Know it when I see it, I don't know what I want but I'll ___; Needs and wants)*

Open-heart surgery, it's not: 1. This is nothing to do with surgical repair of the heart; it's not very complicated. 2. Rather dismissive way of saying that something is dead easy, when it may or may not be; used in a variety of circumstances, but most commonly when a frustrated but poorly-informed senior executive is trying to get some forward motion on a project; invariably followed by the embarrassing realization that the task is indeed quite complicated, albeit probably not as much as open-heart surgery. *(see Brain surgery, it's not; Real teeth, our campaign needs to have ____; Rocket science, it's not)*

Openness: 1. Propensity to be open. 2. Susceptibility to outside influence; open-mindedness; pretence at having these qualities, but with no intention of doing anything other than what you wanted in the first place – a trait common in chief executives. *(see Open; Open door policy; Transparency)*

Opportunity: 1. Chance to do something. 2. Complete rebranding of the word 'problem', probably borrowed from a quote attributed to the author Dorye Roettger: *"There are no problems – only opportunities to be creative." (see Ask, big; Challenges; Poisoned chalice; SWOT analysis)*

Optimal: 1. Another word for optimum; the best possible result, even if it involves compromise. 2. Interesting word that effectively tries to make the most of a bad job by adding an optimistic feel to a state of affairs that usually isn't; the best we can do, all things considered; not really optimal at all – more of a fudge; cracks papered over; not that good; distinctly average; whatever we could knock up in the time; patchy. *(see Bugs, iron out the; Crafting, it needs a bit of; Drawing board, back to the; Satisficing; Sub-optimal)*

Optimize: 1. Take full advantage of; make better; be as efficient as possible. 2. Exploit to the full; squeeze every last drop out of; frantically try to improve; bring up to scratch, if that's possible; scrabble to meet basic entry criteria. *(see –ize; Optimal; Sub-optimal)*

Optionality: 1. State of affairs allowing for options. 2. Euphemism for avoiding decisions, as in: *"Let's keep some optionality in the proposal at this stage." (see Options, explore the)*

Options, explore the: 1. Consider all the possibilities. 2. Look urgently for an alternative, as in: *"F**king hell, is this all we've got?!"*; mildly pejorative suggestion that colleague has not really done their homework properly, as in: *"I seriously think we need to explore all the options, Bernard."*; hastily search for other possibilities; panic; generate a head of steam, be all in a fluster.

-oriented: 1. Suffix meaning designed for, directed towards, motivated by, or concerned with. 2. Trying to suggest direction or some sort of centre of gravity where usually there is none; a close cousin of –centred and –centric; almost invariably redundant and should probably be stripped out of every document or presentation in which it appears. *(see -centred, -centric; -driven; -focused, people-, goal-; Goal-oriented)*

Orchestra model: 1. System in which the boss sets direction and an expert team get on with executing it. 2. Polar opposite of what happens in most companies, due to (a) a boss who is incapable of setting a clear direction and leaving the staff alone or (b) insufficiently skilled staff. *(see Conductor's baton, wave the; Pull out all the stops)*

Organogram: 1. Variously spelt organigram or orgnagram, a diagram of how a company is organized. 2. Impenetrable tangle of reporting lines signifying bugger all; wiring diagram gone haywire; snake's honeymoon; horribly misleading latticework of interrelationships designed to make everyone think they are more senior than everyone else; originator of the dreaded dotted line – source of tremendous confusion and tension, as in: *"I am very much my own man, but I have a dotted line in to Brian." (see Dotted line; Hierarchy; Matrix; Non-hierarchical; Pecking order; Pull rank; Snake's honeymoon; Viper's nest)*

Out, I want him/her: 1. I want them fired. 2. I have no particular reason but they have to go; my ego has got the better of me and I feel threatened; he/she appears more competent than me and I can't have that; get them out, before I'm exposed; call HR immediately and trump up some justification for getting them out. *(see Marching orders, get your)*

Out of office message: 1. Automatically generated email response pointing out that the intended recipient is not there. 2. Brilliant smokescreen for being present when one is patently not; frequently abbreviated to OOO, which adds a frisson of emotion to matters; often accompanied by a throwaway line such as: *"In my absence do contact Gay or Rebecca on extension 3875." (see Hospital pass)*

Outcomes, negative, positive: 1. Things that happen as a result of something else, for better or worse. 2. Thoroughly unexpected developments; unforeseen consequences; stuff you really never meant to happen; dreadful fallout; wishy-washy list at the end of brainstorm suggesting what really should happen, when none of the attendees has the slightest inclination to do any of them. *(see Action, actioned, actioning; Bandwagon, jumping on the negative ___, positive ___; Brainstorm; Outputs: Success, what does ___ look like?)*

Outputs: 1. Things that happen, usually as a result of some inputs. 2. Flabby plural noun to denote something that needs to be done; even worse as a verb, as in: *"Can you output this one please, Marjorie?"*; huge checklist of trivia, none of which has any bearing on the main point; mad ramblings of boss converted into irrelevant action. *(see Action, actioned, actioning; Delivery of outputs; Input, inputs)*

Outsmart: 1. Outwit rival using intellect. 2. Outwit rival using nefarious means, cheating, deception, rank, forces of darkness or pure violence.

Outsourcing: 1. Process of buying in services rather than conducting them in the company; literally, sourcing from outside. 2. Smokescreen for screwing supplier costs and charging a higher mark-up without doing any of the work; excuse to reduce own workforce significantly, reducing the original company to a soulless administrative shell.

Out there: 1. Somewhere away from here, such as outside this building, town, or country. 2. Consummate piece of bullshit added to any sentence to create spurious impression of scale, as in: *"There are lots of opportunities out there, Paul."*; invariably used without any thought as to where 'there' is; general impression that 'there' is vast, scary, intrepid, somehow pioneering or dangerous; nebulous and fictitious catch-all for a place that no one can ever define; in short, total bollocks. *(see Environment, business, challenging; Jungle, it's a ___out there; Space)*

Over a barrel: 1. In a compromising position; powerless. 2. Completely boxed into a corner; nowhere to run or hide; uncomfortably exposed; caged; with no choice at all; damned if you do, damned if you don't; a daily occurrence in most job descriptions. *(see Cocks on the block)*

Over and above: 1. Over, or above, or both, or perhaps more than needed. 2. Needless tautology stressing that something has been delivered beyond what was strictly necessary, as in: *"Gordon has produced a result over and above expectations."* *(see Above and beyond; Team, take one for the)*

Overarching: 1. Forming an arch over; all-encompassing. 2. Perfectly reasonable word in the right context, as in when something is genuinely forming an arch over something else; more commonly used by self-appointed 'brand strategists' to create some sort of tangible basis for an ethereal concept. *(see Architecture, brand___, business___; Brand strategist; Foundations, lay the, firm, shaky; Umbrella)*

Overview: 1. A general survey. 2. Monumentally vague sweeping statement or eye-wateringly-long report that concludes nothing at all. *(see Closer look, stand back and take a)*

Ownership, take ___of: 1. Take responsibility for. 2. Shirk; duck the issue; delegate immediately; claim credit if it goes right; hide if it goes wrong; pretend to add to list of tasks and ignore completely; use as fodder to impress boss and then shove in a drawer; bury; stifle at birth; add to status report and then go to the pub.

Own goal, spectacular: 1. High profile scoring of goal for the opposition. 2. Blatantly counterproductive move; demonstration of gross incompetence; public display of stupidity, usually born out of hubris or pride. *(see Foot, shoot oneself in the; Hoist with one's own petard; Mountain to climb; Platform, eat one's own; Shafted down the river, yourself; Tent, standing outside the ___ pissing in)*

Ps and Qs, mind your: 1. Be careful to behave properly or use the correct language. 2. Say nothing that will incriminate you; say nothing for fear of revealing incompetence or indolence. *(see Gloss over; Keep it dark; Mum, keep)*

Pacesetter: 1. The frontrunner who sets the pace. 2. Foolhardy first mover in any market. *(see Kamikaze; First mover advantage)*

Package: 1. Parcel or box with something in it. 2. Hotchpotch of ill-conceived ideas hastily lashed together to create the semblance of coherence. *(see Raft of ideas, proposals, respondents; Nationwide; World class)*

Pan-global, -European: 1. Across the world, or Europe. 2. Dick-swinging overclaim designed to make a project or company seem bigger than it really is; test market in Tyne Tees hyped beyond all reasonable levels of expectation. *(see Across the board, right; APAC; EMEA; Nationwide; World class)*

Panjandrum: 1. A pompous self-important official. 2. Utter twat who delights in reciting the company policy on anything, while failing to lift a finger to help on the grounds that it's *"more than my job's worth, mate"*. *(see Administrivia; Bread and butter; Bureaucracy; Compliance; Manager; Process; Target manager; Timesheets; Vis-à-vis)*

Pants down, caught with our: 1. Caught on the hop. 2. Caught *in flagrante delicto* with Julia from HR, or Gary from the post room. *(see Drop our trousers)*

Pants, fly by the seat of our: 1. Make it up as we go along. 2. Business as usual. *(see Adhocracy; Gut feel; Must, this is a; SNAFU)*

Paper cup, here's a ___, there's a tidal wave coming: 1. Something very nasty is on its way, and here is something quite inadequate to help you deal with it. 2. Classic approach to hanging an individual out to dry, much loved by sweaty sales directors from the 'school of hard knocks'; implication that torture is somehow character building; woeful under-equipping of staff for scale of task in hand; line often delivered with a knowing wink and a patronizing arm round the shoulder, as though it's a favour; apparent rite of passage, as in: *"There's a tidal wave coming, David – here's a paper cup, I'm sure you'll cope."* (see Eastern front, this is like the ___when the bullets didn't turn up; Head office, I'm from ___ and I'm here to help; Multitasking; Multiskill; Titanic, rearranging the deckchairs on the)

Papering over the cracks: 1. Patching up a bad job. 2. Business as usual. *(see Pants, fly by the seat of our; Turd, polishing a)*

Paradigm shift: 1. Radical change in beliefs or theory, coined by US science philosopher T S Kuhn (1922-1996). 2. Precisely the same old shit we've always done; no real change at all; minor difference pathetically trumpeted as a brave new dawn. *(see Sea change; Step change)*

Parapet, heads above the, keep our head below the: 1. Take responsibility for something, or don't. 2. Pathetic and entirely inaccurate military analogy that fails miserably to convey the insignificance of almost any business action – above or below, it makes no difference whatsoever. *(see High profile; Stand up and be counted; Trenches, in the)*

Park it: 1. Manoeuvre a vehicle into a stationary position. 2. Shut up; say nothing; bury that toxic bit of information immediately in case we're found out. *(see FIMO; Offline, take it; Ring fence; STFU; SUMO)*

Participation: 1. Joining in. 2. Frequently meaning the opposite; exclusion; being kept in the dark; cover-up for not involving someone, as in: *"Make sure we have Gordon's participation on Project Peabrain, Dorothy.";* cynical scheme to overload someone's in-tray by insisting on their 'participation' in every single project you can think of; cause colleague to collapse due to over-participation. *(see Maxed out)*

Partners: 1. Allies; companions. 2. Desperate and rarely successful attempt by suppliers to command an equal footing with their customers; often wrapped up in the soft language of bonding, as in: *"We are delighted to be strategic partners,"* when in fact the company receives a daily whipping and simply does what it's told. *(see Bonding, team; Proactive; Reactive; Strategic alliance; 60:50 relationship, this is the perfect)*

Party, bring to the: 1. Contribute. 2. Oddly childish idea based on kinder-garten tradition of always bringing a balloon or present to a birthday cel-ebration; shades of whoopee cushions, streamers, and paper hats; possi-ble requirement to attend meeting with cake for all, as in: *"If we're going to involve Sharon in Project Wetwipe, I want to know exactly what she's going to bring to the party"*; sometimes used in a broader company sense when considering whether to hire someone, as though their appeal would increase if they had an imaginary friend or a puppy.

Pass the baton: 1. Hand something over, such as a project, as in a relay race. 2. Consummately fail to do precisely that; bugger off with no fur-ther comment; leave company, along with a calamitous collection of half-finished projects; nightmare trail of unintelligible paperwork, or none at all; create the illusion of a comprehensive briefing, when it is anything but; mislead; misdirect; provide no direction at all; obfuscate; delegate hastily with no regard for successor. *(see Buck, pass the; Drop the ball; Hospital pass; Obfuscate)*

Passion, passionate: 1. Keen; enthusiastic; ardently affectionate. 2. Ubiq-uitous piece of wibble vainly attempting to verify that the company and its staff will be dedicated, relentlessly supportive, and there at any sec-ond of the day; rather seedy implication that there will be some sort of sexual relations between customer and supplier, as though that would be a benefit; almost invariably overclaim, as in: *"As you can tell, at Babcock Bored and Bandycoot, we are passionate about the ball bearing market."* *(see Always on; Authenticity; Constantly striving; Expectations, exceeding; Mission statement; Sun, the ___ never sets at; 24/7/365; Values)*

Pathologist's interest: 1. Concerned posthumously, as in a post mortem. 2. Macabre reference to forensically raking over a dead project, or pos-sibly colleague (medical profession only); outside chance of a desire to learn and improve matters next time, but more likely a need to gloat and laugh generally at the trail of incompetence that will almost certainly be uncovered; delight in watching a project unravel; voyeur's interest, for the sole purpose of saying: *"I told you so"*. *(see Eastern front, this is like the ___ when the bullets didn't turn up; Forensic, send it down to the boys in; Look, take a long hard; Paper cup, here's a ___, there's a tidal wave coming; Pulse, check the, finger on the; Titanic, rearranging the deckchairs on the; Tits up, it's all gone)*

Pathway: 1. Another word for path; a route to something. 2. Annoyingly used to describe almost any experience or interaction between an orga-nization and a customer; suggestion of direction and progress, where usually there is none; clichéd fallback position for executives desperately trying to explain a catastrophic collapse in service, as in: *"We have iden-tified some pinch points in the customer pathway and are applying key learnings to rectify them." (see Customer experience, journey; Learnings)*

Paving the way: 1. Laying down flagstones to make the route easier; smoothing the passage of something. 2. Greasing the wheels; putting in the spadework; trying to make something a foregone conclusion; mak-ing all the decisions before the meeting even happens, as is common practice in Japan, thereby derailing all insignificant (and oblivious) col-leagues. *(see Done deal)*

Pay through the nose: 1. Pay an exorbitant price. 2. Significantly overpay, or fleece a client into doing so; much loved practice of companies peddling so-called 'premium' brands, aka cheap tat dressed up as expensive and flogged to reach undiscerning show-offs who don't know any better; phrase often associated with self-obsessed chief executives who think nothing of shelling out inordinate amounts on acquiring another company to boost the value of their shares, as in: *"Anthony did the deal but he certainly paid through the nose for it." (see Merger; Money for old rope; Premium)*

PDQ: 1. Pretty damn quick(ly). 2. Ridiculously fast; now, if not sooner; by yes-terday; annoying and rather sanctimonious acronym typically deployed by bosses with one of two unfortunate characteristics – (a) chronic disorgani-zation, as in: *"I've sat on this for weeks and now it's screamingly urgent,"* or (b) a dismal inability to say no, as in: *"I've had an extremely unreasonable request from a client but I haven't got the balls to talk them out of it so you'll have to do it." (see ASAP; Buck, pass the; ETA)*

Pear-shaped, it's all gone: 1. It's gone badly wrong. 2. Fruit-themed analogy of unknown origin, suggesting somewhat that the design of a pear is in some way undesirable, although no one has ever ventured to suggest why that might be; possible allusion to the sagging figure of an older woman (unverified); severity ranges from a mildly derogatory horticultural refer-ence to an expression of extreme dismay, spanning from *"this has gone a bit wrong"* to *"everything's f**ked and I'm being fired this afternoon". (see AWOL, go; Tits up, it's all gone)*

Pecking order: 1. Seniority sequence. 2. Vindictive chain of bullying, drawn from the avian world, but true of almost every tribe, including those con-taining humans; starting from the top, the CEO bollocks the MD, who bollocks the nearest director, who finds a subordinate to blame, who delegates responsibility to the hapless bastard who ultimately gets fired. *(see Dotted line; Hierarchy; Matrix; Non-hierarchical; Organogram; Pull rank; Snake's honeymoon)*

Penetration: 1. The ability or power to penetrate. 2. Seedy, semi-sexual description of the degree to which something has an effect; much loved by those in advertising and media, as in: *"This campaign will deliver 100% penetration of the target audience"* – a remark likely to get most other people thrown into jail.

Penthouse, furnishing the: 1. Doing all the nice stuff before the grunt work is done. 2. Partial architectural reference to the fact that in most companies the board resides on the top floor, well away from the *hoi polloi*; suggestion that senior people always concentrate on the so-called 'big picture' so as to avoid doing any actual work, as in: *"He's busy furnishing the penthouse and we haven't even laid the foundations yet."* (see Foundations, lay the, firm, shaky; Grunt work)

Percent, give a hundred and ten: 1. Deliver, probably overly so. 2. Mathematically impossible twaddle originating from the world of football and now all-pervasive in business, particularly sales; purveyors of this classic appear unaware of how stupid it makes them sound; staple of sweaty, Terylene-suited sales directors at the annual sales conference, as in: *"I need you to give 110% to Project Beanstalk guys!"* – an exhortation usually followed by the playing of motivational music such as Pink Floyd's *Money*, Tina Turner's *Simply the Best*, or *S.U.C.C.E.S.S.* by Holly Johnson.

Performance review: 1. Assessment of capability; meeting to discuss same. 2. Cursory glance at one's achievements and activities, usually poorly informed; meeting with someone who barely knows who you are or what you do, a role often called 'line manager'; annual meeting that is crucial to you but that is postponed at short notice on several occasions and sometimes never happens at all; sham. (see Appraisal, one degree; Appraisal, 360 degree; Line manager)

Permanently reducing prices: 1. Lowering the cost of something all the time. 2. Idiotic marketing claim that is mathematically impossible; ludicrous suggestion that the price will continue to drop even past the point of being free – in other words, they'll have to pay you. (see EDLP)

Permission marketing: 1. Marketing that checks that an individual or company is happy to be marketed to before embarking on it, a phrase coined by author Seth Godin in his book of the same name. 2. Somewhat self-deluding notion that many people love to be 'marketed to'; laudable idea to ask people first, but often wrapped up in deceptive clothes, such as tick boxes, opt-out clauses, and terms and conditions; in certain cases, marketing without consent.

Peter Principle, the: 1. Principle that in a hierarchy every employee tends to rise to his level of incompetence, coined by Peter & Hull in the book of the same name, in 1969. 2. Although the book was a spoof, it sent shock waves through the business world, who realized with horror that it was true; suggestion that all senior people are merely in transit out of the organization, having themselves reached their level of incompetence. *(see 80/20 rule)*

Phablet: 1. An elision of fabulous and tablet. 2. Continuing a long trend in the gadget market for exaggerating technological love and making the PR industry feel reassured about their inability to function without their electronic devices.

Phone list, go down the: 1. Scan list of company employees. 2. Scan list of employees with the express purpose of getting rid of a large quantity of them; hold 'ABC' session in which all employees are graded and all the C grades disposed of; cull; prune; destaff. *(see ABC session; Axe, face the; Decruit; Dejob; Destaff; Headcount: LIFO)*

Picnic, one sandwich short of a: 1. Somewhat light on foodstuff for an outdoor meal. 2. Not very smart; thick; slow off the mark; useless; a hindrance to the team. *(see AWOL, go; Basket case; Box of frogs, mad as a; Bundle, one stick short of a; Gene pool, swimming in the shallow end of the)*

PICNIC: 1. Problem in chair not in computer. 2. Incompetent person when it comes to matters of technology; the opposite of a geek; completely clueless at interfacing with the interweb.

Pie chart: 1. Circular diagram with segments denoting quantities. 2. Widely abused way of presenting information, often offering a car crash of colour, three-dimensional graphics, and hard-to-read appended figures; deliberate way of disguising the fact that the figures are not very good, or not even interesting enough to warrant a chart at all.

Pigeonhole: 1. Small compartment for papers and letters; to classify in a rigid manner. 2. Application of irrational bias, fuelled by a range of misguided emotions including sexism, racism, jealousy and xenophobia; uncanny ability to stereotype everyone to fit one's own world view.

Piggyback: 1. To ride on someone's shoulders; as an addition to something else. 2. Transparent attempt to bundle two things together, such as workload, responsibility or budget; try to get two things for the price of one; gain cover by joining in with something else; engineer potential scapegoat in case it all goes wrong. *(see Air cover; Hook to hang our hat on; Scapegoat, make a ___ out of)*

Pig's ear: 1. Something badly or clumsily done; 2. Botched job; cockup; piss-poor attempt, as in: *"Bloody hell, Kev, you've really made a pig's ear out of this one." (see Cockup)*

Pillowtocracy: 1: A company run by a husband and wife team. 2. A company where all crucial decisions are made in the bedroom, often with disastrous consequences. *(see Gynocracy; Mediocracy)*

Pilot (vb): 1. To guide or steer. 2. Give semblance of direction and then abdicate all responsibility, leaving subordinates high and dry; pseudo aeronautical term to suggest confidence, competence and skill at speed – characteristics perennially lacking in managers from Buenos Aires to Bolton.

Pink champagne, a lot of ___ has flowed under the American Express card since then: 1. It was long ago, since when we have had many expensive lunches. 2. Glib, semi-nostalgic throwaway observed by a phenomenal lush, such as those prevalent in the aristocracy, the arts, advertising, media, and public relations; largely the domain of someone who has never used their own cash to pay for anything their entire life; credit card junkie, and possibly a soak whose best days were in the eighties.

Pitch: 1. Word with over forty different meanings, but most commonly in business, a sales presentation. 2. Pack of lies; elaborate web of fabrication that bears absolutely no relation to the working reality if lucky enough to win the business; farrago of half-truths and empty promises; piffle; hot air; not worth the paper it's written on; fiction.

Pioneering: 1. Exploratory, truly innovative, genuinely new. 2. Overworked adjective to suggest ingenuity, usually applied to thoroughly workaday stuff. *(see Bleeding edge; Cutting edge; Leading edge; Next-generation)*

Pipeline, in the: 1. Coming soon. 2. Wishful thinking; not really ever likely to occur; improbable; included in a status report to add extra bulk, as when cold-calling agencies report back to their clients; not a cat in hell's chance of seeing the light of day; blocked; baulked; grounded; tightly wedged in and never likely to budge. *(see Done deal; Hopper, pour into the; Leaky bucket; In the bag)*

Pivot: 1. Reorient business direction to improve product or income. 2. Embark on a massive U-turn after significantly cocking it up; much-loved so-called entrepreneur's term for changing tack after embarking on a dead duck. *(see Coming or going, he doesn't know if he's; Evolving to meet customer demand; Tweak; U-Turn)*

Planning: 1. Working out how to do something; discipline or department intended to do the same. 2. Interminable phase of navel gazing from which some products, or indeed whole companies, never emerge; extended excuse to do the square root of sod all, and yet remain under the comfortable banner of 'strategy'. *(see Go round the houses; Navel gazing; Research; Strategy, strategize)*

Plate spinning: 1. Fine art of rotating multiple items of crockery on poles, for reasons best known to those doing it. 2. Having far too much on the go at the same time, with any one element likely to crash at any moment; unfeasible balancing act that will inevitably go wrong; accident waiting to happen; imminent crash or collision. *(see Ball juggling; Balls in the air, on the block, to the wall; Crash and burn; Python, wrestling with a)*

Platform, online, sales, user: 1. Base on which to do something, such as offer technology or interact with customers. 2. Increasingly overused word, seemingly applied to everything from railway stations to websites. *(see Burning platform; Platform, eat one's own; Platform, exceed the)*

Platform, eat one's own: 1. Destroy one's own source of business. 2. Rather eccentric idea of eating an inedible thing, in this case probably made of wood or metal; sales platform notion arguably taken a step too far; cannibalistic instinct possibly overapplied, to the point of killing customer base; short-sighted and inadvisable short-term approach to aggressive sales, thereby putting future customers off for life. *(see Bazooka after a fly, we're not going to send a; Foot, shoot oneself in the; Hoist with one's own petard; Kamikaze; Object, defeating the; Own goal, spectacular)*

Platform, exceed the: 1. Topple over; spill over designated boundary. 2. Completely overshoot; run hot; lose the plot; blow it; overdo it comprehensively; overcook; blow a gasket; drop; explode in all directions; fail to control; run amok; overstep brief, with unpleasant consequences. *(see Bazooka after a fly, we're not going to send a; Drop a Ricket; Feet, to dive in with both; Nut, sledgehammer to crack a)*

Play hardball: 1. Act in a ruthless or uncompromising way. 2. Be macho; take no nonsense; make it clear you are the king of the castle; refuse to back down, ever; be quite sure that you are right, always.

Play out of our skins: 1. Do better than we usually do. 2. Pull off quite a surprise; overachieve for once; perform to the most of our potential; a rare state of affairs.

Play the percentages: 1. Bet a little here, a little there. 2. Cover every angle; fail or refuse to commit one way or the other; play one side off against the other; divide and conquer. *(see Hedge our bets)*

Player, big: 1. Tall or corpulent competitor; influential individual. 2. Narcissistic puffball; overpaid CEO with a reputation for failing spectacularly and generating big personal payoffs; someone who hobnobs with celebrities; tax avoider, or quite possibly evader; sometimes used to refer to an entire company that acts in approximately the same way, and is probably the subject of a major court case at any given moment. *(see Big cheese; Chairman; Fromage, grand; Head honcho; Heavy hitter)*

Playing away: 1. Having a meeting at someone else's office; in league with the competition. 2. Indulging in industrial espionage; married, but nevertheless sleeping with Tracy from production.

Playtex strategy: 1. To lift and separate two elements of the plan, named after the bra advertising in the sixties and seventies suggesting the same effect for breasts. 2. Another in the large lexicon of semi-sexist, usually sweaty and greasy, sales directors who haven't been laid for years; a close cousin of 'the car is like a beautiful woman' school of sales, this phrase likens a strategy to mammary glands, but only for tenuous reasons. *(see Collars and cuffs, I bet the ___ don't match; Get into bed with; Kimono, open the; Matching luggage)*

Plot, lose the: 1. Mislay running order for theatrical production. 2. Miss the point entirely; veer off disastrously; go nuts; lose sense of humour as well as job; go loopy, thereby alienating family, spouse and friends. *(see AWOL, go; Ballistic, go; Box of frogs, mad as a; Bundle, one stick short of a; Gene pool, swimming in the shallow end of the; Midlife crisis; Moon, barking at the, over the, through the; Picnic, one sandwich short of a; Postal, go; Pram, to throw one's toys out of the; Radar, off the; Rails, gone off the)*

Plug into: 1. Join up with; interlock. 2. Rather strange, pseudo-electrical phrase hinting at technology and power; equally used with ideas as with people, as in: *"We need to plug that into the proposal tout de suite,"* or: *"We need to plug into Bruce pretty quickly"* – an act that may well lead to imprisonment for sexual deviancy.

Plug-in impact: 1. Immediate effect. 2. Strangely electrical allusion to making a difference; shades of jump starting, or hitting something with a charged current; daft phrase for potential effectiveness of an advertising campaign. *(see Impact, high, low)*

Point, to your: 1. Following on from what you said. 2. Something quite unrelated to what was just said; something that someone was going to say regardless of all previous comment; showboating; droning on. *(see Builds)*

Poisoned chalice: 1. Seemingly attractive drink containing a nasty surprise; apparently good brief that isn't. 2. Semi-medieval or biblical reference referring to ornate goblet purporting to have been used by the messiah and containing an elixir giving eternal life; task presented in glowing terms by boss or colleague when it is nothing of the sort. *(see Ask, big; Bombs, box of; Hospital pass; Minister for fun; Opportunity)*

Portfolio: 1. Art bag; collection of works. 2. Arty word to suggest a breadth of skills or achievements; oeuvre; portmanteau collection of stuff; client list, often falsified or out of date.

Positioning: 1. Position; point of view. 2. Form of words laboured over for months by so-called 'brand strategists'; nitpicking between clusters of generic adjectives; brand maps, onions, pyramids and so on, claiming to 'capture the essence' of a brand. *(see Architecture, brand___, business___; Brand onion, pillars, pyramid, values; Foundations, lay the, firm, shaky; Marketing; Marketing guru; Overarching; Smoke and mirrors job; Value proposition, judgments)*

Postal, go: 1. Flip completely; walk out, never to return. 2. Go off the deep end; go walkabout; believe oneself to be a tree; take unexplained to trip to Bournemouth to feed the seagulls; stare at the sea for weeks; sell all worldly possessions and live in a tent by the A24; refuse to cut nails ever again; start playing the sitar in meetings; reach just inside the door of board meeting and turn the lights on and off repeatedly whilst leering through the glass from outside and going la-la-la; start supporting Stenhousemuir Football Club when living in Aldershot and with no previous connection to the area. *(see Alarm bells, set the ___ ringing; Arse in alligators, up to my; AWOL, go; Ballistic, go; Basket case; Box of frogs, mad as a; Bundle, one stick short of a; Gene pool, swimming in the shallow end of the; Mid-life crisis; Moon, barking at the, over the, through the; Picnic, one sandwich short of a; Plot, lose the; Pram, to throw one's toys out of the; Radar, off; Rails, gone off the; Riot act, read the)*

Potential: 1. What can be achieved. 2. Polite word for all the things an individual could in theory do, but never has; wish list of unfulfilled promise; gap between claimed performance and reality; uncomfortable shortfall between CV and working truth; ethereal chimera that may never be realized; dream. *(see Maximize)*

Pound of flesh: 1. Required amount or contribution. 2. Grizzly butcher-cum-anatomical reference; visions of sausage meat or a slab in a mortuary; macabre idea that cash or effort should yield a dollop of dermis in return, as in: *"I'm going to make sure Dennis gives me his pound of flesh for this one."*

Powder dry, keep one's: 1. Hold some power in reserve; not mention or reveal something yet; musketeer's necessity, otherwise ignition will not occur. 2. Fail to reveal; deliberately conceal; withhold information in order to compromise a colleague; hold back crucial news to gain an advantage; play cards close to chest.

Power breakfast, lunch, nap: 1. Fast and virile approach to eating or sleeping. 2. Daft notion that if you're really important you simply haven't got the time to do anything for long, when in reality you should have been able to delegate everything and, therefore, generate plenty of time for eating or sleeping at length; essential sham based on the assumption that if you are busy you must be important, when the opposite should apply; concept effectively invented by people who rather like food and sleep.

Powwow: 1. Talk, conference or meeting; North American First Nations ceremony. 2. Huddle where people get together and make it look as though they have something important to discuss; covert gathering; intense gossip session in which all company members, except those present, are right royally slagged off; international awayday at which nothing is decided at all, but a lot of golf is played; management meeting at which staff are graded and selected for firing. *(see ABC session; Axe, face the; Destaff; Headcount; LIFO; Phone list, go down the; Water cooler conversation)*

Practical advice: 1. Helpful suggestions that can be applied effectively in reality. 2. Pointless theory that cannot ever be applied; condescending lectures from companies to customers on how to do or not do things that are blatantly obvious, such as: *"This coffee may contain hot water"*, or: *"To open door, turn handle."*; conversely, hugely unhelpful information such as the instructions to build a flat-packed desk; academic's trope, as in: *"Ah yes, it works in practice, but does it work in theory?"* (see Advisorial; FAQs; Hints and tips; Shell-like, a word in your)

Pragmatic: 1. Practical. 2. Unprofessionally expedient, as in: *"I think we're going to need a pragmatic approach on this one, Derek."*; cutting corners, flying in the face of all thoroughness.

Pram, to throw one's toys out of the: 1. Child's propensity to eject entertainment devices from their bespoke transport vehicle. 2. Lose the plot completely (adult); behave extremely immaturely; throw a wobbly; embark on embarrassing paddy in the office; seethe with anger; lick the windows; snap at imaginary flies; climb the walls; reveal what everyone else already knew – that you have the maturity level of a two-year-old. *(see AWOL, go; Ballistic, go; Big match temperament; Box of frogs, mad as a; Bundle, one stick short of a; Gene pool, swimming in the shallow end of the; Mid-life crisis; Moon, barking at the, over the, through the; Picnic, one sandwich short of a; Plot, lose the; Postal, go; Radar, off; Rails, gone off the; Riot act, read the)*

Pre-crastination: 1. Delaying something, even before delaying doing it. 2. Chronic inability to get round to doing something; continually using displacement activity in order to delay something, sometimes forever.

Predictionizing, predictioning: 1. Predicting. 2. Dreadful bastardization of a perfectly good word. *(see –ize)*

Pre-emptive strike: 1. Doing something before someone else does. 2. Smashing someone straight in the face just because you think they might do it to you first, usually leading to dismissal; rushing a product launch out of the door half-cock, based on the paranoid assumption that the competition is about to do the same; criticism of colleague sent to HR immediately before they file the same complaint about you; submission of resignation letter five minutes before a meeting in which you know you are going to be fired. *(see First mover advantage; First past the post; Retaliation, get your ___ in first)*

Pregreening: 1. Creeping forward while waiting for a red light to change. 2. Jumping the gun; running before walking; suicidal rush for glory, always ending in failure. *(see Greenlit; Redlit)*

Prejudice: 1. Opinion already held and now immovable; bias or dislike. 2. Obnoxious quality prevalent in those who think they know it all; narrow-mindedness; views of chairman's wife. *(see Chairman's wife)*

Premium: 1. Worth paying more for than the standard version. 2. Categorically not worth paying more for; a puffed up product with a trumped up margin; cock-and-bull notion invented by greedy companies and corroborated by show off rich people; brash; showy; myth that 'premium' people buy 'premium' products – clearly not true in the case of premium lager. *(see Commoditized; Enhance, enhancement; Gold-plated; High ground, take the moral ___; Money for old rope; Pay through the nose; Prestige)*

Pre-revenue: 1. Not making any money (yet). 2. Self-deluding descriptor used by many a dotcom company when they have had a madcap idea that no one wants to pay for; period of time that can go on for years before they either jack it all in or sell to some over-rich sucker or other.

Pressure, face the, handle the, under severe: 1. State of being pressed, usually uncomfortable. 2. Apparently near-permanent state of affairs for every member of staff; non-physical, purely mental condition, but none-theless very real to those experiencing it; too much going on, coupled with an inability to cope with it all. *(see AWOL, go; Ballistic, go; Box of frogs, mad as a; Bundle, one stick short of a; Gene pool, swimming in the shallow end of the; Mid-life crisis; Moon, barking at the, over the, through the; Picnic, one sandwich short of a; Plot, lose the; Postal, go; Radar, off; Rails, gone off the)*

Prestige: 1. High status achieved through success, influence or wealth. 2. Ability to gloat at everyone else, especially the *hoi polloi*; greasy adjective used to describe so-called premium brands, as in: *"There's no doubting this is a prestige offering, Rupert."* *(see Commoditized; Enhance, enhancement; Gold-plated; High ground, take the moral ___; Money for old rope; Pay through the nose; Premium)*

Pretailing: 1. Selling a small number of products online to test whether there might be demand for a larger number to be made, often allowing a designer to recoup production costs for a limited manufacturing run. 2. Another in the seemingly endless run of elisions in the marketing world; getting someone else to take the financial risk without exposing oneself, as it were.

Prevaricate: 1. Speak or act evasively with intent to deceive. 2. Daily activity at work. *(see Obfuscation)*

Principle, core: 1. Central tenet. 2. Strongly-held belief spouted loudly and then roundly ignored when it comes to the filthy money, as in: *"These are my principles, but if you don't like them I have others."* *(see Core; Non-core)*

Prioritize: 1. Give priority to. 2. Do in any order that springs to mind; verb much loved by people who badly want to convey the impression that they are highly organized, when they almost certainly are not, as in: *"I'll prioritize that immediately, Bernard"*, invariably followed by complete failure to give any priority to the matter at all; euphemism for putting something to the bottom of the pile or ignoring it altogether. *(see –ize)*

Proactive: 1. Tending to initiate rather than react. 2. Omnipresent adjective in advertising and PR agencies, as in: *"We pride ourselves on taking a* *proactive approach"*, as though a passive or reactive one would be more appealing; pretty much redundant word, and a close contender for worst bull of the lot, along with 'going forward'. *(see Going forward; Reactive)*

Problem, I don't have a ___ with that: 1. It's fine by me. 2. Hugely annoying reverse phraseology meaning it's alright as far as I am concerned; laced with a nasty, power-tripping twist, just reminding you that I could have a problem with this if I wanted to, but this time I'm being nice about it. *(see Buy-in; Green light; Greenlit; Issues , I have ___with that; Redlit; Unhappy, I'm not ___ with)*

Problem, not a: 1. That's fine by me. 2. That's not at all fine by me, but I'll trot out the phrase anyway in an attempt to look helpful, without having any intention of solving the issue at all. *(see Problem, I don't have a ___ with that)*

Process: 1. Method for doing something. 2. Whatever we fancy doing today; random assortment of actions that bear little relation to each other; assorted stuff; much loved by people who have no imagination and must, therefore, fall back on 'process'. *(see Adminsitrivia; Bureaucracy; Jobsworth; Panjandrum; Target manager)*

Product: 1. Item produced by a company with a view to selling for a profit. 2. Term bandied around for any old tat that gets produced, including intangible things such as services. *(see Productize)*

Productize: 1. Turn something into a product. 2. Repellent faux verb denoting 'we desperately need to start making money out of this'; process classically involving drawing a diagram that explains in kindergarten fashion how something gets done; most commonly used by frantic executives in industries that never make much money, or none; a stalwart of so-called 'digital natives' who love farting about on the web but can rarely explain how to get paid, citing the old adage that 'information wants to be free'. *(see Democratize; Digital native; –ize; Monetize; Product)*

Productivity: 1. Amount of product generated. 2. Much abused word hinting at, but not necessarily accurately reflecting, the amount of stuff being made or generated; apparent measure of output, albeit eminently capable of being reported in a highly misleading way; sum total of what a business or country does, which may not amount to much in some cases.

Professionalize: 1. Make more professional. 2. Here we go again – another attempt to –ize something, in this case, professionalism; fundamental contradiction, given that amateurs are not professionals, and vice versa;

strong whiff of charade, inasmuch as a company or executive is either professional or they are not – any effort to 'professionalize' probably indicates a cover-up, or at the very least shoddy behaviour up until now. *(see –ize)*

Profile, raise the: 1. Make more noticeable. 2. Make anyone notice at all; much loved clarion call for PR agencies, particularly with crap brands or Z list so-called celebrities. *(see Z list celebrity)*

Projecting: 1. Portraying an image on a wall or screen. 2. Rather disingenuous euphemism for looking forward; pretending to see into the future; flying in the face of all current information and making up fanciful stories about apparently rosy days to come; generating fiction, as in: *"Robert is just projecting the fourth quarter figures for the air freshener market, going forward."*

Project X: 1. Code name for a task. 2. Hilarious notion that giving something a project name will prevent anyone else from finding out what it really is, particularly the competition; superb opportunity to choose a risible name for whatever nonsense one has been asked to work on, as in Project Slug, Wibble, or Hatstand; unintended playground for amusement months later, as in: *"Project Gazelle will take three years."*

Promise, brand, broken: 1. Claim to live up to, or renege on. 2. Trail of disappointments based on a perpetual sequence of bombast and failure; brand promises something and is found wanting – repeat *ad infinitum*. *(see Brand strategist; Foundations, lay the; Guardian, brand ; Guidelines, brand, corporate; Positioning)*

Promotion: 1. Job elevation; price reduction or other incentive to buy. 2. Twice as much work with exactly the same pay; a new posh title with no material effect on job quality or pay; desperate attempt to persuade someone to buy something when all else has failed; vague suggestion of riches to come, as in: *"If you crack this you'll almost certainly be up for promotion, Darren."*

Proof of concept: 1. Verification that the idea will work. 2. More twaddle from our friends the management consultants, as in: *"Before we give this the green light, Nigel, are we sure we have proof of concept?"*; perfectly valid idea of testing something first bastardized into a phrase that makes it sound as though (a) there's a method to achieve it, and (b) the whole thing is as scientific as a rocket launch or finding a cure for cancer. *(see Acid test; Blue touch paper, light the; Purpose, fit for; Success, what does ___ look like?)*

Prosumer: 1. So-called 'professional consumer'. 2. Hideous elision suggesting that consumers are now fully-versed in all professional matters, particularly communications emanating from corporations; idea based on some unfortunate examples of said corporations being thoroughly caught out while trying to hoodwink their customers – now reverentially referred to as 'prosumers'. *(see Masstige)*

Provenance: 1. Proof of authenticity or origin. 2. Cynical rewriting of history, or naked invention of it, to suggest that a brand has 'authenticity'; pack of lies, such as 'forged in the crucible of time', or 'hand-stitched by Aborigines', when in fact the product was made in Runcorn. *(see Authenticity)*

Proximity: 1. Closeness to. 2. Overused word for anything that needs to be shown to be related to something else, such as: *"These product credentials clearly demonstrate the proximity of the two brands, Robert."*

PRP: 1. Performance-related pay; remuneration that goes up, or possibly down, depending on how well things go. 2. Brilliant device invented by procurement departments to pay less for everything; performance criteria are cunningly designed to ensure no bonus is ever payable; even worse, some contracts demand a refund for poor performance, thereby guaranteeing the supplier will make a loss before they even start work.

Psychic RAM: 1. Ability to remember or absorb mental stimuli; combination of random access memory from the world of semiconductor storage capacity, with a twist. 2. Idiotic collision of the mental and physical worlds; stupid idea that the brain's ability can be likened to the storage capacity of a computer, as in: *"Hey guys, you're using up too much of my psychic RAM!"* *(see Bandwidth, he doesn't have the; Intelligent, if you were any less ___, I'd have to water you once a day; Mental furniture; Obvious, firm grasp of the; Picnic, one sandwich short of a ___; Shilling, not the full)*

Pull out all the stops: 1. Use every available resource. 2. Church organ-style full throttle phrase; go gung ho; go the whole hog; deploy everything, regardless of suitability for the task; overdo it; over deliver; work on all fronts to retrieve situation. *(see All-singing, all-dancing; Conductor's baton, wave the; Go the whole hog; Gung ho; Kitchen sink; Orchestra model; Push the boat out)*

Pull rank: 1. Overrule by citing greater seniority. 2. Create semblance of collaboration and then apply personal bias anyway; intervene and humiliate subordinate; decide on a whim with no suitable evidence; revert to playground approach to decision-making, as in: *"My conker is bigger than yours!"* *(see Gut feel; Hierarchy; Matrix; Organogram; Pecking order)*

Pull the levers: 1. Manipulate handles, for reasons various. 2. Play puppeteer; pull strings; lead a merry dance; try everything in the hope that something works; throw as much stuff at the wall as possible in the hope that something sticks.

Pull your finger out: 1. Remove digit from an unspecified place. 2. Get on with; make an effort for once; put on a sudden burst of sustained endeavour in order to save the day or get the job done, usually after doing nothing for months; finally attempt to work out what one's job truly involves, rather than just sitting around reading the occasional email. *(see Engender)*

Pulse, check the, finger on the: 1. Measure the mood of something; be in tune with what's happening. 2. See if elderly colleague is still alive; establish whether any colleague is awake during phenomenally boring meeting; forensically examine the workings of an entire company to see if there's any life in it at all. *(see Forensic, send it down to the boys in; Pathologist's interest)*

Punch above our weight: 1. Hit harder than a boxer of that size should; do better than expected. 2. Stolen from the boxing world and it's gradation of fighters by weight to determine fairness of a contest; further confirmation of the business world's obsession with sporting competition; suggestion that a company or team are somehow akin to a prize fighter, oiled and ready for action; whiffs of the underdog, as the lesser equipped company heroically beats a bigger rival; David and Goliath re-enacted in Basingstoke to secure a contract for heat pumps, or something rather less glamorous than a fair maiden or a kingdom. *(see Sucker punch)*

Pure play: 1. A company that only does one thing, or one that only exists online. 2. Curious use of the word 'pure' to suggest that clarity of thought is somehow close to godliness; hints of American football manoeuvres; shades of machismo; all in all, rather baffling and contributing little to meaning or understanding.

Purpose, fit for: 1. Capable of doing the job. 2. Utterly pointless phrase querying whether the subject in question will do the job, as in: *"I can see the spec, Brian, but is this product fit for purpose?"*; another gem from the sleazy world of management consultancy, where such phrases are invented for the dual purpose of patronizing clients and charging more. *(see Acid test; Match fit; Proof of concept; Success, what does ___ look like?)*

Pushback (n): 1. Response or feedback, usually proffering the opposite view. 2. Euphemism for outright disagreement combined with the likelihood that one side won't mention it at all; weasel word formed by a rather pointless elision of push and back, in order to generate a new phenomenon – wait for it – the notion of pushing back; mealy-mouthed smokescreen for not having the courage to come to the point and say what you really mean, as in: *"I really think you need to provide some push-back to Adrian on this one."*; in short, any response at all that disagrees with what's been said, usually by a more senior person. *(see Feedback; Quality feedback)*

Push the boat out: 1. Launch something; throw more effort at something than is strictly necessary. 2. Go over the top; overdo it; add a little gloss to something that is essentially workaday; make a song and dance about it; throw everything at. *(see All-singing, all-dancing; Fat man in the canoe; Go the extra mile; Go the whole hog; Hype; In the same boat; Pull out all the stops; Rock the boat, don't)*

Pushing on a piece of string: 1. Trying to get something done carefully. 2. Having to be so diplomatic that it is effectively impossible to say what you truly mean; hopelessly tactful conversation that achieves nothing at all.

Pushing the envelope: 1. Move a piece of stationery across the table; push the boundaries of what is possible, from the aeronautics jargon referring to graphs of aircraft tolerance. 2. Another cracker from the kit box of oleaginous executives who wished they had become a *Top Gun* pilot but never had the skill; notional envelope used to denote Mach number or speed ratio a pilot or plane can endure before passing out or self-destructing; ludicrously applied to the world of business, populated as it is by flabby, Terylene-suited men slumped in warehouses, rather than an elite squad of finely-tuned pilots. *(see Crash and burn; Flying unstable; Maxed out; Needle, moving the; Needle, pushing the; Wheels coming off)*

Put to bed: 1. Tuck a young child in at night, and possibly read them a story; finish the job. 2. Rather odd phrase denoting completion of a task; shades of a nostalgic longing for childhood, perhaps with a Freudian hint of fond memories of one's mother; slight suggestion that since night-time is reminiscent of the end of the day, it somehow represents the conclusion of something. *(see At the end of the day; End of play)*

Putting lipstick on a pig: 1. Applying cosmetics to a porcine beast, presumably to make it look better. 2. Frantically try to make something appear better than it is, usually to no avail; futile cover up effort. *(see GIGO; Jazz hands; Rebrand; RIRO; SISO; Turd, polishing a)*

Pyramidal: 1. Triangular shaped. 2. Ludicrous adjective derived from the noun pyramid, various pronounced pyrameedal or pyramydal; in any event, triangular would be more accurate, given that organizational structures are not 3D. *(see Pyramided out; Triangulate)*

Pyramided out: 1. At full stretch; unable to cope or take on any more. 2. Truly bizarre and wildly off-the-point expression suggesting that someone is all over the place, presumably pulled in a minimum of three directions; conversion of this thought into a piece of twisted geometry, only to end up with a trumped-up verb, to 'pyramid out', or be 'pyramided out'. *(see Maxed out; Pyramidal; Triangulate)*

Python, wrestling with a: 1. Grappling with the largest snake in the world. 2. Trying to cope with a very tricky problem, and probably failing; being attacked on all fronts, as though by many slippery tentacles; dealing with many departments, none of them cooperative; scrabbling to draw multiple components together and make them work; any task in the civil service. *(see Balls in the air, on the block, to the wall; Ball juggling; Plate spinning; Snakepit; Snake's honeymoon; Viper's nest)*

Qualitative: 1. Relating to quality. 2. Biased views and irrational preferences displayed by marketing directors the world over; flying in the face of the numbers; doing a 'gut feel' or going on a hunch. *(see Gut feel; Pants, fly by the seat of our)*

Quality assurance mechanism: 1. System designed to ensure decent quality. 2. Load of guff intended to disguise a lack of quality, such as 'the customer is always right', or 'exceeding your expectations'.

Quality feedback: 1. Accurate comment on the performance of a product or person. 2. Massive bawling out from one's boss about shoddy workmanship, absenteeism, incompetence, poor attitude and range of other defects. *(see Feedback; Pushback; Riot act, read the)*

Quantifiable: 1. Measurable, countable. 2. Unquantifiable; lies and damn statistics; bewildering pie charts containing misleading averages to obscure the true picture. *(see Crunch the numbers)*

Quantitative easing: 1. Reducing pressure on the numbers. 2. Distorting the numbers so they look nicer and everyone can convince themselves that everything is okay. *(see Crunch the numbers; Downsize; Fiscal juggling; Negative growth, profit)*

Quarter, one, two, three, four: 1. Three months. 2. Arbitrary division of the calendar year into pointless chunks to make it easier for mentally-challenged finance directors to understand what is going on; time-wasting excuse for department heads to 'look at the figures this quarter' instead of doing any real work; predictable annual landmark on which the CEO cancels the training budget he approved only two months before. *(see Above and beyond; Fiscal juggling; Tertial)*

Question, million dollar, $64,000: 1. The one question which, if properly answered, will allow some progress to be made. 2. A perfectly pedestrian line of enquiry that should have been looked at as a matter of course, now blown out of all proportion into the golden solution. *(see Silver bullet, there is no)*

Questions, ask the hard: 1. Ask some perfectly normal questions. 2. Say what everyone else is thinking but dare not mention – that the project is a pup and the CEO is a tosser. *(see Team, take one for the)*

Quick fix, there is no: 1. This is going to take a long time and needs to be done properly. 2. We've skimmed this for too long and now it's completely buggered – we'll either have to start again from scratch or give up completely. *(see Easy answers, there are no; Magic ingredient, there is no; Silver bullet, there is no)*

Quiver, what's the strongest arrow in your ___? 1. What is the most powerful thing you can do here? 2. I am having a weird daydream in which we have all been transported back to medieval times, as in: *"Prithee nuncle, ask your fletcher to prepare your finest shaft and dispatch it forthwith!"*, or some such twaddle; a somewhat weaker version of the military metaphor, standing little hope against bombs, rockets and more modern fighting equipment.

R&D: 1. Research and development. 2. Rip off and duplicate.

Rabbit, cutting the legs off the ___ to fit it in the hutch: 1. Changing something just so that it falls in line with another, with unfortunate consequences. 2. Blindly destroying something perfectly fine in order to make it succumb to some other arbitrary construct. *(see Nip in the bud; Roots, take the plant up by the ___ to see how it's growing)*

Rabbit, let the dog see the, let the ___ see the trees: 1. Make the reward evident. 2. Crass animal-cum-hunting metaphor that means next to nothing; standard incentive-based nonsense spouted by sales directors, mainly in Basingstoke.

Radar, off the, under the: 1. Visible or not visible, depending on preference and circumstances. 2. Part of a seemingly never-ending suite of pseudo-military metaphors that make businessmen feel more virile, even if they work in the feminine hygiene category. *(see AWOL, go; Ballistic, go; Box of frogs, mad as a; Bundle, one stick short of a; Gene pool, swimming in the shallow end of the; Mid-life crisis; Moon, barking at the, over the, through the; Picnic, one sandwich short of a; Plot, lose the; Pram, to throw one's toys out of; Rails, gone off the)*

Raft of ideas, proposals, respondents: 1. Some ideas, proposals or respondents. 2. Disparate gaggle of half-baked and semi-witless suggestions knocked up in the cab on the way to the meeting; certainly not presented on a raft, and probably not even near water at all. *(see Package; Tranche)*

Rails, gone off the: 1. No longer on track. 2. Gone totally doolally; flipped; wigged out; lost it. *(see AWOL, go; Ballistic, go; Come a cropper; Moon, barking at the, over the, through the; Plot, lose; Postal, go; Pram, to throw one's toys out of; Radar, off)*

Ramp up: 1. Push something up a ramp, probably a car. 2. Make bigger; exaggerate; overclaim; over hype. *(see Ladder it up, Ratchet)*

Range, product, ___extension: 1. Goods for sale, sometimes new. 2. We are likening the goods we offer to the great expanse of the American Midwest – a vast range of goods and services to cater for your every conceivable need, now available in Guatemalan honey flavour.

Ratchet up: 1. Tighten with a mechanic's tool. 2. Grasp vainly at automotive vocabulary in a futile attempt to make a flimsy programme seem more macho; much loved by sales managers in Birmingham, particularly in the bathroom fittings category. *(see Ladder it up, Ramp up)*

Rationale: 1. Line of argument to explain direction of thinking. 2. Total flimflam and post-rationalization made up on the spot to justify woolly thinking or sub-standard crap. *(see Bullshit)*

Reach out: 1. To contact in some way. 2. Truly horrible way of suggesting any form of interaction with a colleague or associate, offered in an 'arms around the world' sort of tone; visions of two fingers only just touching, à la Sistine Chapel, or a film villain about to drop off a cliff despite vain attempts to hold them back; possibly acceptable if sung by a member of the Four Tops.

Reactive: 1. Only acting in response to something else. 2. Bone idle and incapable of original thought. *(see Proactive)*

Real estate, how much ___does this have: 1. How much lasting value does this idea have? 2. Daft American question trying to compare the long-term price of something with the property market; another in a long line of asinine semi-rhetorical lines of enquiry, such as: *"What does success look like?"*; unanswerable, inasmuch as the question is nonsense. *(see Bench, has this got; Legs, it's got; Success, what does ___ look like?)*

Real teeth, our campaign needs to have ___: 1. Our communications effort needs to be effective; dental structures are crucial to our efforts. 2. Another in a long line of medical metaphors applied to business; mindless application of the word 'real', when patently the teeth in question will not be the real thing; implication that most of the time the campaigns embarked upon do not have any teeth, in any sense of the word. *(see Literally; Open-heart surgery, it's not)*

Realignment: 1. Instance of restoring or changing to a previous or different position. 2. Issue of a direct order to do what you're told or f**k off, as in: *"We need some serious realignment here, Geoff."*; use of the reasonably soft word 'align' as a surrogate for full agreement; alignment thus becomes a seemingly inoffensive word for toeing the party line whether you like it or not; in extreme cases, realignment can include the wholesale firing of anyone who chooses not to 'realign'. *(see Align, aligned; Ducks in a row, get our; FIFO (2); Hymn sheet, singing from the same; Off message; Off-piste; Wildebeest in a row, has the lion got his)*

Reality check: 1. Occasion to consider a matter realistically or honestly. 2. Moment that seldom occurs in business due to too much haste or downright stupidity; sometimes used in pseudo-rigorous way by glib managers, as in: *"I'm broadly in agreement, but I think we need to take a reality check here, Sebastian,"* often accompanied by a broad sweep of the hand or a thoughtful tug of the beard.

Realness: 1. Reality. 2. Shocking use of the 'ness' suffix in a forlorn attempt to lend weight to an abstract (and often woolly) notion; abject failure to use the words 'real' or 'reality' in the correct context; rather high-handed idea that others will be duped by the creation of a word that doesn't actually exist, in order to assert greater intellectual authority, as in: *"Yes Gordon, but what is the essential realness of the brand?" (see Rootedness)*

Real time optimization: 1. Making the best of it, now. 2. Hideous distinction between time and real time, as though the former were not real; much favoured by self-styled digital natives, as in: *"Guys, our real time optimization is so spot-on this offer is whaling!" (see Digital native; Optimize; Whaling)*

Re-baselining: 1. Changing the baseline, or basis of measurement. 2. Shocking collision of baseball terminology, measurement criteria and egregious fiddling of the numbers; different way of saying that we don't like what the figures are saying so we'll change the way we portray them; typically, choosing a different vertical scale, converting currency, shortening or lengthening the time period being analyzed, or re-calibrating in any way that will make things appear different; obfuscating. *(see Baseline; Fiscal juggling; Obfuscation)*

Rebrand: 1. Change name of product, or significantly overhaul the manner in which it is portrayed. 2. Reach the stage where a knackered old product or service is so reviled by customers that it can't go on; spend a fortune talking to self-appointed 'brand strategists' to ascertain what on earth can be done; spend a fortune on 'focus groups', only to find out what you already knew – that people hate it; scour the globe for another way of presenting the same old tat; choose a new name, or invent one entirely from random paper cuttings or pieces of Latin loosely stitched together to suggest authenticity; sit back and wait for results; revert to original name the following week after public outcry of sham and cover up; leave company in disgrace. *(see Authenticity; Brand strategist; Focus group; Look and feel; Putting lipstick on a pig; Redeploy; Redesign; Re-engineer; Repackage; Reposition; Re-purpose; Restructure; Turd, polishing a)*

Recruitment: 1. The hiring of personnel. 2. Time-consuming and futile charade involving interviews, character profiling, psychometric testing and the gathering of fictitious references – candidates are often said to be *"pursuing other options"* three months later. *(see Card, red; Decruit)*

Redeploy: 1. Use somewhere else. 2. Fire. *(see Rebrand; Redesign; Re-engineer; Repackage; Reposition; Re-purpose; Restructure)*

Redesign: 1. Change of specification. 2. Start again; go right back to the beginning; rip up original plan; acknowledge terminal flaw in current version. *(see Drawing board, back to the; Rebrand; Redeploy; Re-engineer; Repackage; Reposition; Re-purpose; Restructure)*

Redlit: 1. Subject to a stop signal; not happening. 2. Repellant past tense of red light, joined together and turned into an adjective, signifying a project on hold or going nowhere. *(see Green light; Greenlit; Issues, I have ___ with that; Problem, I don't have a ___ with that; Unhappy, I'm not ___ with)*

Red meat announcement: 1. Announcement with real substance. 2. Rather misguided phraseology for a political statement that has some proper content for once; usually not true at all, merely referring to the same old guff; curious suggestion that any 'vegetarian' proclamation would somehow naturally lack clout.

Redundancy: 1. Superfluous to requirements in job. 2. Close cousin of being fired, but with slightly different phraseology; helpful catch-all for employers keen to get rid of a large number of people; excessive proliferation or superfluity; too many people doing the same stuff; too many products doing the same thing; too much of everything, leading to significant pruning.

Re-engineer: 1. Restructure a company or part of its operations; generate a new version of a machine. 2. Part of a suite of words with the re- prefix designating changing something because it just isn't working. *(see Rebrand; Redeploy; Redesign; Repackage; Reposition; Re-purpose)*

Reinventing the wheel: 1. Creating something that has already been done somewhere else. 2. Omnipresent phrase for a monumental waste of time; colossal duplication of work; one department doing something identical to the next department; two colleagues doing the same; abject failure to communicate, resulting either in doubling up or having to repeat the whole thing; exasperated cry from managing director, as in: *"For f**k's sake guys, we're not reinventing the wheel here!" (see Left hand, not knowing what the right is for, ___ and second left hand; Wheels coming off)*

Repackage: *(see Rebrand; Redeploy; Redesign; Re-engineer; Reposition; Re-purpose; Restructure)*

Reposition: *(see Rebrand; Redeploy; Redesign; Re-engineer; Repackage; Re-purpose; Restructure)*

Reptilian brain: 1. Cerebral matter possessed by a reptile; part of the brain that is driven to establish and defend territory. 2. Theme much loved by psychoanalysts when droning on about the role of the brain in determining how we respond to things; often linked to hard-to-prove theories about lizards and dinosaurs; somewhat miraculously used to suggest how people should behave at work; overall, a slightly daft concept that leaves one wondering whether a human brain might not be preferable.

Re-purpose: *(see Rebrand; Redeploy; Redesign; Re-engineer; Repackage; Reposition; Restructure)*

Research: 1. Systematic investigation to establish facts or principles. 2. Seemingly endless process of trying to find out what on earth is going on; starting from scratch when knowing sod all about a subject; playing catch up; wading through mountains of data in the futile hope of finding something enlightening; revisiting the same idea again and again, with little progress; sitting through interminable debriefs; posing a huge set of bland questions and receiving a similar quantity of equally dull answers; gathering vast quantities of information and then not knowing what to do with it. *(see Go round the houses; Navel gazing; Planning)*

Respect, with: 1. Pay attention, I'm about to disagree with you. 2. Two very dangerous words presaging a flaming row, as in: *"With respect Michael, you're talking bollocks." (see Enlighten me; Follow, do you; Lips, read my; Teach your grandmother to suck eggs, don't, would never, would you; Warts and all)*

Rest on our laurels: 1. Be satisfied with past achievements and cease to try any more. 2. Standard state for pompous, arrogant organizations; trite component of any chairman's statement, as in: *"This has been an exceptional year of achievement, but be assured we will not rest on our laurels.";* announcement frequently followed by catastrophic collapse of share price due to resting on laurels.

Restructure: *(see Rebrand; Redeploy; Redesign; Re-engineer; Repackage; Reposition; Re-purpose)*

Results-driven: 1. Motivated by the outcome. 2. Completely pointless phrase, as helpful and informative as a human who is oxygen-driven or a car that is fuel-driven; as ever, this piece of nonsense fails to register that if someone is doing something, they are more likely than not going to be interested in what happens as a result of their efforts; much loved by recruitment consultants as a crass way of describing a person who will probably get the job done, as in: *"Julian is a results-driven individual who will undoubtedly add value to any organization."* *(see -centred, -driven; -centric; -focused, people-, goal-; –oriented; Task-oriented; Value-add, value-added)*

Retaliation, get your ___ in first: 1. Do something before it gets done to you. 2. Fantastically circular idea that someone can predict when someone else is going to take revenge on them, even before anyone does anything; hilarious notion that getting your own back is a good thing to do in the business world; hints of battleground vengeance, vindictive action and an overall eye-for-an-eye mentality; interesting idea that an all-out brawl in the office would be beneficial, even when no one knows why. *(see First mover advantage; First past the post; Pre-emptive strike; Rise above it)*

Return on involvement: 1. You get back what you put in, even in a non-monetary sense. 2. Touchy-feely (or highly cynical) notion that a brand or company that gets involved with their community will garner a better return on their financial investment; excuse for chairman or similarly senior personnel to host fundraisers, mill about in schools or art galleries, and generally show off while in fact simply pursuing their favourite hobby at someone else's expense. *(see ROI)*

Reverse gear: 1. Going backwards. 2. Hasty retreat; sudden change of heart; manoeuvre similar to Italians in Second World War; spectacular U-turn; total policy change, often disguised as a small adjustment. *(see Evolving to meet customer demand; Tweak; U-Turn)*

RFP: 1. Request for proposal. 2. Highly abusive system in which companies ask suppliers to submit ideas, usually via email and without ever meeting;

blanket communication from procurement department that is desperately trawling the market for cost comparisons and ideas, with little or no intention of ever awarding a contract; a nasty process best avoided by all. *(see Commercial wife-beating)*

Ride, bumpy, along for the, roughshod over: 1. Journey of varying types – uneven, free, or at the expense of others. 2. Highly adaptable suite of phrases to suit many needs; preparatory briefing suggesting hard times to come, as in: *"Hang on tight guys, we're in for a bumpy ride!"*; plaintive remark related to not just making up the numbers, as in: *"We're not just along for the ride here, guys!"*; defiant comment on interference from unwanted colleagues or other departments, as in: *"If they think they can ride over us roughshod, they've got another thing coming."* *(see Handrails, hold the; Last chance saloon, drinking at the; Saddle, cycling with no)*

Riding the razor blade: 1. Caught in an uncomfortable position. 2. A truly eye-watering image for either sex, implying lacerated genitals at the slightest wrong move; visions of careening down the banister only to come a cropper near the end; gung ho behaviour often followed by a nasty ending; living unnervingly close to the edge; sailing close to the wind; risking everything; cavalier attitude to personal and career safety. *(see Coals, walk on hot; Handrails, hold the; Last chance saloon, drinking at the; Saddle, cycling with no; Rock and a hard place, caught between a; Wind, sailing close to the)*

RIF: 1. Reduction in force. 2. Fire a large number of people. *(see Decruit; Dejob)*

Right arm, give your ___ for: 1. Make significant sacrifices to gain something; be prepared to do almost anything. 2. Extreme personal gesture to get something done; as severe as losing a limb or possibly sawing it off oneself; serious desire to get something; obsession; irrational objective that cannot be shifted; near-insane death wish. *(Kamikaze; Left hand, not knowing what the right is for)*

Right shoring: 1. Having or putting people in the right country, usually for nefarious tax purposes. 2. Firing a large number of people, regardless of where they are located. *(see Nearshore; Offshoring)*

Right-size (vb): 1. Make the right size; make something fit. 2. Silly way of pointing out that if something is going to work or fit properly then it needs to be the right size; unnecessarily turned into a verb.

Ringfence (vb): 1. Put a fence around something; cordon something off. 2. Annoying phrase that allows someone to point out that they don't want to talk about something now and would rather deal with it later, as in:

"It's a fair point, Mary, but let's ringfence it and take it offline."; delaying or stalling tactic, dressed up as modern parlance; evasion. *(see Marker buoy, Let's stick a ___ on that; Offline, take it)*

Riot act, read the: 1. Warn or reprimand seriously, originally from the 1715 English statute stating that people committing a riot had to disperse within an hour of the reading of the act by a magistrate. 2. Bawl out comprehensively, frequently in front of colleagues for maximum humiliation; tear off a strip; go ballistic; go crimson with rage. *(see Appraisal, one degree; Ballistic, go; Postal, go; Pram, to throw one's toys out of the; Quality feedback)*

RIRO: 1. Rubbish in rubbish out. 2. Simple principle that if you start with crap, then you'll probably finish with it, the moral being to use good ingredients. *(see GIGO; Putting lipstick on a pig; SISO; Turd, polishing a)*

Rise above it: 1. Don't let it bother you, usually of adverse conditions. 2. Suggestion of some kind of elevation, probably not physical; find a higher plane; don't retaliate; don't get involved. *(see High ground, take the moral ___; Retaliation, get your ___ in first)*

Risk-averse: 1. Not prone to taking any chances. 2. Inherently conservative; weak-willed; unadventurous; lily-livered; scared; not likely to do anything that might cause any trouble; ineffective; possibly not worth having around; a bit useless; not helping much; preferring to stay at one's desk rather than get up and do something. *(see Jobsworth)*

Risk management: 1. Discipline claiming to be able to manage risk. 2. Not a cat in hell's chance of managing anything, given that the future is unpredictable and events are so often random. *(see Black swan)*

Roadmap: 1. Cartographical device to find out where you are going. 2. Irritating way of suggesting that a company or project has some direction; attempt to attach geographical substance to an amorphous concept; part of the extensive arsenal of all rhetorical-question askers when trying to appear organized or authoritative, as in: *"Thanks for the detailed rundown, Nigel, but what is the roadmap for Project Begonia?"*

Robust: 1. Strong; hardy. 2. Odious adjective when misused, most commonly when referring to numerical information, as in: *"How robust is this data, Geoff?"*

Rock and a hard place, caught between a: 1. On the horns of a dilemma. 2. In a nasty situation, with all choices being unsatisfactory; state of affairs intentionally generated by a colleague to humiliate you, or self-generated due to naivety or incompetence. *(see Riding the razor blade)*

Rock and roll, let's: 1. Let's go; let's make a start. 2. Hilarious attempt by middle-aged, corpulent or bald executives to appear like rock stars; stealing vernacular from a more sexy industry imbues them with a sense of youth and vigour, while their colleagues observe them with all the disdain of watching their dad dance at a disco. *(see Lock and load, let's; Match fit)*

Rock the boat, don't: 1. Don't upset anything or anyone; don't make a fuss. 2. Say nothing; we know it's all wrong, but the chief executive thought it up so don't complain; we know it's rubbish, but it's the best we've got; I invented this and am not prepared to admit that it's poor; I'm your boss so shut up and get on with it. *(see Fat man in the canoe; In the same boat; Mum, keep; Push the boat out; Rowing in the same boat, direction; SUMO)*

Rocket science, it's not: 1. It's not very complicated. 2. I haven't a clue what rocket science is, but I want to use a patronizing phrase that highlights my superior intelligence; much loved by poorly educated sales managers struggling to appear intellectual; frequently applied to issues that are in fact quite complex; it may not be rocket science but it may well be beyond the understanding of your tiny brain. *(see Brain surgery, it's not; Open-heart surgery, it's not)*

ROI: 1. Return on investment – almost never proven. 2. Acronym usually deployed by industries that have real difficulty in proving that they generate any return on investment at all, such as advertising and PR; intended to add some heft to otherwise flimsy projects with little financial rationale; also used as a humiliation device when a decision is required on whether a project is going ahead or not, as in: *"I can see the business case for Project Madras, Gerald, but can we really prove the ROI?"* *(see Effectiveness)*

Roll-out: 1. Full launch of something that was previously only a test or in a pilot phase. 2. Much abused word-pairing designed to give a bit of clout to something otherwise quite functional, such as making a product launch occur; shades of royalty, as in rolling out the red carpet, which presumably lends a monarchic flavour to humdrum projects; hints of national, and sometimes international, domination, as in rolling out across the nation, as though on some kind of glamorous tour; shades of grandeur, as in: *"Victoria, could you drop by with the roll-out plans for project Tiny Tim this afternoon please?"*

Root-and-branch review: 1. Survey conducted on a large scale and without discrimination. 2. Colossal witch-hunt to find someone to blame for monumental cockup; process that sometimes alights on one individual who is then ceremonially fired, or an entire department, who are then humiliated and subject to ridicule by all concerned; semblance of a thorough investigation but with absolutely no intention of changing anything at all. *(see Deep dive; Drains up, have the; Lift up a rock; Look, take a long hard; No stone unturned; Roots, take the plant up by the; Witch-hunt)*

Rootedness: 1. Not present in any conventional dictionary, but probably trying to convey a degree of anchoring or stability. 2. Part of a long line of twisted words that add 'ness' to the end in the vain hope of suggesting something more rigorous; patently thin; not rooted at all; flapping free in the breeze; most commonly parked on a childish chart alongside a tree, possibly with a watering can over the top. *(see Realness)*

Roots, take the plant up by the ___ to see how it's growing: 1. Break something that was perfectly fine by fiddling with it. 2. Marvellous horticultural metaphor involving the destruction of a perfectly healthy plant by pulling it up to see how it works; tremendous parallels in business, mainly from the 'if it ain't broke, don't fix it' school; salutary lesson to micromanagers intent on meddling with anything they can get their hands on, often with unfortunate results. *(see Micromanaging; Rabbit, cutting the legs off the ___ to fit it in the hutch)*

Ropes, know the: 1. Have a thorough understanding of something. 2. Well-versed in nautical rigging, or possibly the fine art of macramé; be able to navigate the lethal corners of a political organization; understand how not to get fired; duck and dive; bob and weave; keep one's head down and let someone else take the fall. *(see Knitting, stick to the; Neck of the woods)*

Rose-tinted: 1. Excessively optimistic. 2. Charming adjective usually used to describe those with an overly favourable view of the past, or a rather naïve perspective on the current position; sometimes used in dismissive fashion, as in: *"I think you need to take off your rose-tinted glasses here, Nigel."* *(see Halcyon days; Marriage made in heaven)*

Rottweiler: 1. Breed of large German dog with a reputation for toughness. 2. Hard-as-nails operator; ballbreakingly tough executive; character who always believes they are right and simply will not back down; frequently narrow-minded and blinkered bully who treads all over subordinates without a care. *(see Ballbreaker; Ferret on amphetamines; Nutcracker; Open door policy)*

Rowing in the same boat, direction: 1. Pulling together and aiming at the same goal. 2. Athletic-cum-aquatic phrase exhorting everyone to work as a team; usually rolled out when people are patently not working as a team; exasperated comment on bitter in-fighting, back stabbing, front stabbing and all-out internecine warfare between colleagues; plea to squabbling executives, as in: *"Come on guys, we're all rowing in the same boat here!" (see Back stabbing; Bus, who's driving the; Fat man in the canoe; Front stabbing; In the same boat; Push the boat; Rock the boat, don't; Train, who's driving the; Wavelength, on the same, not on the same)*

RTFM: 1. Read the f**king manual. 2. You have clearly had no basic training in the use of this equipment and lied at interview. *(see CV; FOFO; SOP)*

Rubber hits the road, when the: 1. When things really start happening. 2. Rather curious automotive reference implying somehow that before anything happens the rubber is not on the road; unclear position of rubber until that point; suggestion of a car being dropped suddenly from a height; semi-macho racing driver reference, as in: *"We need to be firing on all six when the rubber hits the road, guys." (see Firing on all six, on all cylinders; Hit the ground running)*

Rubber stamp: 1. Approve without challenging. 2. Implication that there will be no trouble getting something approved – not always a wise assumption; on the nod; passed without difficulty; blessed from on high without question. *(see Run it past)*

Rule of thumb: 1. Rough and practical approach based on experience. 2. Pure guesswork, with no basis in fact or experience at all; finger-in-the-air stuff.

Rules of engagement: 1. Code by which two sides will abide when coming together, sometimes in war. 2. Apparent set of principles that everyone roundly ignores; chaos or free-for-all; trite question asked by ill-informed person trying to catch up in a meeting, as in: *"Just remind me, Julian, what are the rules of engagement here?" (see Unfair advantage)*

Run it past: 1. Ask for someone's opinion. 2. Politically astute consultation to see if something is likely to meet with approval or not; canny effort to save enormous amounts of wasted effort by establishing whether an idea is effectively dead in the water before it starts; experienced nod to the way things work round here, as in: *"I think we better run it past Norman before we proceed." (see Buy-in; Rubber stamp)*

Run-of-the-mill: 1. Ordinary; average. 2. Relentlessly undistinguished colleague or product; boring; bland; dull; dreary; not worth having around; beige. *(see Mediocracy; Vin ordinaire)*

Runway, on the: 1. Ready to take off. 2. Aeronautical reference to suggest potency; power in reserve; visions of jets about to take off; revving engines, clearance awaited; *Top Gun*-style remark that makes sales executives feel particularly virile, as in: *"It's great to have Project Catflap on the runway at last, Graham."*

Russian roulette: 1. Game of chance in which each player spins the cylinder of a revolver loaded with only one cartridge, and presses the trigger when pointing it at his own head. 2. Any act which, if repeated, is likely to have disastrous consequences; precisely what many companies and individuals do – repeat the same hazardous approach again and again, in the vain hope that something will work out better next time; abject failure to learn from experience; glib comment on risk taking, as in: *"I'm simply not going to play Russian roulette with you on this one, Kate."*

Sabbatical: 1. Period of leave granted to staff or academics, usually after seven years of service. 2. Mad, drug-fuelled excursion round the globe under the approximate guise of charity fundraising. *(see MBA)*

Sacred cow: 1. A person, institution or custom beyond criticism. 2. Subject matter absolutely out of bounds due to the extreme entrenched views of the chairman, or his wife – usually based on fanaticism, elitism, sexism, chauvinism or some equally undesirable trait. *(see Aunt Sally)*

Saddle, cycling with no: 1. Proceeding without the appropriate equipment. 2. Eye-watering analogy to portray the lonesome act of being woefully under-equipped, whether of resources, technology or intellect, for the job in hand. *(see Hand rails, hold the; Last chance saloon, drinking at the; Riding the razor blade)*

Same page (vb): 1. Make people agree with each other. 2. Egregious generation of a verb from a noun, as in: *"It's vital that we same page the troops, Vernon."* *(see Hymn sheet, singing from the same)*

Sanity check: 1. Period of brief reflection to see if common sense has prevailed. 2. Horrible moment of realization that common sense has certainly not prevailed, usually occurring moments before a crucial presentation or product launch.

Satisficing: 1. Curious elision of 'satisfy' and 'suffice' coined by American professor of computer science and psychology Herbert Simon to describe the manner in which people do just enough research before buying products. 2. Dreadful compromise brought about by chronic lack of resources and talent. *(see Optimal; Sub-optimal)*

Scalable: 1. Capable of being made bigger; capable of being climbed (of a wall). 2. Tragic Americanism designed to make hard-pressed managers feel they are on course for world domination. *(see Upscale; World class)*

Scapegoat, make a ___ out of: 1. Single out for blame. 2. Cynically select an individual or department who had nothing at all to do with the disaster that has just occurred; spend inordinate amounts of time and energy putting a case together that proves it was all their fault; report to managing director with comprehensive dossier, saying you're very sorry but the truth had to be revealed and you felt it was your duty. *(see Heat, take the; High jump, in for the; Let's not go there; Piggyback; Team, take one for the; Witch-hunt)*

Scenario, best-case, nightmare, worst-case: 1. A summary of the plot of a play; a predicted sequence of events. 2. Situation, almost always disastrous; prediction, almost always wrong. *(see Armageddon plan; Doomsday scenario)*

Scope, scope out: 1. Work out what to do. 2. Spread out vast amounts of paper on the boardroom table in a desperate attempt to make sense of it all, often resulting in resignation or dismissal; alternatively, resort to an impenetrable last-ditch diagram that is so convoluted that no one else will admit they don't understand it. *(see Last chance saloon, drinking at the)*

Scorched earth policy: 1. Warfare policy of removing absolutely everything to do with the enemy, usually by fire. 2. Wanton slash and burn approach deployed by Kamikaze managers, often in high churn businesses such as telecommunications – there are rarely any survivors. *(see Armageddon plan; Doomsday scenario; Efficiency drive; Kamikaze)*

Scraping the barrel: 1. Using one's last or weakest resource. 2. Winging it; just getting by; gathering anyone in the company who could possibly join in, including the tea lady; presenting the most useless material ever; thin, cliché-ridden proposal; not a cat in hell's chance of winning. *(see Ambulance chasing; Bottom feeding)*

Scratch my back and I'll scratch yours: 1. Do something helpful for me and I'll reciprocate. 2. Mantra much loved by corrupt executives on the take in disgraceful incestuous arrangements that are entirely for their own benefit. *(see Get into bed with; Kimono, open the)*

Screw it, let's do it: 1. What the hell, let's get on with it – a philosophy espoused by Richard Branson in the book of the same name. 2. Reckless, cavalier approach adopted by unscrupulous salesmen in order to hit this month's target.

Screwed: 1. Fastened by a screw; had sex with; in an awkward position. 2. Fired; destroyed; humiliated; incapable of redeeming self-esteem or employment. *(see Shit creek, up ___ without a paddle)*

Sea change: 1. A seemingly magical change, originally coined by Shakespeare in *The Tempest*. 2. Pray desperately for a total change of fortune, such as increased sales or salary. *(see Paradigm shift; Step change)*

Seagull manager: 1. Manager who flaps around a lot, makes a big noise, and dumps on everyone from a great height. 2. 90% of all managers.

Seals, left them clapping like: 1. Elicited a delighted reaction from an audience. 2. Vainglorious report from a sales meeting, almost always over optimistic; hubristic analysis of chances of winning, rarely correct; inflated self opinion manifested in a belief that one is a superb presenter and really rather brilliant. *(see Beavers, defending it like; Done deal; In the bag)*

Seamless: 1. Continuous or flowing. 2. Ubiquitous word now applied to anything that needs to look as though it hangs together; almost certainly used in connection with things that patently do not hang together, but must be made to appear so if the company is to have any chance of success. *(see Connectivity; End-to-end; Hit the ground running; Joined-up thinking; Solutions, end-to-end)*

Search and destroy: 1. Track someone down and eliminate them. 2. Aggressive approach to 'killing' the competition much loved by macho executives; similar approach to identifying scapegoats who can be blamed for any failing, so long as it is clear that the fault is not yours. *(see Take no prisoners)*

Segue: 1. To proceed from one section to another without a break, usually in music, from the Italian *seguire*, to follow. 2. Egregious way to suggest everything working beautifully together, used both as a verb and a noun; hilariously, frequently spelt 'segway' by those stretched to the limits of their linguistic capabilities when trying to be just a bit too smart for their own good. *(see Connectivity; Joined-up thinking; Seamless; Tranche; Vis-à-vis)*

Set in stone: 1. Fixed. 2. Not really fixed at all; shades of Excalibur and Arthurian tales; often used in the reverse, as in: *"Of course, Nigel, these proposals aren't completely set in stone."*

Setback: 1. Something that has gone wrong, usually causing delay. 2. We're absolutely f**ked; it's all over; that's the end of it; surrogate for admitting that it'll never happen; much loved by chairmen when discovering an utter disaster, as in: *"We have suffered a setback but we remain determined* to launch Project Vortex as soon as circumstances allow." *(see Fat lady, it's not over until the ___ sings; Learnings)*

Shafted down the river, yourself: 1. Done oneself a disservice. 2. Superb collision of aquatic and sexual-cum-spear-wielding imagery to engineer a state of affairs where a person (gender unspecified) has managed to 'shaft themself', for reasons unknown. *(see Appraisal, one degree; Appraisal 360 degree; Foot, shoot oneself in the; Own goal, spectacular; Shit creek, up ___ without a paddle)*

Share and air: 1. Show what you've been doing and discuss it with colleagues. 2. Showboat; gloat that your stuff is better than theirs; gerrymander judging criteria so that all your material wins in-house awards. *(see Show and tell)*

Shark, keep moving like a, waiting for the sharks to circle: 1. Maintain forward motion, or be surrounded by aggressive competitors. 2. Macho, or perhaps *mako*, notion that to be a success in business you always have to be doing something, when in fact most studies show that consistency is more effective; phrase based completely incorrectly on the belief that sharks need to keep swimming in order to breathe, which is nonsense, as demonstrated by the nurse shark which remains stationary for sustained periods; sense of panic as though surrounded by bloodthirsty carnivores. *(see Wagon, the Indians have surrounded the)*

Sharpening a sword with your cock: 1. Lengthy and somewhat futile attempt to describe a process that is going way over time. 2. Wince-inducing genital metaphor that proposes an unholy collision between one's manhood and a lethal steel instrument of war; expression of intense dismay in overlong meeting, as in: *"Oh for f**k's sake guys, this is taking longer than sharpening a sword with your cock."* *(see Cocks on the block; Riding the razor blade; Saddle, cycling with no)*

Shell-like, a word in your: 1. I'd like a private word with you. 2. You're really in the shit this time; something has gone spectacularly wrong, and all fingers point to you being the culprit. *(see Advisorial; Hints and tips)*

Shift, put in a: 1. Work hard; pull one's weight. 2. Mark of respect; acknowledgement that team member has really contributed. *(see Heavy lifting, do the)*

Shilling, not the full: 1. Less than the required amount; not all there. 2. Totally batty; prone to garrulous outbursts of drivel at all the wrong times; overly loquacious; an embarrassment; can't be taken anywhere; not clever; a liability. *(see Bandwidth, he doesn't have the; Intelligent, if you* *were any less ___, I'd have to water you once a day; Mental furniture; Moon, barking at the, over the, through the; Obvious, a firm grasp of the; Psychic RAM; Picnic, one sandwich short of a ___)*

Shit creek, up ___ without a paddle: 1. In a hopeless position. 2. Deep in the brown stuff; absolutely knackered; with no hope of reprieve; state of affairs that can be self-inflicted or due to Machiavellian behaviour by a colleague, or several of them. *(see Machiavellian; Screwed; Shafted down the river, yourself)*

Shit hits the fan, when the: 1. The moment when it all goes wrong. 2. Charming image of excrement being thrown at an air cooling device, only to find that it is catapulted all round the office; images of fair proportions of it ending up on you, and certainly all over your desk; mildly-threatening rebuke, as in: *"Bloody hell Steve, thanks to you the shit has really hit the fan." (see Air cover)*

Show and tell: 1. Demonstrate and explain to colleagues the nature of your work. 2. Twee lunchtime sessions designed to improve team bonding; hapless staff are tempted by the promise of free cheap sandwiches, and always accept due to chronically low pay and lack of foodstuffs in the fridge at home; thinly-veiled showboating session in which the organizer gets to explain how clever their work is and how brilliant they are. *(see Bonding, team; Share and air)*

Showcase (vb): 1. To show. 2. Redundant verb that merely makes the perfectly adequate verb 'to show' four letters longer, with no gain in understanding; when something has been shown, it may have been part of a showcase, or perhaps even put in one.

Show the door: 1. Point out the features of a hinged dividing panel; fire. 2. Quaint way of saying that someone has been asked to leave; non-specific with regard to where the said person is leaving; has come to mean leaving the building, for good; part of a range of options for exiting the office. *(see Defenestrate, defenestration)*

Sidetracked on all fronts: 1. Not concentrating on anything specific. 2. Spatially-challenged phrase to denote utter confusion; comprehensive ability to be distracted; butterfly mind; daydreamer; self-styled creative type who refuses to knuckle down under the pretext that they are 'thinking'.

Silos, working in: 1. Conducting one's business affairs from inside a silage storage container. 2. Daft pseudo-agricultural term to signal that everyone is doing their own thing and not talking to each other – standard practice in most companies; even worse as a verb or adjective, as in: *"We don't want to silo the accounts department,"* or *"production has really become siloed, don't you think Jane?"*

Silver bullet, there is no: 1. There is not one simple and effective answer. 2. Truly bizarre idea that if one did have a silver bullet it would help in some way; shades of the wild west or perhaps an assassin's brief for a hit; all-round bafflement that such a ballistic item cannot be found, as though there really should be plenty of them in an office environment. *(see Easy answers, there are no; Magic ingredient, there is no; Question, million dollar, $64,000; Quick fix, there is no; Smoking gun)*

Silver lining, every cloud has a: 1. Fanciful idea that this desperate or unhappy situation may lead to something better. 2. Misleading blind optimism that is rarely justified in companies that continue to limp along from one crisis to another.

Single-minded, single-mindedly: 1. Being of one mind; doing something without hesitation. 2. Nastily over-used adjective suggesting that there has never been any doubt about this at all – a highly improbable state of affairs; heavy suggestion of autocratic decree, as in: *"The CEO single-mindedly pushed this one through."*; strong indicator of blind pursuit of a direction without heed to anyone else. *(see Willful blindness)*

SISO: 1. Shit in shit out. 2. Wise and eternally verified notion that if you put poor data or other effort into something the result will be just as bad as the crap it always was. *(see GIGO; Putting lipstick on a pig; RIRO; Turd, polishing a)*

Situation: 1. State of affairs; circumstance. 2. Sorely abused word added to pretty much any sentence you can imagine, with no discernible improvement in understanding; no-win situation; global situation; anything situation; cornerstone word for any meaningless wibble, as in: *"Well clearly, Graham, as you see, this is where this area fronts up to this situation."* *(see Solutions, end-to-end; Space)*

Six feet straight in the soup: 1. Rapid descent into murky waters, possibly hot. 2. Fantastic notion of somehow taking a six-foot run up straight into an enormous bowl of soup, as though that were normal procedure; dramatic collision of culinary and acrobatic metaphor; candidate, perhaps, for a new circus act. *(see Come a cropper)*

Six-Week Sprint: 1. Concentrated burst of activity to get something done. 2. Opposite of what most companies do, until it's too late. *(see Hundred Day Plan; Spin Cycle, Twenty-Mile March)*

60:50 relationship, this is the perfect: 1. This relationship is imbalanced. 2. Superbly exasperated expression of being set upon in a lopsided partnership that is supposed to be equal. *(see Partners)*

Skeleton staff: 1. The fewest number possible to do what needs to be done. 2. An even lower number; not enough people at all; hard-pressed workforce in dire need of rest and more resources; underfed and losing weight fast, possibly on the verge of becoming genuinely skeletal.

Skeletons in the cupboard: 1. Nasty information about the past that could return to cause trouble. 2. The history of every company in the world, and their directors. *(see Smoking gun; Sucker punch)*

Skill set: 1. Capabilities. 2. Stupid pairing of words that reduces a person's talents to something sounding like a primary school pencil case.

Skin in the game, they need to have some: 1. We would like them to have a vested interest. 2. Truly a crown prince among the candidates for worst piece of drivel in the world, this phrase really takes the biscuit; apparently based on the frankly mind-boggling principle that one might embark on a game that involves flaying oneself in some way, or perhaps gluing a part of your epidermis to another person; even better, the person making this ludicrous request clearly believes this would be a perfectly reasonable thing to ask someone to do; chuck-across-the-room dreadful.

Slam dunk: 1 Scoring shot in basketball in which a player jumps up and forces the ball down through the basket. 2. Fast and completely conclusive result, unless claimed by a self-deluded salesman returning from a meeting and wanting to sound impressive, in which case it could be anything but. *(see Done deal)*

Small stuff, don't sweat the: 1. Don't worry about the detail. 2. Glib imprimatur from lax boss giving subordinate *carte blanche* to ignore all the practical stuff; invariably leads to the client asking for more detail, or failing to award the business on the grounds that it was 'all too big picture'.

Smarketing: 1. Smart marketing; or, sales and marketing (precise origin unclear). 2. Repulsive elision designed to denote either marketing that is smart, or the apparent unification of sales and marketing; both suggestions are flawed, in that marketing is most usually not at all smart, and the sales and marketing departments invariably refuse to talk to each other. *(see Insperience; Internecine warfare; Turf wars)*

Smirting: 1. Smoking and flirting at the same time. 2. A new approach by young office workers since smoking indoors was banned – many now take up smoking just so they can chat people up in windy doorways or on fire escapes.

Smoke and mirrors job: 1. An illusion. 2. Any pitch by an advertising agency; work of fiction; things that will almost certainly not come to pass; spectacular feat of storytelling. *(see Behavioural economics; Ether, float into; lost in the; Marketing; Transparency)*

Smoking gun: 1. Proof that a killing occurred only recently; evidence of wrongdoing. 2. Lethal material locked in the chairman's safe, or that of a journalist with a point to prove. *(see Silver bullet, there is no; Skeletons in the cupboard)*

SNAFU: 1. Situation normal, all f**ked up. 2. The standard state of affairs is that nothing works; Royal Air Force acronym generated as a pat response when the captain asks for a status report; nothing functions properly, but what's new? *(see AFLO; Armageddon plan; Fear; FUBB; Lose-lose; Negative growth, profit; Pants, fly by the seat of our)*

Snake oil salesman: 1. Disreputable salesperson offering a cure-all for every need. 2. Account executive in advertising or public relations. *(see Balanced scorecard; Vin ordinaire)*

Snakepit: 1. Depression containing serpents. 2. Open plan office; vicious collection of rivals and desperadoes intent on killing each other; gaggle of secretaries surrounding chairman in a cordoned-off area at office party. *(see Office party; Python, wrestling with a; Viper's nest)*

Snake's Honeymoon: 1. Tangle of wires; complex intertwining of issues. 2. Chaos on all fronts; IT nightmare often found under desk with too many computers; vivid analogy for company or individual with far too much going on; diary car crash; impossible overlap of timelines on several projects that will undoubtedly lead to disaster. *(see Action list; Framework, operating, overarching; Matrix; Organogram; Pecking order; Pull rank; Python, wrestling with a; Touchpoints; Viper's nest)*

Socialize: 1. Get on with people. 2. Fail to get on with people, but smile anyway. *(see Commoditize; Diarize; Democratize; Monetize)*

Soft area: 1. Trendy collection of bean bags and curious furniture quite unlike anything else in the office. 2. Location of lunchtime detritus, such as old crispy bit of Pot Noodle, found unnervingly down the side of a lime green sofa; scene of inappropriate gossip after the boss has left; venue for occasional snog after Friday drinks; designer showcase that rapidly becomes grubby and dog-eared, rather like the office bike. *(see Bean bags; Breakout groups; Come on people; Hot desking; Huddle; Office bike)*

Solus: 1. Alone; separate. 2. Truly odd word meaning just the one; often used to describe just one execution in advertising, as in: *"Okay so we haven't got the budget for several posters, Darren, so we'll just crack this one out solus."*

Solutionism: 1. The belief that all problems have solutions. 2. Rather self-evident idea that difficulties can often be solved; adopted as a trite endline by one particular international technology and science company in the form of: *"Solutionism. The new optimism."* Enough said.

Solutions, end-to-end: 1. Totally pointless addition to almost any word, as in painting solutions (painters), marketing solutions (marketing), and even food solutions (food); often end-to-end, as in 'seamless'; now parent of the awful bastard son 'solutionism' – spawn of the devil. *(see Seamless; Situation; Space)*

SOP: 1. Standard operating procedure. 2. How we normally do it round here; semblance of process that may or may not be written down; if written, it is expected to be followed to the letter; if not written, staff are expected to know anyway; sometimes called culture, although no one can ever define what that is. *(see Building the plane as we fly it; Culture, company; Fly by the seat of one's pants; RTFM; SNAFU)*

Space: 1. Area or market. 2. Pathetic new use of a perfectly good word, as in: *"We want to be leaders in the technology space."*; as redundant as 'situation', 'solution', and 'out there'. *(see Out there; Situation; Solutions, end-to-end)*

Space cadet: 1. Idiot. 2. Vacant colleague.

Spaghetti junction: 1. Motorway interchange with many underpasses and overpasses; nickname of Gravelly Hill Interchange in Birmingham. 2. Absolute pandemonium in the work place; Brownian motion; briefs and projects flying everywhere without any control; utterly bereft of process; jobsworth's idea of hell; carnage; abject absence of procedure; free-for-all; business as usual in an advertising agency. *(see Jobsworth)*

Spanish archer, he got the: 1. He was fired. 2. Euphemism for being fired, based on one of the worst puns ever, as in: *"He got El Bow"*, a pidgin-Spanish version of 'he got the elbow', hence El Bow, the Spanish Archer; truly dreadful.

Speak to: 1. Refer to, or reference. 2. Nasty twist on a perfectly good word pairing whose correct meaning is to address someone; mutated into an attempt to address a subject, as in: *"I'd like to speak to the issues in the haircare market, Sebastian."*

Spear, fall on one's: 1. Impale oneself; resign on a technicality. 2. Make a mistake and have to go; be forced to go as an example to others; have to leave because the chairman cocked up but he wants to stay; act as scapegoat. *(see Fall on your sword; Lamb, sacrificial; Scapegoat, make a _ _ _ out of)*

Spin cycle: 1. Fast activity cycle, typically six weeks. 2. Peculiar laundry-based analogy, perhaps suggesting rinse, launder, or the use of an unspecified white powder. *(see Six-Week Sprint, Twenty-Mile March)*

Spondulix: 1. Slang for money, of unknown origin. 2. Another word used to make the perfectly ordinary deployment of a budget sound more exotic, as in: *"We're spending serious spondulix on Project Bedpan you know, Derek." (see Wonga)*

Spots, stripes, or a bit of turbo: 1. Any of a range of options. 2. General confusion based on a vague brief, as in: *"I don't know what you want – spots, stripes or a bit of turbo?" (see Turbo-charge)*

Sprat to catch a mackerel: 1. Use a small incentive or loss leader to land a bigger prize. 2. Discount so heavily that you don't have any chance at all of making a profit; bend over and take it; ensure the company will go bust within the year; misjudge and mismanage; fundamentally underestimate size of task and cost accordingly. *(see BOHICA; Drop our trousers; Herring, chasing a different)*

Square the circle: 1. Attempt the impossible, based on the insoluble mathematical problem of constructing a square with exactly the same area as a given circle. 2. Conundrum faced by managers of failing businesses every day; conjurer's trick that can't be pulled off in the real world; Catch-22. *(see Box, think outside the, try and put a _ _ _ round that one; Catch-22)*

Squeeze the lemon in both directions and drive the swine to market: 1. Meaning unknown, despite extensive research. 2. Comprehensive gobbledegook mixing three metaphors, combining fruit with livestock, and trying to make a point at the same time; genuinely staggering.

Stacked, completely: 1. Piled high comprehensively. 2. Incapable of taking on any more work; not coping; snowed under; stuffed; under the cosh; on the verge of a breakdown; in need of medical assistance, both mental and physical. *(see Back-to-back; Cocks on the block; Under siege; Wall-to-wall)*

Stakeholder: 1. Person or company with shares in an organization, or some other kind of vested interest. 2. Horribly abused word for any Tom, Dick or Harry who wants to have a say; particularly abhorrent when manacled to another word, as in stakeholder interests, stakeholder values, or stakeholder issues; the phrase 'increasing stakeholder value' invariably means the opposite, or is a smokescreen for increasing value only for the company directors. *(see Engage, engaged, engagement; VC; War chest)*

Stand up and be counted: 1. Take responsibility. 2. Take responsibility, for once in your life; get it in the neck; reap what you sow; endure the consequences of one's actions. *(see Parapet, heads above the, keep our head below the)*

Static: 1. Transmission interference. 2. Similar confusing noise made by chairman. *(see Background noise; Blue-sky thinking; Communication, lack of, plan, skills; Waffle; White noise)*

Status report: 1. Regular report explaining state of play on a range of jobs. 2. Utterly pointless tome that no one bothers to read; copied in to scores of uninterested parties around the world; time-wasting activity that takes a hapless junior executive the whole of Friday every week to produce; ragbag of meaningless updates from around the company; work of fiction only fit for burning.

Step change: 1. Significant change or improvement. 2. Very rare in business, in fact almost never seen, despite management claims in annual reports. *(see Paradigm shift; Sea change)*

STFU: 1. Shut the f**k up. 2. Stop talking immediately. *(see FIMO; Park it; SUMO; Word dump)*

Stick that, some American is going to jet in and tell you exactly where to: 1. You may well be overruled by a foreign executive. 2. Frank admission that one's boss in New York holds all the strings; slap on the wrist for managing director of regional office when the big guns arrive in town. *(see Head office, I'm from ___ and I'm here to help; Where the sun don't shine, shove it)*

Stickability: 1. Ability to stick around (of person or issue). 2. Quality often associated with members of staff who appear unfireable; web content that just won't go away. *(see Bodies are buried, where the ___; Skeletons in the cupboard; Smoking gun; Sticky)*

Sticky: 1. Covered with an adhesive substance; having the property of sticking to something. 2. Somewhat trite word hi-jacked by digital natives (qv) to denote online material to which people come back again and again, as in 'sticky content'; now very much part of glib lexicon used by semi-earnest web folk, tugging their beards, juggling skateboards, and asking in a slightly condescending way: *"Yeah, but how sticky is this site, Dan?"* *(see Chasing eyeballs)*

Still heading west: 1. Restless. 2. Reference to pioneers who arrived in California but still wanted to keep travelling; 'never satisfied' quality desired by some organizations looking for a bit of pep to spice up otherwise limp workforce. *(see Head off at the pass; Wagon, the Indians have surrounded the)*

Strategy, strategize: 1. What you intend to do. 2. Broad canvas for endless wibbling about what you intend to do, wrapped up in arcane phraseology, reams of diagrams, trite statements, research debriefs, and countless meetings; favoured domain of the indecisive. *(see Big picture; Brand strategist; Game Plan; Go round the houses; Methodology; Planning; Research; Wall-to-wall)*

Strategery *(pronounced Stratee-gery)*: 1. The art of putting a strategy together. 2. Much loved in the advertising planning fraternity, as in: *"We've revisited the strategery and it all adds up."*; hideous way to describe piss-poor lobbing together of random ideas to make up an incomprehensible document full of diagrams.

Strategic alliance: 1. Mutual agreement between two companies. 2. Agreement between two companies who will later screw each other and end up in court, both claiming the other reneged on the deal. *(see Bonding, team; Partners)*

Straw man: 1. Outline or example for discussion that will never be enacted. 2. Pointless proposal that takes the same time to prepare as a proper proposal, but which will never be executed; utter waste of time dumped on you by your boss to pad out a meeting; much loved by bosses who recite the disgraceful mantra: *"I don't know what I want, but I'll know it when I see it."* *(see Aunt Sally; Know it when I see it, I don't know what I want but I'll ___)*

Stretch target: 1. Number that is bigger than the real target. 2. Increased target produced under pressure from aggressive finance director; figure that will never be achieved in a million years; arbitrary addition of 20% to any realistic number supplied by the person who knows the nature of the work best; annoying line of interrogation in sales meetings, as in: *"Yes*

William, I can see the spreadsheet, but what's your stretch target?" (see Flexible, flexibility; Target, hit the___, miss the point, miss the ___ left, right and centre, moving; Target manager)

Stuffocation: 1. Suffocation by stuff. 2. Amusing elision depicting drowning in trivia. *(see Administrivia)*

Style Nazi: 1. Person who insists on an immaculate office environment. 2. Politically incorrect descriptor of fastidious individual who spends their entire time wandering around the office tidying up and criticizing the habits of others, thereby earning the sobriquet of Little Hitler, or similar; precise, vain individual whom no one particularly likes, but can't afford their designer clothes or interminable purchasing of the latest gadgets.

Sub-optimal: 1. Not good enough. 2. Woolly hyphenated word to say this is a bit crap. *(see Bugs, iron out the; Drawing board, back to the; Crafting, it needs a bit of; Non-verbal; Optimal; Satisficing; Underperformance)*

Success, what does ___ look like?: 1. How will we know if we have achieved anything? 2. Absolutely disgraceful rhetorical question that has crept into the language in the last few years; truly banal, inasmuch as success doesn't look like anything at all, being an abstract concept; flip query to team in session to suggest some sort of measurement will be needed, and aren't I jolly clever for being the one to point it out; errant twaddle of the first order. *(see Bench, has this got; KPIs; Legs, it's got; Outcomes, positive, negative; Outputs; Proof of concept; Purpose, fit for; Real estate, how much ___ does this have)*

Sucker punch: 1. Sudden, unexpected knockout blow. 2. Swift development that ruins a product or business, catching the management completely unawares; scandal; sexual revelations in the boardroom. *(see Double whammy; Left field, from; Punch above our weight; Skeletons in the cupboard)*

SUMO: 1. Shut up, move on. 2. Get over it; stop whining. *(see Coming from, where I'm; FIMO; GUGOI; Park it; Rock the boat, don't; STFU)*

Sun, the ___ never sets at: 1. We are always open for business. 2. Dreadful never-ending promise to attend to a customer's every need, as in: *"The sun never sets at Sunshine Desserts."*; impossible-to-deliver claim; world domination theme. *(see Always on; Constantly striving; Expectations, exceeding; Global, globalization, globally; Passion; 24/7/365; Work-life balance)*

Swingeing cuts: 1. Punishing, severe reduction in budgets or staff levels. 2. The grim reaper arrives at your office, swinging his scythe; scenes akin to satanic mills and purgatory; depression all round; marching orders for everyone. *(see Across the board, right; Draconian; Internal communications; Marching orders, get your)*

SWOT analysis: 1. Strengths, weaknesses, opportunities, threats; analysis usually made before taking a product to market. 2. Flawed exercise that no one ever completes properly because they don't have the humility and realism to declare the weaknesses and threats properly; such meetings then become peppered with self-deluding narrative such as: *"Of course there are no threats, Robin, only opportunities"*, or the truly derogatory: *"There are no threats, Caroline, only challenges." (see Challenges; Opportunity)*

Synergy, synergies, synergize: 1. Acting together. 2. Lazy catch-all for anything lumped together in an amorphous blob; often used for components that have no relationship at all; horrible as a plural: *"We are looking for serious synergies here, Mervin."*, and even worse as a verb, as in: *"We are looking to synergize our offer with yours, Malcolm." (see Harnessing synergies)*

Ts and Cs: 1. Terms and conditions. 2. Slack abbreviation for all the technical detail that could derail the entire deal; contract; modus operandi; process and pricing structure; basis for making a whopping loss after the euphoria of winning the business has died down.

Table, bring to the: 1. Carry towards a piece of furniture on which items can be set. 2. Overly serious phrase for someone contributing something to a discussion, as in: *"Are you sure we need Jeremy in the meeting? What's he going to bring to the table?"*

Tail wagging the dog: 1. Unlikely scenario of a canine being vibrated to and fro by its own appendage; something less important influencing a greater component. 2. Queasy realization that all the wrong priorities are being pursued; feeling of being taken to the cleaners by a lesser power; underdog beating the professionals; tiny detail confusing the main point; usually couched as a question, as in: *"Surely this a case of the tail wagging the dog, Roger?"*

Take on board: 1. Absorb; pay attention to; take into consideration. 2. Rather highfaluting quasi-nautical term to let someone know that you acknowledge their point; partial suggestion that the person in question is captain of a ship and has a considerable crew at their disposal; suggestions of luggage or ballast, inasmuch as taking something on board would presumably involve a crane or an embarkation ticket at the very least; broad brush phrase for hearing something but having absolutely no intention of doing anything about it, as in: *"That's fine Mr Chairman, I've taken all your points on board."*

Take no prisoners: 1. Be uncompromising and determined in one's actions. 2. Blame everybody and destroy everything; dismantle projects and departments willy-nilly; utter annihilation caused by macho gung ho behaviour in the office; hell-bent on retribution; barnstorming bravura performance by power-crazy managing director determined to find a scapegoat; slash and burn, and hang the consequences. *(see Search and destroy)*

Talent, war on: 1. Sustained effort to find high quality staff. 2. Baffling phrase reminiscent of political or military campaigns such as the *War on Terror* or *War on Drugs*; comprehensive failure by all parties to realize that it is physically impossible to wage war on a concept, be it an inclination to blow people up, distribute illicit narcotics, or be a skilled practitioner in the workplace; an additional flaw in the notion becomes apparent upon noticing the use of the word 'on' rather than 'for', rather suggesting that companies would like to engage in battle with the very people whose skills they covet. *(Know-how; Knowledge management, transfer)*

Talk it through: 1. Discuss it. 2. Blether uncontrollably with no particular outcome in mind. *(see Brain dump; Off the top of my head; Word dump)*

Talk the talk, walk the walk: 1. Make your actions match your words. 2. Trite rhyming axiom for delivering what you claim; presumably born of intense frustration with the large number of people who don't; often directed at those who waffle interminably but never do anything, or entire companies who do the same, as in: *"Forget all the bluster, Rod, if you're going to talk the talk you'll need to walk the walk."*

Talking out loud: 1. Saying something audible. 2. Tautological twaddle that fails to spot that talking intrinsically involves making some kind of noise in order to be effective; staple phrase of dimwits incapable of formulating a point of view before opening their mouths, as in: *"I'm just talking out loud here, Joe."* *(see Bullshit; Non-verbal; Off the top of my head; Word dump)*

Talk track, open a new ___: 1. Start a new conversation. 2. Confused notion that dialogue is somehow physical, and thus capable of being initiated by opening something tangible; hints of trainspotting, with some suggestion that a piece of track can be bought with which to communicate; overall, most odd.

Tangent, returning to the: 1. Discussing once again something that was irrelevant in the first place. 2. Approach much favoured by wafflers who are incapable of sticking to the point; not content with having veered off the subject in the first place, they then insist on coming back to off-brief material again and again; deeply irritating for all present. *(see Marker buoy, Let's stick a ___ on that; Mental lay-by)*

Tap into: 1. Hammer a plug into a barrel to siphon off some booze; put a nail into a wall, fairly gently. 2. Steal; act like a parasite; nick; divert source to one's own advantage.

Target, hit the ___, miss the point, miss the ___left, right and centre, moving: 1. Achieve an objective, fail to do so, or change it entirely. 2. An obsession for almost everyone in business – the need to hit a target – although almost no one explains why this might be important; arbitrary figure or deadline chosen by the chief executive for the hell of it, or to increase the value of his own personal share portfolio. *(see Aims; BHAG; Objectives; Stretch target; Target manager)*

Target (vb): 1. Aim at or for something. 2. Nasty bastardized verb, now almost ubiquitous in any marketing or media discussion; lazy catch-all dressed in action-oriented clothes, as in: *"We need to target 20-35 year olds without alienating teenagers and pensioners." (see Demographic; Stretch target; Target, hit the___, miss the point, miss the ___ left, right and centre, moving; Target manager)*

Target manager: 1. Person whose job description is to ensure that other people hit their targets. 2. Truly bizarre governmental creation; idea that hitting an arbitrary figure will somehow make the quality better; loathsome individual who is the subject of intense ridicule; focal point of concerted attempts to play the system, as in seeming to hit a target when the working reality is horribly different; pointless process of hitting the target while comprehensively missing the point. *(see Administrivia; Bread and butter; Bureaucracy; Jobsworth; Panjandrum; Process; Target, hit the___, miss the point, miss the ___ left, right and centre, moving; Vin ordinaire)*

Task-oriented: 1. Concerned with a job. 2. Completely redundant descriptor that for some reason feels the need to highlight that someone is concerned with getting the job done; begs the question: *"Why are you bothering to point this out?"*; linked implication that some people do not concentrate on the matter in hand; at its worst when used as a headhunter's fawning piece of praise, as in: *"Gordon is a task-oriented operator who would be a tremendous asset to the company." (see Results-driven)*

TBH: 1. To be honest. 2. Acronym that often precedes a statement that is not strictly honest. *(see IMHO)*

Teach your grandmother to suck eggs, don't, would never, would you: 1. Try to tell somebody something they already know. 2. Preach; showboat; hold court; pontificate; drone on; state the bleeding obvious; repeat oneself; waffle; patronize; condescend; assume everyone is a dullard except for you. *(Enlighten me; Follow, do you; Respect, with)*

Team, take one for the: 1. Selfless personal sacrifice in the interests of the greater good. 2. Flagrant brown-nosing in the desperate hope of peer recognition or promotion; be nominated as a scapegoat and dismissed immediately. *(see Above and beyond; Anonymize; Ask, big; Brown-nosing; Can, carry the; Flag up; High jump, in for the; Lamb, sacrificial; Scapegoat, make a ___ out of)*

Team, there's no I in ___ : 1 Axiom suggesting that teamwork cannot function properly if ego is involved. 2. Tired mantra much loved by HR personnel; deployed whenever someone wants to humiliate a certain individual, or spitefully squash an example of personal individuality; commonly followed by the addition of the person's name and a patronizing raising of the eyebrows, as in: *"There's no I in team, Bernard."* *(see Motivation, lack of, team; Troops, the)*

TEAM: 1. Together everyone achieves more. 2. Patronizing mantra parroted by gung-ho HR personnel in a desperate attempt to foster unity in a gang when there is none; futile effort at deflecting internecine warfare. *(see Back stabbing; Front stabbing; Internecine warfare; Team, there's no I in ___)*

Techno-babble: 1. Unintelligible technical talk. 2. Impenetrable nonsense spouted by the IT department. *(see Chatty dolphin; Obfuscation; Technorati)*

Technorati: 1. People who are highly knowledgeable about technology. 2. Portmanteau word combining technical with literati to generate an apparently untouchable elite who know what the bits and bytes do. *(see Techno-babble)*

Teflon: 1. Trademark name for *polytetrafluoroethylene*, used for nonstick cooking vessels; person to whom nothing bad sticks. 2. Annoying colleague who gets up to all sorts of nefarious deeds but never gets caught; bright-eyed favourite who always gets the credit; hugely annoying person and source of much office envy.

Teleconference: 1. Conversation on the phone between more than two people. 2. Hilarious opportunity to muck about or do sod all; includes amusing rigmarole involving narrating passwords to a robot, as though the conversation were so hush-hush it requires security; chance to pick fluff out of one's navel and drop in the odd obtuse remark such as: *"That'll never fly, Brian.";* extended breather in which you can catch up on your personal emails. *(see Videoconference; Webinar)*

Telescope, we have to look at this from both ends of the ___ : 1. We need to look at this from both sides of the argument, or from every possible angle. 2. Spatially-challenged request that defies most of the conventions of vision; misguided idea that looking into a telescope from the wrong end will yield any helpful image; invariably uttered by someone who (a) has no grasp of even the basics of such a piece of equipment, nor (b) has ever even looked into one. *(see Closer look, stand back and take a; Dolly back; Focus; Helicopter view)*

Template abuse: 1. Failure to adhere to a template. 2. Willful disregard for company decree concerning portrayal of typeface, colours, logo and so on when making a presentation; insistence on inserting one's own clip art into a chart, thus subverting the so-called 'integrity' of the brand; nemesis for self-appointed 'brand guardians' everywhere. *(see Guardian, brand)*

Tent, standing outside the ___ pissing in: 1. Urinating into camping apparatus; ruining one's own chances. 2. Hilarious, mildly scatological imagery denoting someone who keeps sabotaging everyone's best efforts; self-destruct mode; death wish; corollary of standing inside the tent and pissing out – presumably a more hygienic state of affairs; theme for exasperated intonation, as in: *"Oh for God's sake, Barry, just for once can't you stand inside the tent and piss out?"* *(see Knee-jerk reaction; Own goal, spectacular)*

Tent pole: 1. Long and slender piece of wood or metal for holding up camping equipment. 2. Stupid word pairing to describe any spike in sales as depicted on a graph; even more stupid when applied to a non-graphical item, as in: *"Do you think this campaign is going to tent pole, Roger?"*

Tertial: 1. A four-month period. 2. Perverse way of dividing up a financial year into three tertials rather than four quarters; fun technique for annoying finance directors in sister companies or other countries, particularly France and the USA, who then have to convert all the numbers back to quarters so they can compare like with like. *(see Fiscal juggling)*

Test-drive: 1. Assess capabilities and limitations, usually of a car. 2. Give it a go, flying in the face of all sensible advice; attempt something but fully expect the wheels to fall off; enact in private, fully aware that it will probably be a disaster. *(see Act out; Wheels coming off)*

That's what this is called: 1. Needless repetition of the name of something. 2. Hugely irritating tautological trait much loved by dimwitted executives, as in: *"That's called quality, that's what this is called."*

There by the grace of God go I: 1. That could have been me. 2. Pseudo-religious admission that one has got away with it; commonly used when observing an equally-qualified colleague being hauled over the coals or given the boot.

Things, bigger and better: 1. Hypothetical place where ambitious people go when they leave. 2. Euphemism for admitting that the person leaving was far better than the company; mealy-mouthed admission that the company is crap at retaining staff, due to low morale, lousy products and bad pay; staple of all-staff memo explaining why someone has gone, as in: *"Graham has moved on to bigger and better things,"* but without wanting to say what.

Think do: 1. If you think of something, do it immediately. 2. Good advice for all procrastinators; get on with it.

Think-tank: 1. Group of specialists convened by a business to undertake intensive study of a problem. 2. Any random gang of hapless attendees charged with sorting out something that has gone badly wrong. *(see Brainstorm)*

Thought canoe: 1. Metaphorical place where everyone agrees on an idea. 2. A bizarre and truly abstract concept, this one; staggeringly odd notion in which a gang of people are urged to draw their thoughts together and place them in a mythical 'canoe', as in: *"Come on guys, quit your daydreaming and get on board the thought canoe." (see Fat man in the canoe)*

Thought leadership: 1. Idea that if you don't have the resources to be the true market leader, you can at least have ideas befitting one. 2. Weasel phrase much loved by also-rans, has-beens and no-hopers; charming idea that if you're not number one, you can nevertheless think you are and somehow all will be fine. *(see Challenger brand; Leader, category, market, thought; Market-leading; World class)*

Thought shower: 1. Politically correct alternative to brainstorm. 2. Ludicrous outcome of someone in a council somewhere deciding that the word brainstorm was offensive to anyone with mental difficulties; abject failure to notice that the majority of those attending so-called thought showers are themselves deeply challenged, summoned as they are to a nasty room to solve an unsolvable problem. *(see Brainstorm)*

Thread-centred: 1. A story adhering to a consistent narrative 'thread'. 2. Awful adjective from the world of storytelling, as in: *"What's our thread-centred message, Barry?"*; usually heard when there isn't really a message at all. *(see –centred; -centric; -driven; -focused)*

Tick all the boxes: 1. Fulfill all desired criteria. 2. Phrase which should in theory convey complete satisfaction, but which in reality rarely does; often used in the negative by earnest procurement types, as in: *"I'm afraid you didn't win the business because you failed to tick all the boxes."*

Tight as a cow's arse in fly time: 1. Very tight indeed. 2. Australian outback phrase usurped for conceptual use, such as describing the intellectual integrity of a proposal or briefing document; also used to bemoan horrible looming deadline or frugal budget, as in: *"Blimey Craig, this quote is as tight as a cow's arse in fly time."*

Time-poor, time-rich: 1. Having plenty of time, or not enough. 2. Modern pairing of phrases to describe use and availability of time; loosely based on the 'time is money' concept by equating poverty or wealth to the number of available hours in a day; often coupled with other –rich/-poor criteria, as in: *"This audience is information-rich and time-poor."*; lingo much used by media types and self-appointed 'brand strategists'. *(see Brand strategist)*

Timesheets: 1. Record of number of hours spent on a particular task or client. 2. The bane of staff the world over; subject of doleful comments around the office about needless administration; worst enemy of procrastinators who fail to fill them in for months and then complain it will take them all weekend to catch up. *(see Administrivia; Panjandrum; Vis-à-vis)*

Time-suck: 1. Laborious, time-consuming task. 2. Laborious, time-consuming task that sucks.

Tin, does what it says on the: 1. A product or person that does what it claims it will. 2. Rare occurrence in the over-hyped world of marketing; a pleasant surprise to encounter the unadulterated truth for once; usually attributed to Ronseal, who use it as their strapline.

Tipping point, the: 1. Moment at which a phenomenon or craze 'tips', moving from little-known to highly popular, coined by Malcolm Gladwell in the book of the same name. 2. Widely abused term to be found most frequently in the political and PR worlds; hard to articulate, let alone generate; a notion that is as rare as hen's teeth. *(see Must-have)*

Tissue session: 1. Meeting at which rough concepts are discussed. 2. Touchy-feely expression which is a close cousin of the 'chemistry' meeting; dangerous opportunity for a client to write their own ads in front of the ad agency who should be doing it themselves; classic chance for a committee to design a camel by taking elements from several campaign ideas and nail them all together in an unholy mess.

Titanic, rearranging the deckchairs on the: 1. Futile tinkering when the ship is already sinking. 2. Macabre metaphor for marginal manoeuvres when all is doomed. *(see Eastern front, this is like the ___ when the bullets didn't turn up; Paper cup, here's a ___, there's a tidal wave coming; Pathologist's interest)*

Tits up, it's all gone: 1. Breasts now pointing skywards. 2. A close cousin of belly up, it appears all is not well when parts of the anatomy point to the heavens; possible allusion to being on one's back on a mortuary slab. *(see Pathologist's interest; Pear-shaped, it's all gone)*

TLA: 1. Three-letter acronym. 2. Rather peculiar idea of describing an acronym with an acronym, with barely any gain in brevity; often favoured by large corporations who love to suggest that they are 'in the know' when you clearly aren't; annoying habit of lawyers, accountants and other so-called specialists, of generating an impenetrable argot to obfuscate what they are up to. *(see Obfuscation)*

TLC: 1. Tender loving care. 2. Trite acronym denoting showing even a modicum of sympathy in a business context; often used in a condescending way by thoughtless managers, as in: *"Given the fact that Julie has just lost her father, I think we should give her a little TLC."*

TLDNR: 1. Too long – did not read. 2. Exasperated acronym generated by overworked executives determined to get to the point; a salutary lesson to keep it short.

TMI: 1. Too much information. 2. Too much information for my tiny brain; too intellectual for me; sorry, I just don't get it.

Ton of bricks, subtle as a: 1. As heavy-handed as a large quantity of rubble. 2. With all the finesse of a gung ho sales director careening into a meeting unprepared, calling the client a wanker, and thundering out again. *(see Gung ho)*

Ton of bricks, you can see through that like a: 1. Totally obvious. 2. Not visible or obvious at all; hideous metaphor collision in which construction material is strangely confused with glass; effectively indecipherable.

Tools, management, unique: 1. Systems that help business owners and managers understand what is happening, almost never unique. 2. A continuing obsession with construction instruments in a vain attempt to suggest precision and craftsmanship where there is precious little. *(see Collateral; Crafting, it needs a bit of; Woodwork, spanners in the, spanners jumping out of the)*

Topline: 1. Very sketchy summary. 2. Very sketchy summary open to massive misinterpretation; seeds of regular confusion as everyone gets the wrong end of the stick; originated by impatient managers desperate to hear the results but unable to wait for a detailed report; hugely misunderstood in a financial context, where the topline is nastily juxtaposed with the bottom line; the topline figure may be relatively healthy, while the bottom line may reveal a whopping loss; occasionally customized into the odious 'top topline', which is presumably so brief that it reveals absolutely nothing. *(see Bottom line)*

Top of mind: 1. In someone's thoughts, ideally all the time. 2. Nirvana for all marketers and advertisers, who desire this as a permanent state for their brands; presumably similar to the frame of mind of an obsessed lover who thinks of nothing other than their new love all day, as though that were likely for a brand of teabags; little reference to bottom of mind, thus raising the tacit assumption that the brain somehow organizes thoughts by physical height.

Tout de suite: 1. At once, immediately (French). 2. Dismissive way of saying that something is needed now; rather pathetic attempt to introduce a soupçon of Gallic flair to an otherwise humdrum subject; rarely written, and if so, usually misspelled. *(see ASAP; PDQ; Vis-à-vis)*

TQM: 1. Total quality management. 2. The apparently revolutionary idea that controlling quality should not be left to a quality controller, but should be the responsibility of everyone involved; pioneered by the very-efficient Japanese in the sixties; blindingly obvious piece of management consultancy twaddle that even your grandmother could have told you.

Touch base: 1. Arrive in time at a baseball base to prove you are not out; say hello; update. 2. More sports verbiage, with businessmen all over the world now 'touching base' regularly, even though they have probably never played the game, and possibly never even seen a match; slightly flip reference to staying in touch, often deployed when gathering papers together and finishing a meeting, as in: *"Okay Malcolm, we can touch base on Project Bugle later."* *(see Baseline; Re-baselining)*

Touchpoints: 1. Number of occasions, or different media, used by brands and customers to interact. 2. Rather silly modern word invented to cope with proliferating media channels; unnecessary in an age when television, press, radio, cinema and posters was all there was; now the hub for unintelligible spider diagrams showing hundreds of interactions and purporting to be able to control them all, even though consumers do what the hell they want regardless. *(see Look and feel; Snake's honeymoon)*

Touchy-feely: 1. Sensitive; aware of emotions. 2. Mildly derogatory hyphenated adjective to poke fun at those in companies who deal with the soft stuff, typically the not-remotely-softly-named human resources; a regular stomping ground for hard-nosed sales people, deriding the appraisal process and raising their eyebrows to the heavens, as in: *"I suppose when we review Marcus we'll have to do some of the touchy-feely stuff."* (see Bonding, team; Emotional intelligence; Human resources; Open door policy)

Traceability: 1. Ability to trace something. 2. A concept that fills all corporate flannellers and charlatans with utter dread; horrible realization that one might indeed be found out, despite consistent attempts to deny all responsibility and cover all tracks.

Traction, gain, give it: 1. The act of drawing or pulling; being pulled; adhesive friction between a wheel and its surface. 2. Idiotic contemporary phrase denoting gaining any foothold whatsoever; most commonly applied to ethereal concepts such as campaigns and ideas, which palpably can never gain traction with anything, being intangible; shades of county fairs and traction engines, being slow and lumbering, like most ideas that people want to 'gain traction'; consummate nonsense.

Trailblaze: 1. Cut a path through the jungle; pioneer in a particular field. 2. Epic-sounding verb almost always used by a shrinking violet who barely left Basingstoke; not trailblazing at all, in fact probably rather ordinary; typically deployed to add a touch of flair to something really dull, as in: *"Colin, I'm convinced that the new XL variant of our panty pads range will trailblaze the market."* (see Vin ordinaire)

Train, who's driving the: 1. Is this an automated transport vehicle or operated by a person?; Who's in charge here? 2. Classically used when there is total chaos and it is apparent that no one is setting direction at all. *(see Bus, who's driving the; Rowing in the same boat, direction)*

Tramlines: 1. Lines on which electrically driven public transport vehicles run. 2. Constraints; parameters; any kind of direction at all would be helpful frankly; often uttered by exasperated executives given no brief whatsoever, as in: *"Dave has told me to progress Project Ringpull, but he hasn't given me any tramlines at all."* (see Guidelines, brand, corporate)

Tranche: 1. Portion or installment, especially of a loan or share issue, from the French word for slice. 2. Supercilious way of saying 'a piece'; unfortunate and generally unwanted spill over from the financial world, with our old culprits the management consultants very much at fault too; another classic in the lexicon of averagely-educated executives who never passed

O-level French but are determined to add a whiff of Gallic flair to proceedings. *(see Raft, of ideas, proposals, respondents; Segue; Vis-à-vis)*

Transparency: 1. Openness. 2. Modern obsession with 'being transparent', without having any intention of shedding light on what the company gets up to at all; closed shop; secret order; shady dealings behind the scenes; smokescreen; so-called 'corporate social responsibility' charter with no meat and no action. *(see CSR; Open; Open door policy; Openness; Smoke and mirrors job)*

Trawl for it: 1. Rummage deeply for an item, such as a particular chart in a presentation of over a hundred. 2. Scrabble to find information in an unholy mess; make reference to a point buried somewhere and be conspicuously unable to find it; attempt similar exercise on one's own chaotic desk; regret mentioning the point in the first place.

Trenches, in the: 1. Doing the dirty work. 2. Another one from the overworked military school that tries to imply that business is akin to warfare; under the cosh; doing all the work while others are swanning around. *(see Parapet, heads above the, keep our head below the; Troops, the)*

Triangulate: 1. Form of trigonometry that measures lengths, lines and angles. 2. Ludicrous verb created for the sole purpose of describing three people meeting, as in: *"You, me and Derek need to triangulate on this later."* *(see Dialogue; Pyramided out)*

Trilemma: 1. Energy industry buzzword to describe a triple problem, in this case reconciling the need to be green, affordable and reliable, all at the same time. 2. Issue that simply cannot be resolved, no matter how loud anyone shouts or employs hectoring behaviour.

Trititasking *(pronounced Try-tee-tasking)***:** 1. Doing three things at once. 2. Highly contrived non-word that really doesn't work; failure to grasp the basic hierarchy of doing one, two, three or many things; whoever invented this must presumably feel the need to refer variously to tasking, uni-tasking, mono-tasking, duo-tasking, double-tasking, quad-tasking, *ad infinitum*; crass beyond belief. *(see Multitasking)*

Troops, the: 1. The people who do the work. 2. Overworked and underpaid workforce, often referred to dismissively by management as though they were some sort of military battalion. *(see Motivation, lack of, team; Parapet, heads above the, keep our head below the; Team, there's no I in; Trenches, in the)*

Trouser leg, pissing down your own: 1. Performing an action distinctly to one's disadvantage. 2. As the saying goes, it may initially provide a nice warm feeling but doesn't help in the long run; wilful self-destruction. *(see Foot, shoot oneself in the; Hoist with one's own petard; Own goal, spectacular; Tent, standing outside the ___ pissing in)*

Trousers, still in short: 1. Still immature or inexperienced. 2. Throwaway phrase normally used to denigrate a trainee or less senior colleague; frequently uttered by people who are themselves pretty naïve but wish to cover up the fact by pointing out that someone else is a no-hoper.

Truffle (vb): 1. To forage around; delve into. 2. Feeble attempt to liken the actions of a tame French pig searching for expensive fungi with the act of investigating something in business, as in: *"We're truffling around the issue to assess consumer confidence, Brian."*

Tub thumping: 1. Making a racket. 2. Making a racket, often for no reason at all; clarion call hammered out by oppressed chief executive with hapless and disinterested workforce; blast of invective delivered by sales director whose team is underperforming horribly; physical destruction of boardroom table when stridently making a point and somewhat overdoing it. *(see Bang the drum)*

Turbo-charge: 1. To inject extra energy or pace into an engine or an activity. 2. Classic macho word pairing redolent of racetracks, the Grand Prix, thundering down the motorway in a sports car, picking up women, and so much more; only ever used by people who haven't had a shag for years, typically Terylene-suited salesmen from Bolton. *(see –driven; Spots, stripes or a bit of turbo)*

Turd, polishing a: 1. Attempting to smarten up excreta; futile exercise to make something fundamentally bad look marginally better. 2. Profoundly frustrating process of being told to improve something when it's effectively dead in the water; scatological imagery reminiscent of having one's hands deeply in the doo-doo while simultaneously having to put on a brave face and pretend everything is alright. *(see Destigmatize; GIGO; Jazz hands; Ladder it up; Putting lipstick on a pig; Rebrand; RIRO; SISO)*

Turf wars: 1. Battles between different factions in business. 2. Outright warfare, most commonly between departments vying for their slice of the budget, but sometimes between rival companies pitching for their share of a contract; blatant disregard for professional etiquette; underhand tactics; occasional violence in car parks when emotions run too high. *(see Collaboration)*

Turfismo: 1. Mixture of turf wars and machismo. 2. Extreme aggressive/defensive behaviour, not solely the preserve of men. *(see Turf wars)*

Tweak: 1. Tiny adjustment. 2. Monumental U-turn. *(see Coming or going, he doesn't know if he's; Evolving to meet customer demand; Pivot; Reverse gear; Turd, polishing a; U-turn)*

Twenty-Mile March: 1. Consistent effort over a controlled period. 2. A perfectly good pacing concept from Jim Collins, unless used in the wrong context. Amundsen beat Scott to the pole by consistently marching 20 miles a day. In bad weather he did it anyway, and in good he stopped at 20 to save energy for the next day. Scott either stayed in his tent or overshot and wore himself out. Companies should go for similar consistency. *(see Hundred Day Plan; Six-Week Sprint; Spin Cycle)*

20/20 hindsight: 1. Brilliantly accurate when it comes to what has already happened. 2. Hugely annoying trait of many politicians and business folk who appear fantastically lucid and well-informed after the event; as helpful as saying: *"I wouldn't have done that if I were you".*

24/7/365: 1. Permanently open or available. 2. Aggravating numerical sequence depicting hours, days and months; spawn of the internet age in which nothing ever closes; excuse for companies to make their people work all hours. *(see Always on; Amber, treat every ___ as red; Constantly striving; Expectations, exceeding, failing to achieve, living up to, managing, meeting)*

Twinternship: 1. An internship where the student's mission is to promote the company and its brands using social media such as Twitter. 2. Tacit acknowledgement that the company knows sod all about anything modern such as the interweb, and must, therefore, hire a savvy teenager to help them out. *(see Digital native)*

Two-faced: 1. Deceitful; insincere; hypocritical. 2. Janus-like, as in the Roman god often depicted on doors looking in opposite directions, depicting looking back to the old and forward to the new – hence the month of January; utterly untrustworthy; unreliable; slimy boss who talks a good game and then does something completely different; crowd-pleaser who says yes to everything and then does nothing.

Typo: 1. Typographical error. 2. Every third word in a press release; woeful grammatical skills displayed in the majority of business paperwork.

Umbilical cord, cut the: 1. Sever all ties. 2. Deny all knowledge of; abdicate all responsibility; bail out; do a runner; leave hanging; hang out to dry; hide in cowardly fashion; be thoroughly attached to, and then disappear without trace; announcement of severing a relationship, as in: *"I think we're going to have to cut the umbilical cord on this one, Veronica."*

Umbrella (vb): 1. Rain protection apparatus; overarching cover. 2. Peculiar verb to denote overall protection; since migrated into a strangely active verb, as in: *"We need to umbrella these proposals, Derek.";* approximately meaning to draw together under one theme. *(see Overarching)*

Unbundling: 1. Process of disaggregation. 2. Dismantling into component parts; going back to basics; unravelling a product or service that was always far too complicated; realizing that something was massively confusing and needs to be simplified. *(see Granular, let's get)*

Under siege: 1. Surrounded by the enemy. 2. Surrounded by the enemy at work; snowed under; stacked; coming in from all sides; short of food and getting weaker by the minute; comprehensively outvoted by colleagues; in a minority of one. *(see Balls in the air, on the block, to the wall; Stacked, completely; Wagon, the Indians have surrounded the; Wall-to-wall)*

Underperformance: 1. Sub-standard showing. 2. Mealy-mouthed word to highlight that things have not gone well; attachment of under- prefix to a word that normally suggests a decent result, as in a performance. *(see Sub-optimal)*

Undressing in public: 1. Removing clothes in the presence of others. 2. Pat phrase much used in the city to describe the process by which public companies report their performance to analysts and investors; off-hand remark about the horrors that may be revealed at such an announcement, as in: *"Well, since they have to undress in public twice a year, you'd have thought they'd have got their house in order by now, don't you think Gerald?"*

Unfair advantage: 1. Improved success, through nefarious means. 2. Frankly bizarre phrase suggesting that winning can be achieved by cheating or somehow bending the rules, as though that were acceptable in business; a notion that raises the question as to whether a fair advantage would be equally acceptable; nonsensical request to staff, as in: *"We need to generate an unfair advantage on this one, guys!"* *(see Failure is not an option; Forces of darkness, deploy the; Level playing field; Rules of engagement)*

Unfun: 1. Not fun. 2. Despicable US tradition of adding the un- prefix to any word they can find; often used when someone becomes overexcited and is on a roll with other words legitimately having the un- prefix, as in: *"Guys, this whole thing is unethical, unnecessary and unfun!"*

Unhappy, I'm not ___ with that: 1. I am happy with that. 2. Crass use of a double negative to stress that you are perfectly fine with something; mini-bullying phraseology that reminds the other person that you could be unhappy if you wanted to; reassertion of authority by pointing out that you could veto this if you had a mind to; part of an arsenal of similar phrases in the power mind games lexicon. *(see Buy-in; Green light; Greenlit; Issues, I have ___ with that; Problem, I don't have a ___ with that; Redlit)*

Unquantifiable: 1. Incapable of being measured. 2. A perfectly good adjective if used to describe something that truly cannot be measured; more often used inappropriately to exaggerate when something can in fact be measured, as in: *"This offer is whaling so much it's unquantifiable!"* *(see Quantifiable; Whaling)*

Unthinkable, think the: 1. Have an original idea. 2. Absolutely pathetic piece of contradictory twaddle that ignores the fact that if something is unthinkable then it cannot be thought; truly ridiculous request often heard at brainstorms, as in: *"I need us to think the unthinkable here, guys!"* *(see BHAG; Brainstorm; Failure is not an option; Greatest imaginable challenge; Impossible, nothing is)*

Up for it: 1. Ready for the challenge. 2. Rather macho statement of preparedness; hints of a call to arms; keen; enthusiastic; full of spunk and energy; fist-clenching and tub-thumping; braced for action.

Upcycling: 1. Process of converting waste materials or products into new ones of better quality or for better environmental value, via recycling. 2. The marketing elision bandwagon rolls on. *(see Intrapreneur; Pretailing)*

Upscale: 1. Make bigger; more expensive. 2. Aggravating use of up- as a prefix, when 'scale up' would be more suitable; interchangeable as a verb or an adjective as in: *"This needs to be more upscale Bill,"* as well as: *"We need to upscale this Amanda."*; strong chance that neither of these phrases means anything much at all; make bigger; increase willy size, for no apparent reason. *(see Scalable; Upsizing; Upskill)*

Upside: 1. Advantage; the pro to the con; the bit where things go right. 2. Likely benefit; the good bit, usually offset by an unwanted bad bit; rough and ready measurement system, as in: *"That's the upside, Steve, but what's the downside?"* *(see Downside)*

Upsizing: 1. Making bigger. 2. More machismo based on scale. *(see Upscale; Upskill; Upweight)*

Upskill: 1. Hire more people who can do the job properly; train existing staff to be better at what they do. 2. More up- prefix twaddle, suggesting a northerly direction for skills; euphemism for pointing out that the current workforce is crap and can't do the work effectively; stupid word to convey the need for more capable people. *(see Upscale; Upsizing; Upweight)*

USP: 1. Unique selling point. 2. Utterly generic point, which may or may not lead to sales; lazy acronym much used in advertising to pinpoint the reason why a customer might possibly buy a product; desperate scramble for uniqueness, invariably resulting in the usual old claims such as 'washes whiter'; hackneyed cliché that rarely motivates.

Up the ante: 1. Increase gambling stake; increase risks or considerations involved in taking an action or reaching a conclusion. 2. Throw everything at it to call the other person's bluff; gamble on a large scale; chuck in the kitchen sink; petulantly bet on a winning outcome by deploying every possible resource at the same time; macho power play, as in: *"I think we need to up the ante on this one, Malcolm."* *(see Kitchen sink)*

Up-to-the-minute: 1. Latest. 2. Probably out of date; somewhat tired; lacklustre; old; obsolescent.

User experience: 1. What a customer has to go through when using a product or service. 2. Catalogue of frustration; phrase much loved by so-called 'brand strategists' and digital natives, especially in connection with mobile devices and internet products. *(see Brand strategist; Digital native; Free-roaming experience; On-rails experience)*

Utilize: 1. Use. 2. Pointless longer version of the verb to use.

U-turn: 1. Complete reversal of stance. 2. Embarrassing turnaround frequently propagated by roguish politicians and indecisive companies; visions of hurtling down the road in one direction, slamming on the brakes, and suddenly turning round to head the other way; total change of mind, for reasons often left unexplained; bare-faced lying, often refusing to admit a change of direction at all; self-deluding insistence that nothing has changed at all, and that it is simply business as usual, when everyone else can see the about turn. *(see Coming or going, he doesn't know if he's; Evolving to meet customer demand; Pivot; Reverse gear; Tweak)*

Upweight: 1. Make more weighty. 2. Yet another pointless up- prefix culprit. *(see Upscale; Upsizing; Upskill)*

Valuable: 1. Of value. 2. Often not of any value at all, as in: *"Thanks for those valuable insights, Mr Chairman." (see Insights; Value-add, value-added)*

Value-add, value-added: 1. Addition of value. 2. Deeply annoying piece of management consultancy jargon; variously used as a noun, as in: *"What's the value-add here, Geoff?"*, and as an adjective, as in: *"This is a value-added proposition, Martin, as you can clearly see."*; based on the counterintuitive notion that anyone worth their salt would attempt to add no value at all. *(see Results-driven)*

Value chain: 1. Bundles of activities, described by original proponent Michael Porter as building blocks that design, market, deliver and support a product. 2. Massively misinterpreted management tool that few people really understand, including possibly the author; MBA concept that allows for the generation of significant amounts of hot air, as in: *"Of course, Derek, we need to examine the value chain in detail,"* when no one really knows what it is. *(see Value creation)*

Value creation: 1. The art of building a company that is actually worth something. 2. Ponderous and seemingly never-ending academic debate about what the true value of a company really is; variously measured via stockmarket value, balance sheet, expectation of future performance, cash in the bank, or the chairman's wife's middle name; pointless hypothetical figure based on fabricated evidence. *(see Chairman's wife; Value chain)*

Value proposition, judgments: 1. Statement that has some worth; decisions based on a set of principles. 2. Nothing of the sort; cliché-ridden piece of piffle using the same old words, and interchangeable between products the world over; flabby set of platitudes that no one cares much about and has no intention of emulating; nothing to do with value, more likely long-winded pontification about this and that in order to fill a space on the boardroom wall. *(see Positioning; Vision, visioning)*

Valued customer: 1. Someone buying our product that we care about. 2. Someone buying our product that we couldn't give a toss about, so long as we've got their money; fawning, oleaginous phrase beginning a sales letter, as in: *"Valued customer, you'll recall you bought a sofa from us last year and we are writing to let you know that the no-stain guarantee we flogged you under duress has now expired."* (see Expectations, exceeding, failing to achieve, living up to, managing, meeting)

Values: 1. Principles a company holds dear. 2. Rambling set of adjectives defining a perfect world that no one can hope to live up to; typically containing a description of the perfect partner, as in passionate, innovative, and world class. *(see Change drivers; Innovation, innovative, innovatively; Mission statement; Passion, passionate; Vision, visioning; World class)*

Variable (n): 1. Item that can vary. 2. Catch-all word for any component of anything, as in: *"So what variables are we actually dealing with here, Fiona?"*; hints of mathematical rigour where there is none whatsoever, as in the correct meaning of having a range of possible values; variable indeed, as in very vague.

VC: 1. Venture capitalist. 2. Shady organizations and individuals who lend money with a smile and then demand it back at an inconvenient moment while holding a large firearm; greasy posh blokes with braces and a penchant for leaning back in chairs and holding court; windbags; usurers. *(see Stakeholder; War chest)*

Vehicle: 1. Conveyance for transportation, taking various forms. 2. A word now strangely usurped to denote almost anything in business, particularly intangible items such as plans and frameworks; suggestion of solidity where there may be none, as in: *"Which communications vehicle are we using in this campaign, Rupert?"* (see Mechanics)

Vertical market, ___integration: 1. A specific market; merging two businesses that are at different levels of production. 2. Overly posh phrase for two companies getting together because they each need what the other has; completion of a previously patchy service; 'vertical market' adds a particularly pointless dimension to what should otherwise simply be a market, especially when abbreviated to 'verticals', as in: *"Charlie, can you give me a rundown on the verticals in the telecoms market please?"* (see Integrate, integral, integration)

VFM: Value for money. 2. Patently not value for money, as in: *"Where's the VFM in this , Nigel?"*

Vibing: 1. Talking about nothing much in a lively sort of way. 2. Talking utter bollocks, often when off one's head on booze or drugs; riffing randomly on any topic that comes to mind; content of many brainstorms, as in: *"Oh, we'll just vibe around that particular thought."*

Videoconference: 1. Discussion in which each attendee is visible to the other via a video screen. 2. Hilarious method of non-communication; opportunity to investigate nasal hair of boss in remote city; chance for office wags to hide just out of screen and suddenly dive in with a remark, thus scaring the pants off unwitting colleagues in far-off countries. *(see Teleconference; Webinar)*

Vin ordinaire: 1. Standard but not very exciting table wine. 2. A distinctly average kind of person; dull; beige; wan; bland; mediocre; Colin in accounts; civil servant. *(see Balanced scorecard; Jobsworth; Mediocracy; Run-of-the-mill; Snake oil salesman; Target manager; Trailblaze; Vis-à-vis)*

Viper's nest: 1. Home of many poisonous snakes. 2. Certain departments traditionally housing gossips, feckless layabouts, and ne'er-do-wells; spiteful gathering of vituperate pessimists, hell-bent on slagging off everything and everybody; occasionally embodied in just one person, such as Bernadette from HR; hot bed of bad blood, negative rumour and poor morale. *(see Hierarchy; Matrix; Organogram; Python, wrestling with a; Snakepit; Snake's honeymoon)*

Vis-à-vis: 1. In relation to; regarding (from the French face to face). 2. Ultra smug way of saying 'in relation to' or 'regarding'; risible attempt to add a dash of Gallic flair to proceedings, or suggest an education rather more elevated than is truly the case; usually perpetrated by panjandrums, as in: *"Stephen, I need to talk to you vis-à-vis your timesheets." (see Panjandrum; Segue; Timesheets; Tranche; Vin ordinaire)*

Vision, visioning: 1. Ability to see; dream of how things could be. 2. Over-blown statement of what a company wants to do, now turned into a labour-consuming process and imbued with all the qualities of black magic; puffery; nothing much at all; series of staid platitudes nailed to boardroom wall or tired-looking reception area; even worse, turned into a horrible verb, as in: *"Darren, when you've finished visioning we'll take it to the board." (see Change drivers; Mission statement; Value proposition, judgments: Values; Voodoo, corporate)*

Voice mail: 1. Electronic system for leaving a message. 2. Perfect way to delegate and do a runner; arch coward's way of breaking bad news without doing it in person. *(see BCC; CC; Email)*

Voodoo, corporate: 1. The spirit of a company. 2. Daft ethereal phrase along the lines of defining someone's 'mojo'; shades of black magic or casting of spells, as though that were standard practice in conventional business; hard-to-bottle essence; strident chief executive's character directly reflected in a petrified bunch of subservient employees. *(see Forces of darkness, deploy the; Mission statement; Vision, visioning)*

VUCA: 1. Volatile, uncertain, complex, ambiguous (military). 2. Really dangerous; constantly shifting; unpredictable; best avoided because you'll definitely get it in the neck. *(see FUBB; Scapegoat, make a ___ out of; SNAFU)*

Ww

Waffle: 1. Combination of words that amount to very little. 2. Piffle; static; white noise; nonsense; twaddle; wibble; hot air; bullshit; most of the contents of this dictionary. *(see Bullshit; Doughnut rather than the hole, it would be wise to concentrate on the; Drive it home; Obfuscation; Off the top of my head; Static; Talking out loud; White noise; Word dump)*

Wagon, the Indians have surrounded the: 1. The game is up. 2. Evocative cowboys and Indians imagery as Americans First Nations personnel beset some hapless pioneers, possibly on their way to California; visions of tomahawks flying and Davy Crockett-style acts of derring-do; in other words, quite unlike any office you have ever seen. *(see Head off at the pass; Shark, keep moving like a, waiting for the sharks to circle; Still heading west; Under siege)*

Wake up and smell the coffee: 1. Stop sleeping and inhale the scent of roasting Arabica beans; pay attention. 2. US phrase imploring someone to stop daydreaming and realize the true extent of what's going on; usually deployed on very naive individuals, as in: *"Oh come on, David, when are you going to wake up and smell the coffee?!"*

Walking wounded: 1. Damaged but not dead. 2. Severely battered staff, usually after a horrible setback such as a round of redundancies or the loss of a major contract.

Wall-to-wall: 1. Carpeting that covers the entire floor; a room so full of goods it's almost impossible to move; desk in a similar state. 2. Overworked with little hope of reprieve; snowed under; not coping; unable to say no to requests to do even more; possibly micromanaging. *(see Back-to-back; Micromanaging; Stacked, completely; Strategy, strategise; Under siege)*

Wantrepreneur: 1. Someone who wants to be an entrepreneur, but hasn't made it. 2. Abject failure; total ho-hoper. *(See Entrepreneur; Intrapreneur; Inventrepreneur)*

War chest: 1. Box full of kit ready for battle; cash stockpile ready to be used for acquisition. 2. Macho stash amassed to embark upon world domination plan; VC contribution gathered for same purpose; springboard to massive payday for a privileged few; no cash at all, merely borrowings to facilitate all the above using someone else's money. *(see Stakeholder; VC)*

Warts and all: 1. With all blemishes evident. 2. Frequently shocking revelation of the true state of affairs in a company; nasty picture, with no holds barred; frank analysis of doomed set-up; precursor to news you really don't want to hear, as in: *"Okay Keith, I'm now going to give you the full picture, warts and all."* *(see Drains up, have the; Respect, with)*

Wash its face: 1. Pay its own way; break even. 2. Curious ablution reference to describe a project or budget reconciliation, as in: *"I'm happy to proceed with Project Sideboard, so long as it washes its face."*

Wash our hands of it: 1. Take no further part, nor responsibility. 2. Do a runner; bail out; pretend we were never involved; pass the buck; hand over, regardless of stage reached; pay a forfeit just to be shot of something. *(see Buck, pass the; Hospital pass)*

Wash up meeting: 1. Post mortem. Post mortem in which the project/client/colleague has indeed sometimes expired.

Watch the boards light up: 1. Hope to observe a positive reaction. 2. Asinine expression drawn from the world of telecommunications, in which lights appear on a switchboard when callers connect; shades of some mad villain surveying a child-like model of an empire, with lights denoting various outposts; fairground drama mirroring the rather more mundane process of customers buying some product; overly macho enthusiasm for something relatively humdrum, as in: *"Of course Barbara, as soon as we launch the new barbeque flavour we can really watch the boards light up."* *(see Flagpole, run it up the ___ and see who salutes)*

Watch this space: 1. Keep an eye open because something is going to happen. 2. Obtuse way of saying things are moving pretty rapidly and you'd better be sufficiently on-the-ball to keep up; much loved by project managers working on something mind-numbingly dull who wish to convince themselves that their work is actually rather dynamic; implication of being in-the-know when you're not, as in: *"I can't reveal all the details yet, Martin, but what I can say is watch this space."*

Watchout, I've picked out a: 1. I have identified something we need to keep an eye on. 2. Deeply aggravating conversion of the two words 'watch' and 'out' into a one-word noun; hints of danger and imminent peril when in fact people are just sitting in a room staring at some fairly boring data; overly histrionic intervention in a meeting, as in: *"Hang on guys, I've just picked out a watchout from the Tyne Tees figures."*

Water cooler conversation: 1. Chat with a colleague when collecting a thirst-quenching beverage. 2. Phenomenal opportunity to gossip indiscreetly and waste vast amounts of time; exchange of views concerning football results, what was on the television last night, and how hot the temp on reception is; relating of unfortunate drinking stories, as in: *"You'll never believe it, but Colin overshot on the shandy and threw up on Victoria's briefcase." (see Office, the; Powwow)*

Wavelength, on the same, not on the same: 1. Listening to the same radio station; in tune generally, or not. 2. Broad theme for a complete communication breakdown; collapse of relations; propensity to take a call from the Mumbai office, or ignore it completely; internecine refusal to help colleague; spite; obduracy; total failure to agree. *(see Ducks in a row, get our; Hymn sheet, singing from the same; Rowing in the same boat, direction; Wildebeest in a row, has the lion got his)*

We are where we are: 1. Our geographical location is beyond dispute. 2. Intensely annoying statement of the bleeding obvious; last bastion of all small-minded colleagues who like to suck air through their teeth, decry a state of affairs, and yet offer no constructive advice at all; overtones of having an opinion or even offering to help, while simultaneously providing neither. *(see It is what it is; Jobsworth; Obvious, a firm grasp of the; Panjandrum)*

Webinar: 1. Seminar held on the web. 2. Theoretically helpful medium for discussing information online, but much abused; forum for a succession of idiotic questions that must be endured by large numbers of better-informed individuals; opportunity to daydream and count the number of nasal hairs sported by the presenter. *(see Teleconference; Videoconference)*

Well I know what I think: 1. I am announcing that I know my own mind, without actually doing so. 2. Truly brilliant pronouncement that creates the impression of having an opinion while in fact doing no such thing; after making the statement, all that is needed is to sit back, listen to the opinions of others, and agree with them; a masterful phrase in the arsenal of the sycophant.

WFH: 1. Working from home. 2. Can't be arsed to go to the office. *(see OOO; WTF)*

Whaling: 1. Killing large marine mammals; an online offer that is selling in much higher quantities than normal. 2. Monumentally banal American expression for offer that is 'going off the scale'; highly inappropriate allusion to the death of one our most impressive beasts, applied to the rather less important world of social media; even more tragic in office patter, as in: *"I see that the 2 for 1 cinema tickets offer is really whaling, Chris."* *(see Killer whale; Off the scale; Unquantifiable)*

Wheels coming off: 1. Falling apart; about to crash; not going well. 2. Everything going wrong; on the verge of collision, or total annihilation; spectacularly shit; badly handled; incompetence in action; project about to be terminated due to lack of professionalism; company in the same position. *(see Crash and burn; High risk; Maxed out; Needle, moving the; Needle, pushing the; Nero syndrome; On ramps; Off ramps; Pushing the envelope; Nightmare, utter; Reinventing the wheel)*

When the chips are down: 1. When the gambling is about to begin; when it comes to the crunch. 2. Macho betting phrase that tries to lend a little frisson of danger to the most boring of subjects, such as the pet care and personal hygiene markets; perpetuation of the ridiculous notion that shifting air conditioners from a warehouse in Purley is somehow as glamourous as playing James Bond in *Casino Royale*. *(see When the going gets tough, the tough get going)*

When the going gets tough, the tough get going: 1. When things are difficult, decent people come to the fore and take responsibility. 2. The polar opposite of what happens in most companies; when the going gets tough, most senior executives are nowhere to be seen, often having gone on holiday deliberately to avoid criticism; parroting of clichéd Billy Ocean song title as a pathetic motivational speech by hackneyed sales directors, as in: *"Well Sebastian, when the going gets tough, the tough get going!"* *(see When the chips are down)*

Where the sun don't shine, shove it: 1. Stick it up your arse! 2. Profane rejoinder conveying complete disdain for the request and the requester; approximate translation: *"If you seriously expect me to do that, you can f**k right off!"* *(see Brown-nosing; Stick that, some American is going to jet in and tell you exactly where to)*

White elephant: 1. Elaborate venture that proves useless. 2. The majority of all projects undertaken by companies. *(see Elephant in the room; Wild-goose chase)*

White noise: 1. Electrical sound with a wide continuous range. 2. General racket from which no helpful sound can be discerned; boardroom discussion about car parking spaces or share allocation; annual general meeting at which disgruntled shareholders are rioting in response to invidious director's pay awards; gaggle of secretaries in local bar drinking Martinis and talking bollocks at high pitch; chairman's speech. *(see Background noise; Blue-sky thinking; Communications, lack of, plan, skills; Static; Waffle; Word dump)*

WIBGI: 1. Wouldn't it be good if...? 2. Fanciful notion that something can be much better than it truly is; pie in the sky; crazy delusion about likelihood of success. *(see Holy grail)*

Wild-goose chase: 1. Absurd or pointless pursuit of something unattainable. 2. The majority of a company's activities every year; dead end; blind alley; cul-de-sac; directionless effort; waste of time for everybody; chimera; vain hope; managing director's doomed *cause célèbre*; ship of fools, bound for nowhere. *(see Goal posts, move the; White elephant; WOMBAT)*

Wildebeest in a row, has the lion got his: 1. Do we agree on this? 2: Staggeringly ridiculous wildlife reference suggesting a decent working knowledge of the savannah, while simultaneously revealing colossal ignorance of same; quaint implication that the king of the beasts would do what comes naturally to every apex predator, that is to say line up his prey in a neat row before embarking on an attack. *(see Beavers, defending it like; Ducks in a row, get our; Hymn sheet, singing from the same; Loose cannon; Off message; Off-piste; Realignment; Wavelength, on the same, not on the same)*

Wilful blindness: 1. Ignoring the obvious due to dangerous convictions, 'just following orders', ignorance or prejudice. 2. Lethal frame of mind that can lead individuals or entire companies to 'do an Enron'; utter conviction that one is in the right. *(see Single-minded, single-mindedly)*

Win or lose, we're in with a chance: 1. Contradictory nonsense probably attempting to convey that it's not over until it's over. 2. Utter bollocks, inasmuch as if you have won or lost then you have indeed won or lost, and are therefore no longer in with a chance, since the element of chance has now been comprehensively removed. *(see Fat lady, it's not over until the ___ sings; Winners and losers, there are always)*

Wind, sailing close to the: 1. At full tilt and in danger of capsizing. 2. Travelling perilously fast; careening; losing it on the chicane; overcooking it; at full throttle and most likely to crash and burn. *(see Crash and burn; Flying unstable; Riding the razor blade)*

Window of opportunity: 1. Chance to do something. 2. Peculiar imagery suggesting that a chance to do something is somehow akin to a pane of glass or aperture to look through; shades of voyeurism, as in peeping through a window to sneak a glance of something salacious, such as the chairman shagging the new receptionist over the boardroom table.

Windowseated (vb): 1. Placed next to the window in an airplane. 2. Rather quaint expression to point out that someone has been fired or frozen out of a position, believed to have originated in Japan, as in: *"He's out of the company now – he's been windowseated."*

Windsurfing in peanut butter: 1. Attempting something nigh on impossible. 2. Brilliantly inventive vision of tackling an unachievable task, but valiantly so; invokes the retort *"smooth or crunchy?"*

Winners and losers, there are always: 1. Someone will win and someone won't. 2. Comprehensively self-evident platitude much loved by small-minded and obtuse salesmen; totally pointless waste of anyone's time, as though some earth-shattering insight has suddenly been revealed; trite twaddle spouted by office bore, as in: *"Of course, Jane, there are always winners and losers."* *(see Win or lose, we're in with a chance)*

Wins, quick, easy, there are no easy: 1. We can succeed fast; there is no way to succeed fast. 2. Glib throwaway hinting at prior knowledge or implying experience where there may be nothing more than guesswork; mildly hectoring tone, as in: *"Of course there are no easy wins in this market, Sally."* *(See Low-hanging fruit, go for the; Win-win)*

Win-win: 1. Advantageous or successful in more than one way; both sides can benefit. 2. Irritating word pairing from our persistent culprits the management consultants; patronizing ruse to suggest that this is not just one victory, but two or more; hoodwinking idea that no one actually loses; deep joy, we all win!; smug aside in meeting, usually accompanied by a knowing wink, as in: *"This looks very much to me like a win-win, Geoff!"* *(see Lose-lose; Wins, quick, easy, there are no easy)*

WIP: 1. Work in progress. 2. Euphemism for it hasn't been done. *(see Always in beta; Development; Flatline)*

-wise: 1. Relating to whatever precedes this. 2. Horribly overworked suffix stuck on to the end of pretty much any word people can get hold of when they haven't expressed themselves clearly, including hardy perennials such as company-wise, control-wise, country-wise, product-wise, market-wise, and many more; not wise at all, in fact, rather ignorant. *(see –ise)*

Witch-hunt: 1. Rigorous campaign to round up or expose dissenters on the pretext of safeguarding the safety of the community. 2. Comprehensive search for someone to blame; no expense spared in finding a culprit, having deployed no funds so far in helping to make something a success; vindictive finger pointing; accusatory activity; methodical search for a scapegoat, followed by public humiliation or dismissal. *(see Backlash; Blame culture; Deep dive; Lift up a rock; Look, take a long hard; No stone unturned; Root-and-branch review; Scapegoat, make a ___ out of)*

Within our gift: 1. In our power. 2. Dismissive phrase usually trotted out when something can't be done, or when someone wants to abdicate responsibility for doing something helpful; pompous, rather archaic way of saying I don't have the authority to do that, as in: *"I'd love to give you a pay rise, Julian, but it is simply not within my gift."*

WOMBAT: 1. Waste of money, bandwidth and time. 2. Financially futile, not worth the mental effort, nor the hours needed to do it; pointless; suicidal; baseless; any project that should never have been commissioned. *(see Bandwidth, he doesn't have the; White elephant; Wild-goose chase)*

Wonga: 1. Informal term for money, possibly from the Romany word for coal, *wongar.* 2. Term much loved by people who want to make budgets sound more impressive, as in: *"We're spending serious wonga on this product launch, Nigel."* *(see Spondulix)*

Wood, can't see the ___ for the trees: 1. Unable to see the overall picture due to too much detail, or unable to see the specifics due to too much vagueness. 2. Near-permanent state of affairs whenever anyone in business is staring at data; inability to understand what on earth is going on. *(see Closer look, stand back and take a)*

Woods, not out of the ___ yet: 1. We are not yet in the clear. 2. Ominous warning of complacency or celebrating too early; suggestion of getting away with something, or not being rumbled; common in companies that are skimming it or flying by the seat of their pants. *(see Fly by the seat of one's pants)*

Woodwork, spanners in the, spanners jumping out of the: 1. Unexpected problems arising. 2. Strange collision of carpentry and mechanical tools; no justification as to why spanners might be relevant to woodwork at all; worse still, suggestion that they might reside inside the woodwork – a physical impossibility; even more ludicrous, suggestion that they might jump of their own accord; overall, outright gobbledegook. *(see Crafting, it needs a bit of; Tools, management, unique)*

Word dump: 1. Spontaneous outburst of verbiage enacted in front of someone else. 2. Nasty trait of people who can't think for themselves; sudden pouring out of half-baked drivel, perpetrated on hapless colleague on the way to the toilet; verbal diarrhoea ejaculated without warning. *(see Bounce ideas off; Brain dump; Criteria, key; Data dump; Drive it home; Enlighten me; Human wind tunnel; STFU; Waffle; White noise)*

Word of mouse: 1. Information disseminated on the internet. 2. Dismaying word play turning word of mouth into its online cousin.

Word on the street: 1. Opinion generally held. 2. Hip, down-with-the-kids saying used by executives who want to show that they are in touch with a customer base or group of colleagues; phrase usually used by *nouveau riche* executives who have rarely left their gated community, let alone listened to anything on the street.

Work cut out for us, we've got our: 1. We have a lot to do. 2. We have too much to do and we'll never make it in time.

Worklessness: 1. Unemployment. 2. Truly disgraceful replacement for the word 'unemployment'; odious avoidance of the plain fact that someone has no work; cowardly twisting of words to skirt round the truth; deliberate inclusion of the word 'work' in order to suggest that there is some. *(see Frontofmindness; Here-and-now-ness; Negative growth, profit)*

Work-life balance: 1. Sensible ratio of work and free time. 2. Complete inability to achieve any balance between the two at all; chronic over work, comprehensively encouraged by one's employer for no particular tangible benefit; exploitation; slave labour; abject failure to see partner or family for weeks on end; obsession with projects that any other person would find dull and unimportant; all night work for sustained periods, followed by lengthy absence through illness; vacillating horribly between two extremes; lack of balance. *(see Always on; Constantly striving; Expectations, exceeding; Sun, the ___ never sets at; 24/7/365)*

Workshop (vb): 1, To conduct a meeting, usually to come up with some ideas. 2. Unsatisfactory verb that covers a multitude of sins; almost certainly nothing whatsoever to do with a workshop in the artisan or craft skills sense; random collection of unsuitable people idly toying with an apparently important business issue; group of international colleagues exchanging banter and achieving f**k-all; marathon consumption of biscuits and coffee, at someone else's expense; humiliation by smug facilitator; horrible participation in childish 'team bonding' exercises, to no discernible end; futile solution to almost every business challenge, as in: *"I think we need to workshop this one, Shaun." (see Awayday; Brainstorm; Executive retreat; Off-site)*

Workshy: 1. Not inclined to work. 2. The majority of employees in the world.

Workstream: 1. Stuff to do. 2. Modern exaggeration of stuff to do, enlarging workflow into a body of water, somehow suggesting greater quantity; implication that everybody knows what direction the project is heading in, which is rarely the case.

World-beating, -changing: 1. The best there is; revolutionary. 2. Truly breathtaking piece of arrogant twaddle; suggestion that a project or product can change the world, or beat everyone else; arrogance on a staggering scale; rank self-aggrandisement; words to be avoided at all costs in company reports and mission statements. *(see Mission statement; World class)*

World class: 1. As good as any comparable product or service in the world. 2. Almost certainly nothing of the sort; decidedly average; impossible to measure, since no satisfactory metric of 'world class' has ever been developed. *(see Challenger brand; Market-leading; Mission statement; Scalable; Thought leadership; World-beating, -changing)*

Wow factor: 1. An element of a proposal or product that evokes the reaction "wow!". 2. Derisory piece of histrionics designed to distract the audience from the fact that the proposal has no substance, or that the product is distinctly sub-standard. *(see FMF; Jazz hands; X factor)*

WPMF: 1. Worth paying more for. 2. Nasty acronym deployed by marketers in an attempt to make their product sound more appealing in strategy documents, when usually it is pretty much identical to all the others. *(see Premium; USP)*

WTF: 1. What the f**k? 2. Crikey, that's a surprise; oh shit, the game is up.

WILF (vb): 1. What was I looking for? 2. Pointless pursuit of shoppers in shops or online; abject failure to know what one is doing generally; ridiculous idea of wishing to spend without actually needing anything.

WYSIATI: 1. What you see is all there is. 2. Daniel Kahneman's acronym explaining how people jump to conclusions based on the only limited evidence they have; true of almost every hard-pressed executive working at speed and using just the narrow information they currently have to hand.

X factor: 1. Mysterious ingredient that makes something brilliant. 2. Disastrous television programme that provides a national platform for contestants to humiliate themselves in front of the largest possible audience. *(see FMF; Magic ingredient, there is no; Wow factor)*

Y2K: 1. The year 2000. 2. Pointless mnemonic deployed at the start of the millennium by smug executives in a futile attempt to sound impressive.

Yes man: 1. A male who always says yes. 2. Obsequious and fawning subordinate of either sex who has no opinion of their own and so always does what they are told, regardless of the consequences. *(see Brownnosing; On message)*

Yield compression: 1. Producing less. 2. Weasel phrase to point out that less money is being made than was formerly the case; possibility that no money is being made at all, or that there is a whopping loss; appalling attempt at a smokescreen to disguise woeful performance, as in: *"It was behind budget with significant yield compression retarded by squeezed inputs." (see Negative growth, profit)*

Z list celebrity: 1. Barely-known person. 2. Unknown person wanting to be known. *(see Profile, raise the)*

Zee, we've covered everything from A to: 1. We have thought of everything. 2. We've done sod all, but are claiming that we have been hard at work; we are gratuitously using the American Zee rather than the English Zed to let you know we are thoroughly in tune with our friends across the pond. *(see A-Z; Chapter and verse; Full Monty, the)*

Zero in on: 1. Home in on; make a specific target. 2. Suggest precision where there may be scarcely any; liken business dealing with being a crack ancient warrior aiming a spear at an enemy. *(see Clarity; Focus)*

Zero tolerance: 1. Refusal to tolerate anything that the rules don't allow. 2. Refusal to tolerate anything that I don't like, because I am in charge; random, whim-based decree denouncing whatever the chief executive can't stand this month; juvenile idea that if I say it mustn't happen, then it certainly won't happen, as in: *"We have a zero tolerance to sexism in this company,"* followed swiftly by revelations that said chief executive has been shagging the receptionist behind his wife's back, and refusing to pay all female executives the equivalent to their male counterparts. *(see Failure is not an option; Nero syndrome)*

Zombie: 1. Company that is bust in all but name, but kept alive for tax dodging purposes. 2. Member of staff with similar qualities.

Zone, in the: 1. In contention; in the running; concentrating properly. 2. Frankly nowhere, but grasping yet another phrase from American sport to suggest that we are on the case. *(see Ballpark figure; Cover all the bases)*

ABOUT THE AUTHOR

KEVIN DUNCAN is a business adviser, marketing expert, motivational speaker and author. After 20 years in advertising and direct marketing, he has spent the last fifteen years as an independent troubleshooter, advising companies on how to change their businesses for the better.

Contact the author for advice, training, or speaking opportunities:

kevinduncanexpertadvice@gmail.com

www.expertadviceonline.com

Add your own examples and stay posted at **www.bulldictionary.com**